Exploring E-commerce, Global E-business, and E-societies

Craig Fellenstein
Ron Wood

Prentice Hall PTR
Upper Saddle River, New Jersey 07458
www.phptr.com

ISBN 0-13-084846-8

90000

9 780130 848468

Library of Congress Cataloging-in-Publication Date

Fellenstein, Craig.
  Exploring e-commerce, global e-business, and e-societies / Craig Fellenstein, Ron Wood.
    p. cm.
  Includes bibliographical references and index.
  ISBN 0-13-084846-8 (hardcover)
  1. Electronic commerce. I. Wood, Ron, 1949- II. Title.

HF5548.32.F45 1999
658'.05--dc21   99-055178

Editorial/Production Supervision: *Benchmark Productions, Inc.*
Acquisitions Editor: *Karen McLean*
Cover Design Director: *Jerry Votta*
Cover Design: *Anthony Gemmellaro*
Manufacturing Manager: *Alexis Heydt*
Editorial Assistant: *Michael Fredette*
Marketing Manager: *Kate Hargett*
Project Coordinator: *Anne Trowbridge*

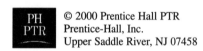

© 2000 Prentice Hall PTR
Prentice-Hall, Inc.
Upper Saddle River, NJ 07458

Prentice Hall books are widely used by corporations and government agencies for training, marketing, and resale.

The publisher offers discounts on this book when ordered in bulk quantities.
For more information, contact: Corporate Sales Department, Phone: 800-382-3419;
FAX: 201-236-7141; E-mail: corpsales@prenhall.com; or write: Prentice Hall PTR,
Corp. Sales Dept., One Lake Street, Upper Saddle River, NJ 07458

All rights reserved. No part of this book may be
reproduced, in any form or by any means, without
permission in writing from the publisher.

Printed in the United States of America

10 9 8 7 6 5 4 3 2 1

ISBN 0-13-084846-8

Prentice-Hall International (UK) Limited, *London*
Prentice-Hall of Australia Pty. Limited, *Sydney*
Prentice-Hall Canada Inc., *Toronto*
Prentice-Hall Hispanoamericana, S.A., *Mexico*
Prentice-Hall of India Private Limited, *New Delhi*
Prentice-Hall of Japan, Inc., *Tokyo*
Pearson Education Asia Pte. Ltd., *Singapore*
Editora Prentice-Hall do Brasil, Ltda., *Rio de Janeiro*

To my wife and children—who are definitely more important than e-commerce. Thank you for your unconditional love, patience, and never-ending support. —Craig Fellenstein

To my wife, children, and grandchildren. . . I want to thank each of you for your perseverance, love, encouragement, and patience. I dedicate my contributions in producing this book to each one of you. To my wife, a special thanks for your insights and constructive criticisms. —Ron Wood

Contents

Part 2
E-commerce Channels to Generate Profitable Revenues   75

Part 3
Structured Transformations Through E-commerce   107

Part 4
Global Segmentation   165

Preface

Why is it that new e-commerce companies are causing huge swings in our global stock markets—swings that are realized with both positive and negative indicators? The notion of electronic commerce, or e-commerce, is one that has been present for decades. If we accept this electronic practice as a topic that is not so new, then why is it that constant introductions of new e-commerce technology innovations and Internet-related solutions are causing such dramatic changes in how we live and work each day? What are the characteristics of an e-society? Will e-commerce soon become a tethered electronic medium that everyone just accepts as a normal daily routine part of one's day? Compare this new e-commerce evolution to that of the past few decades. What is it that actually defines the term e-commerce? What is an e-business? Is it merely a form of e-commerce? Which e-commerce technologies, when properly synchronized, define an e-business opportunity? What e-commerce roles do global corporations play?

This book will explore many of these questions by providing an analysis of the business issues, the business dynamics, and suggestive societal impacts that are a direct result of the introduction of e-commerce. This new electronic frontier, referred to quite simply as e-commerce, has introduced tremendous change into our business and social structures around the world. Many e-commerce technological challenges have forced global corporate enterprises to acquire faster and better communications capabilities. This suggests an important question: To what end are global corporations having to rethink their own core business approaches, contrasted to new, innovative e-commerce solutions?

These global e-commerce marketplaces include business-to-business, business-to-consumer, government-to-business, government-to-public sector, and business-to-both suppliers and consumers. Each of these areas has been touched in some form by e-commerce. In fact, if an enterprise is to be competitive and profitable in today's electronic economy, it is safe to assume that the enterprise is either fully engaged in some form of e-commerce or the enterprise is seriously considering the internal changes required to become more effective at leveraging utilities of e-commerce.

The term *e-commerce* has forsaken itself into several forms, with several variations of the definition. In general, however, e-commerce is a particular state of business, comprising a series of simple and complex electronic business transactions. An e-commerce transaction implies that computer-based, and network-based, electronic transactions have to be successfully executed. Solutions in e-commerce often leverage the Internet, and its many vast subnetworks, to enable a particular technological action to occur. For instance, solutions involve advertising a product or service, purchasing (via electronic means) a product or a service, being billed for a product or a service, paying for a product or a service; and then (not so straightforward) determining the logistics involved in the manufacturing and delivery of that product throughout the entire supply chain. These manufacturing and delivery environments will leverage technologies of e-commerce to competitively perform in their daily business, as suppliers of many types of products and/or services. Based on these concepts, the term e-commerce is not so difficult to understand; in simple terms, e-commerce is an electronic business transaction that utilizes a network. It is the complexities of events that need to occur, in a synchronized manner, that seem to complicate the exact meaning of the word "e-commerce."

In this book we will explore the various meanings of the term "e-commerce," and we will also explore many useful designs and approaches that lead to excellent e-commerce solutions. The Internet world of e-commerce has yielded many innovative solutions that display outstanding characteristics of *Design Quality*. These are characteristics that are actually built in to the final e-commerce solution set. These design successes occur not by accident, but through careful planning and execution of a timely, global business marketing strategy, tightly coupled to a fast and effective technical Internet development team.

There is another important term that falls within the scope of e-commerce. This term is referred to as *e-business*. The term "e-business" implies performing day-to-day business transactions, using specific combinations of e-commerce technologies that are designed to allow for intercompany commerce. The notion of an e-business may, in fact, be thought of as a combination of e-commerce technologies (or utilities) combined to form the e-business. For example:

- Web-enabled interfaces to a company's product or service line(s)
- Electronic catalogs and hosting of various other types of information content
- Application interfacing to back-end office systems to accomplish A/R functions
- Forms of Web-based electronic data interchange services
- Simple graphical screen design metaphors for comfortable user interfaces
- Customer care interfaces for registration, service delivery, and support

These combined design quality features tend to attract and retain a larger population of Internet end users over longer periods of time. How does this all integrate to work together as a single e-commerce environment? In technical terms, certain types of computers (referred to as servers) are the actual machine engines of e-businesses. These servers can host (and cooperate with) many other e-commerce functions available across the Internet (for example, credit card billing services, payment services, and catalog viewing) on many other servers. So, in simplest terms, servers merely "serve up" information content and deliver various business functionalities associated with that specific content. This serving of consumer-related services is very attractive to many businesses, and also to many consumers across every sector of industry. Many social systems seem to be creating environments that are enabled through specific approaches of e-commerce. This has shown both positive and negative effects.

Many global Internet-oriented businesses are capturing this new type of e-commerce, as *idea-share,* and some of these companies have moved their own stock market share holder values up (some in the course of a day's time) as much as 50 to 200 points (for example, Netscape, Yahoo!, Amazon.com, AOL, eBay—and there are plenty more). We suppose that one line of exploratory thought could be based on corporate mergers in the Internet and technology sector(s). This notion of "mergers" seems to be occurring in many areas of technology, especially the e-commerce forms of technologies. The assertion here might be that it is simple to negotiate corporate buy-outs and mergers, with highly inflated stocks (like Internet stocks) that have yet to consistently demonstrate apparent revenues. What a paradox this seems to be; it is happening, though, each week in many countries around the world.

The Internet, in practice, and many applications of e-commerce, combined, have the unique potential to evolve into very important *change agents* of social, global change. These change agents are stimulating a change that will last for many decades, if not permanently. Changing the way we perform commerce around the world is, and will continue to be, a significant shift for many cultures. Changing the way we operate within our own homes, for instance, can be very exciting for many individuals. These are just a couple of areas where change is happening now, through implementations of various forms of e-commerce. The impact of e-commerce and the Internet will become even more pervasive throughout all facets of our global societies (businesses, governments, private sectors, educational systems, practices of medicine, personalization devices), as we progress into the next decade. Many of these fascinating and thought-provoking ideas are worthy of a more in-depth treatment, which is provided throughout the chapters of this book.

Consider that the term "e-commerce" technically implies electronic devices and complicated networks (like the Internet) to be able to work together to complete commerce-related tasks. Since the earliest designs of the Internet (in 1969) its growth toward enabling e-commerce transactions to occur has been nothing short of spectacular. The Internet was initially limited to several thousands of network end users (or, end points), and these end users were mainly located throughout North America. Today, Internet end users exceed several millions around the world, and the numbers continue to increase daily. Estimates indicate that approximately 60,000–70,000 end users per day join the Internet. Some other estimates claim that approximately 1.2 servers are connected to the Internet each minute. These are significant numbers.

The original team involved in the invention of the Internet, recognizing its potential benefits and networking brilliance, was concerned from the start that this might one day turn into an unregulated global frontier. Much of the exact history of the Internet, and some fundamental views of the intended operations of the Internet, can be found at http://www.isoc.org, *The Internet Society's* Web site. There are some fascinating topics to consider when studying the history of exactly *how* the Internet was originally designed and created.

Today, the number of Internet end users in North America has grown to well over 80 million. This suggests a growth rate of approximately 340 percent during 1996 into 1999; prior to that, only 18 million end users logged on to the Internet. This has been a phenomenal and unprecedented growth in many positive ways—positive in the sense that, by virtue of the Internet and all of its global subnetworks, it allows for unprecedented forms of social (global) change to occur. Positive in the sense that, by virtue of this same newly discovered worldwide community, and all of its openness and freedom, we are constantly challenged in a way that effects changes across several different dimensions of our personal lives and daily business practices.

This global phenomenon called *e-commerce*, combined with the Internet, has rapidly introduced itself into several geographies around the world. As an example, approximately 25 percent of companies in Europe are operating with some form of access to the Internet. Finland is one of the most technologically-centered countries in the world. Many global industries are already claiming significant revenues through utilization of e-commerce business solutions. Overall, 60 percent of all global companies now have access to the Internet, with 20 percent more currently planning to gain access during the next year.

Several of the leading countries in Europe continue to be successful in adopting practices of e-commerce, and they have moved ahead in several significant areas, both industrially and socially. It is estimated that 46 percent of all companies with Internet access are already conducting electronic business, using "utilities" of e-commerce, in conjunction with the Internet. Spain is followed by France and Germany, while companies in the U.K., Netherlands, and Italy also appear to be introducing many diverse innovations of e-commerce. The majority of industries strongly believe that adaptations of e-commerce will be important to their industry. Most global industries expect the amount of electronic business (or e-business) they do "online" to increase next year. Telecommunications technologies, and the cost of entry for many industries to enhance their own telecommunications capabilities, seem to be a prevailing challenge across many global industries. The cost of higher-speed infrastructures, attached to higher-speed telecommunications services, is significant. These must be present before any e-commerce solution can be considered—unconstrained. Conversely, companies cannot afford the high costs of introducing enhanced telecommunications capabilities unless this cost is amortized across a diverse set of customers seeking this same service utility. This customer set is being aggressively pursued by almost every industry.

As a result of this new electronic environment, appropriately referred to as e-commerce, many global enterprises are beginning to develop strategies that embellish the use of e-commerce technologies as their fundamental means of conducting business. In fact, many small businesses have also been able to establish significant presence points in worldwide markets, all by virtue of deploying e-commerce technologies within their organization. This premise of technologically empowering both suppliers and consumers has emerged as somewhat of a highly competitive, virtual landscape. This notion applies across many desktop computer manufacturers, networking technology suppliers, and a multitude of other hardware and software manufacturers.

Many of the global industry segments are now actively pursuing various *missions* in e-commerce. To remain competitive and profitable in our emerging global e-commerce economy, business enterprises must create virtually connected organizations that leverage e-commerce technologies that significantly accelerate their go-to-market initiatives. Competitive corporations must enhance their business processes to improve their capabilities in acquiring timely business intelligence, higher-quality designs in their products and services, and electronic business capabilities in a safe, secure, and private environment.

The projected growth in the e-commerce market space is expected to exceed $327 billion by 2002. The creative business enterprises have finely tuned strategies that utilize e-commerce technologies as a principal medium of conducting business for both the supplier and the consumer. Consider the evolution of e-commerce. This new environment is one that enables a virtual market space to introduce new competitive approaches and a computer desktop dominance enabling vast networking connections in many countries of the world.

The business enterprises that are buying and selling over commercial networks must use certain *push* and *pull* technologies to gain access to desktops. These technologies allow the business enterprise to appropriately interact with key decision makers. Consequently, there are ensuing battles to dominate access to and from the desktop of industrial enterprises, public sectors, and governments, both small and large.

Consider the different changes imposed across global societies by various e-commerce technological solutions. Observe the subtle momentum where these technological factors have rendered their benefits. Likewise, it is intriguing to analyze and observe the tactics used by the various combatants involved in this struggle for Internet desktop dominance.

This book is truly an *exploration* of a vast number of provoking thoughts and subject areas one can consider while contemplating the world of electronic commerce. We hope that you find this book both interesting to read and more than remarkable in its content and suggestion. Although this material is not necessarily a "handbook" for e-commerce designs and applications, it certainly helps to establish some of the basic underpinnings necessary to engage in specific endeavors of global, regional, or even localized forms of e-commerce.

Acknowledgments

We would both like to thank Dan Curtis and Jack Williford for their extraordinary efforts in reviewing this material, and for their excellent suggestions to help us write this exploration of e-commerce. We hope that our fellow business leaders, practitioners, academicians, and researchers will view the results as visionary, practical, and insightful. A special thank you to Forrester Research for its insightful information.

The field of e-commerce, as well as the global Internet and all of its complicated subnetworks, are a direct result of many great accomplishments from thousands of highly skilled researchers, technicians, academicians, corporate executives, and politicians throughout the world. The incredible change realized worldwide from the Internet has been provided by the accomplishments of these individuals and their own management of innovation and skills. It is due to this incredible mass of innovation that we have been able to co-create, sustain, and nurture the global infrastructure known as the Internet. The Internet is a pioneering worldwide infrastructure that, alone, enables e-commerce technologies and other creative forms of global electronic trade.

We would like to thank those individuals who, in so many different ways, have contributed to the marvels of the global Internet and e-commerce. We hope that this work will inspire others to share their insights and research, as we continue to move forward in the various fields of e-commerce. May we offer our compliments and thanks to all of the global e-commerce practitioners, researchers, academicians, and business leaders for a job well done!

Part 1
What Is E-commerce?

This section of the book serves as the beginning to an exploration of several topics in electronic commerce, or e-commerce. It covers the notion of worldwide e-societies and growth trends around the world indicating that many corporations are taking advantage of worldwide e-commerce solutions. In simple terms, e-commerce is the ability to integrate electronic network solution elements into a particular problem resolution. These can be many different types of electronic solution elements, from billing interfaces, to order management elements, to supply chain elements, to even the spoken language environments of the computer design itself. Many of those achievements that contribute to establishing a fundamental networking infrastructure around the world are considered to be contributing to e-commerce types of technologies. Some of these global networking solutions alone will help us to enable new dynamic capabilities for change and growth for many global societies. Presidential candidates announce their candidacy utilizing the Internet (U.S. Presidential Candidate Steven Forbes, March 1999 announcement). Where else can the Internet play a valuable role? Throughout history change has proven to be inevitable, and if one considers any single change agent alone, none is more impressive than the global Internet infrastructure and its worldwide subnetworks. These complex networks are the single key to the success of e-commerce and an electronic expansion of our global economies.

In the following chapters we will describe several foundations of the Internet and e-commerce, including the distinction of e-commerce solutions from e-business solutions, the business elements required to compete in e-business, and many other key factors to consider about global e-commerce.

Electronic commerce (hereinafter referred to as e-commerce) has been defined in a number of ways. For example, e-commerce can be defined as the transaction, pre-transaction, and posttransaction set of activities that are performed by buyers and sellers through the Internet (or an intranet), where there is a clear intent to buy or sell. This e-commerce definition embraces an evolving set of technical designs, technical implementations, and advanced (or reengineered) business practices.

There are many packaged software and network-based applications that link multiple enterprises and consumers for the purpose of conducting e-business (for example, presales, sales, and postsales). There are also many corporate e-business strategies aimed at optimizing these types of relationships between businesses and between businesses and consumers—through the utilization of Internet technologies. There are commonly noted strategies involving business processes (for example, procurement, selling, auctions, order status, checking accounts, securities accounts, payment processes, shipping methods) that frequently cross enterprise sectors or have common boundaries from one business to another.

Online "service" environments where e-commerce technologies—universal messaging, internetworking, collaborative networking environments, pervasive computing, and many other types of applications—enable individuals to use the Internet. Large corporate enterprises (and other entities) seek to conduct their own business practice(s) utilizing the Internet. Today, many tools and consulting and systems integration services are directly involved as part of enabling these e-commerce types of environments. Many of the large corporation's business strategies, enhanced business processes, and altered business environments have been implemented utilizing Internet technologies.

It is important to point out that e-commerce is becoming a fundamental way of processing transactions between buyers, sellers, and suppliers worldwide. The fundamental stimuli driving this evolution to a state of global e-commerce is that e-commerce is new and perceived as a much simpler way to grow. Everyone seems to agree that e-commerce is quickly altering the dynamics of many of our global business models. This new shift is a fundamental requirement of those global enterprises that strive to achieve global commerce and trade, which will require (and it is almost here now) faster and more efficient telecommunications methods from both their suppliers and consumers. This will be an important milestone in enabling many forms of innovative trading environments, throughout the global e-commerce market.

The current global business environment is extremely competitive and requires faster, more attractive responses to its diverse customers communities. This results in the need for a more timely delivery of their goods and services.

Generally speaking, e-commerce has the need for businesses to manage global trade, leveraging their own intranets, in conjunction with the Internet, and many types of other Internet commerce technologies. This notion connects the definition of e-commerce with the exchange of many forms of data. Some examples of data exchange scenarios might be buying patterns, purchase orders, invoices, shipping documents, billing information, currency, medical information, taxation information. Many other forms of electronic data are required by trading partners (for example, buyers and suppliers) to electronically conduct business over the Internet.

One example of a traditional technology that has carried over to Internet technologies utilized in e-commerce, is Electronic Data Interchange (EDI). There are several Internet-based approaches to conducting EDI utilizing the Internet. Thus, companies are preserving some of the already well-established and highly structured methods of electronic data interchange and its formats of intercorporate information. There are also examples of "back-office" methods that have been enhanced, as a direct result of utilizing certain e-commerce technologies within a company's own Intranet infrastructure. A few examples are accounting and general ledger processes, billing, supply chain management, and security.

The e-commerce environments in many cases enable an automated displacement of a manual, labor-intensive set of processes. One can imagine the potential savings in a simple example of exchanging transaction documentation electronically, resulting in reduced business cycles, fewer errors, higher volumes, and lower costs. This helps the enterprise remain competitive.

Consider e-commerce as an evolutionary set of innovative technological solutions, virtual applications, and networked interbusiness processes. These connections enable the electronic transfer of vast amounts of e-business functionalities, for instance, procurement (both suppliers and consumers), order entry and audit services, high-volume transaction processing, electronic bill presentment and payment services, production and supply chain services, inventory and warehousing services, order fulfillment and logistic services, workflow management, and customer support and support services (Gartner Group, 1997, *Electronic Commerce Strategies (ECS) Strategic Analysis Report*).

A European definition of e-commerce, according to Dr. Reinhold Büescher of the European Commission, "is simply doing business electronically." Dr. Büescher suggests that a fundamental technology for processing business transactions today, using electronic e-commerce approaches, is by means of electronic EDI. It is estimated today that approximately 120,000 of the 2 million companies in the United States are EDI trading partners; only about 6 percent of the companies that could be using EDI are using EDI.

The EDI technology utilizes highly standardized electronic transaction formats, often using dedicated lines or value-added networks (VANS). EDI formats are carefully tailored to industry-specific standards. Many global enterprises are beginning to integrate the use of e-commerce into their ongoing business application interfaces. This approach allows for the integration and reuse of many other stabilized application environments (for example, back-office processes, accounting, general ledger, EDI, order management) that will predictably emerge as an electronic interaction, or e-commerce transaction, between businesses.

The definition of e-commerce suggested by the United Nations is doing business electronically. This includes the sharing of various forms of business information by any electronic means (such as electronic mail or messaging, World Wide Web technology, electronic bulletin boards, smart cards, electronic funds transfers, and electronic data interchange) among suppliers, customers, governmental agencies, and other businesses in order to conduct and execute transactions in business, administrative, and consumer activities.[1]

---

[1] Adopted in December 1997 by the United Nations' CEFACT (Centre for Facilitation of Procedures and Practices for Acquisition, Commerce and Transport.

One recent commentary highlights the different views of e-commerce critics. The article suggests that some sources portray it as a revolutionary set of technology applications that will turn the Internet into a transformational engine for global economic growth. Others see e-commerce as a highly optimized channel for interacting with suppliers, business partners, and customers. The article suggests that both views are correct. It seems to reason that the latter premise is probably the more notable scenario of the two; however, the term "revolutionary" is better stated as "evolutionary."

This same notion purports that e-commerce is changing the nature of fundamental business transactions. For example, today we are able to use several forms of online payment systems to buy goods in a store, payment validations by telephone, and other options. Now we have the Internet with a practical minimum transaction cost that sometimes averages 20 cents per transaction. Basically, this means that the process of transferring, verifying, authorizing, and debiting the payment takes at least 20 cents from the margin of any given product or service. In many cases, the current systems and massive networking protocols used for payments can raise total transaction costs to as much to as $1.00. For example, think of an automated teller machine (ATM) utilized for banking transactions. With e-commerce as a new set of technologies we will find that emerging banks will bring online transaction costs to well under 1 cent (possibly as low as 1/10 or 1/100 of a cent) by early in the next century. These e-commerce technologies are what make it possible for businesses (such as banks) to charge perhaps as little as one-quarter of a cent (or less) for services, while still providing a profit margin. This opens the doors for new and faster ways for an enterprise to interact with its consumers—a win-win situation. The ubiquity of the global network, using e-commerce technologies, can quickly turn a continual stream of nickels into a river of dollars. While faster machines and more advanced e-commerce technologies will do their part to lower transaction costs, the impact may then be relatively small. In the end, technology will increase the speed and rate of transaction processing, but the issues that need be proven are whether it will indeed lower the cost, while continuing to make the transaction profitable. Does this hold true as we progress into the 21st Century?

A very high-level definition of e-commerce simply states that a company or individual is doing business, utilizing predominately electronic (Internet) methods. E-commerce solutions might include the use of many different types of online facilities for doing business: order registration, electronic catalogs, billing and presentment systems, and more. Online Design Quality approaches might include the Internet, intranets, extranets, and private networks—and possibly, other commercial grade networking facilities that enable end users to communicate with other end users. "Doing business" in effect becomes a set of buying and selling activities, primarily of specific goods and/or services; this makes up the overall e-commerce transaction. Complicated perhaps, but not complex.

The communication between buyers and sellers merely initiates e-commerce: E-business processes of shopping from e-catalogs, buying, billing, supplying, and other customer services are now commonly found as Internet e-business practices. The broader definition of e-commerce can often support transactions between businesses and between business and consumers for almost any type of goods—hard, soft, and digital. It is estimated that 67,000 new people each day become new users of the Internet. Timing is therefore prudent for any company to ask themselves, "What can we do that we are not already doing to improve our Internet presence?" Another important consideration is, "What will make our customers want to return to our site, daily, to utilize our site for their own e-business needs?" Also, "What will attract new end users to our Internet site, daily, even hourly, or even by the minute, to take advantage of our company's services or products?" If consumers do not have a need for us, our products, or our services, then, of course, they will probably not return. If the consumer does, in fact, have a need for the products or services offered by your site(s), then what separates your Internet site(s) from competitive sites? Why will consumers remember your site and then return? And never forget, consumers of Internet-based businesses are usually only one mouse click away from leaving your business, only to explore the offerings of your competitors. This is the reality of operations within the Internet environment, and it is in part a virtue in the Internet, unsurpassed by any other marketing method. Surfing the Web—who would have thought of this back in the 1950s? What is in store then for the year 2020? Let's continue to explore this futuristic notion throughout this book, appropriately entitled an "exploration" of e-commerce.

1

E-commerce: An Historical Perspective

....

During 1969, a special United States government project was initiated that has since been marked as the birth of the Internet. Why is the Internet important to the history of electronic commerce? It is primarily the advent of the Internet, and all of its global subnetworks, that enables so many different forms of e-commerce utilities. The United States Department of Defense sponsored the Internet development initiative as a special project of the Advanced Research Projects Agency (ARPA). The original purpose of this ARPA project was to link various computer systems located in widely dispersed geographies, enabling the sharing of academic, scientific, and military data. The notion of Internet forms of electronic commerce was not even a consideration of primary importance. Since that time, the United States Department of Defense gradually allowed commercial computer users not only to utilize, but also to ultimately control network traffic over the Internet (by assimilation of a vast number of interoperable networking rings).

The development of the Internet as a strategic means for conducting electronic commerce, or e-commerce, was caused (in part) by the need of many businesses to overcome the limitations of their own private networks. The results have been the Internet's emergence as a conduit for many innovative commercial uses: e-mail, electronic bill presentation and payment environments, electronic catalogs of products and services—all designed for consumers with Internet access. The Internet is currently being shaped as a global *information repository* using a variety of *push and pull* technologies to reach all Internet end users, globally.

THE INTERNET USED FOR BUSINESS

Today, the Internet is very active in business-to-consumer, consumer-to-consumer, and government-to-consumer contexts. The use of the Internet in a business-to-business context appears to be rapidly gaining momentum. In recent years, the Department of

7

Defense has turned the Internet over to commercial users. As a result, its current use has increased significantly in business-to-consumer transactions and in business-to-business transactions. These rapidly growing transaction volumes have been accommodated by value-added network providers or other private corporate networks. One of the Internet's main commercial applications has been advertising, by presenting electronic catalogs of products and services to a vast number of potential buyers and suppliers.

INTERNET HISTORY

Technically speaking, the Internet is a computer-based network of multiple interconnected public and private networks that are connected together throughout many areas of the world. It started in 1969 as a project of the Advanced Research Projects Agency (ARPA) of the U.S. Department of Defense, for the sole purpose of linking various kinds of computer systems, at that time installed and scattered all over the world. Its original purpose was to create a global, electronic, collaborative environment that would be used primarily by scientists, key military personnel, and educators.

The Internet has the potential to evolve into a significant agent of social change. Its impact is pervasive throughout all facets of our societies (for example, business, government, education, medicine, manufacturing, supply chain management, and distribution). It has grown into a major conduit for the distribution of data and knowledge, by creating many network computing environments distributed around the world. Critical applications are transported to where they will be the most effective. Networked collaborative computing environments continue to empower global enterprises and consumers' homes, by placing more power in the hands of the key decision makers who can adapt to the ever-changing market conditions.

The attractiveness of the Internet and Internet commerce is growing significantly throughout global business communities. These communities generally comprise customers, suppliers, and organizations such as banks, government agencies, and shipping companies—with whom an enterprise does business on a regular basis. The Internet provides the transport mechanisms for the mutual exchange of electronic information, which includes orders, invoices, shipping instructions, material specifications, engineering drawings, product catalogs, shipment status, and other product-related data. It is this trend of applying e-commerce technologies that has transformed business practices into a new environment for customers and suppliers. For instance, it is now fairly straightforward to monitor many changes in a particular marketplace, thus inviting the introduction of faster, more efficient, and more effective supply chains.

The recent surge in Internet use has nurtured the introduction of, and the expansion of, global e-commerce environments. This development in itself has been nothing short of phenomenal.

Several 1998 statistics measure this growth pattern: 70.5 million (34.9 percent) of the 202 million adults in the United States now (that is, as of month year) use the Internet regularly. Almost 80 million people in North America are online, an increase of 21 million in 9 months. Internet use has increased 340 percent since 1995, when 18 million were online. More than 50 percent of those aged 16 to 34 are active Internet users, and 20 million people have made online purchases, up from 10 million just 9 months ago. It is now estimated that 48 million people use the Internet to shop. Furthermore, 71 percent of those end users making the actual purchases online are men. It is estimated that 17 percent of those aged 50 (and over) are actively online, representing approximately 13 million people in North America. Included in this growth of Internet use are senior business executives and high-level government leaders. In fact, during 1999, a presidential candidate announced his appointment to the candidate race on the Internet (Steve Forbes).

The statistics come from survey studies that investigate Internet use by senior corporate executives. These survey results indicate that 90 percent of CEOs, CFOs, and CIOs around the world have Internet access. Additional statistics also indicate that 71 percent of this executive group use many Internet sites for business purposes at least once a week. Furthermore, 45 percent of senior government officials and 35 percent of corporate executives are comfortable using the Internet.

A primary reason for this exponential growth of e-commerce is its convenience and variety, which can be of great value in our daily decision-making processes. Many e-commerce technology providers are now trying to rapidly develop applications and services to address the many diverse requirements of global businesses. Problem resolution endeavors include these efforts: reducing time-consumption for simple electronic transactions, increasing availability while providing faster telecommunications capabilities worldwide, and faster reactionary capabilities to address indicators of *change* in both global and local markets. Other problems areas with e-commerce relate to shoppers' expectations for telecommunication speed and the lack of access for less advantaged people, especially those in less developed countries. One constant challenge of e-commerce is information privacy and security, which were once considered primary flaws in Internet global networks. Tremendous strides have been made in each of these areas, and progress will continue as the Internet continues to evolve.

THE INTERNET'S POTENTIAL FOR E-COMMERCE

The evidence supporting e-commerce growth and potential can be staggering when one considers the accomplishments in this field just over the last few years. In 1997 19.7 million Americans visited retail Internet sites from their homes. United States e-commerce transactions resulted in $707 million dollars in revenue in 1996, increasing to an impressive $2.6 billion dollars in 1997, and to an incredible high of

$5.8 billion in 1998. It is estimated that e-commerce infrastructures are expected to generate, or enable, $34–$37.5 billion dollars in revenue by the year 2002.

Active Internet shoppers rated convenience as the number one reason they prefer to shop online. Approximately 54% of American businesses are estimated to have e-commerce Internet pages.

Small businesses use the Internet to increase their business reach each and every day. They are creating Internet sites by deploying e-commerce and e-business services, thus enabling them to increase their visibility and find new customers. The Internet helps provide potential customers with information about their products, services, and support in any particular region of the world. Statistics show that of many of the small businesses in the United States, approximately 46 percent of those business owners feel that their Internet sites are absolutely worth the effort, time, and money invested.

This phenomenal growth of Internet e-commerce has a potential reach into many geographic regions in the world, including Asia, Europe, the Pacific Rim, Latin America, and more. As one example, the China Internet Corp. (CIC) is planning to deploy the Internet (with Microsoft) to the 1.2 billion people in China. The CIC currently collects news from Reuters and Bloomberg, which it in turn sends to Beijing for translation into Chinese; the information is then made available to CIC's online services. Today, it is estimated that 1.18 million people are using the Internet in mainland China. It is estimated that nearly 80 percent of Chinese Internet users have purchased merchandise over the Internet. This same end-user community regularly acquired information about entertainment, sports, and businesses.

The incredibly vast amount of information available on the Internet is fostering the need for information repository management and information brokerage services. Information brokers are now able to quickly search directories, scan indexes, and develop complex search procedures, using many global information repositories—in order to obtain critical information for their clients and, conversely, about their clients. Information brokerage services are becoming one of the major growth industries evolving from the emergence of e-commerce over the global Internet.

The Internet is the main platform for widespread distribution of e-commerce solutions, enabling millions of daily systematic transactions to occur. Each day, more and more e-commerce technology providers are resolving key concerns and business requirements, demanded by global consumers and businesses. These providers are developing their own innovations into highly valued end-user Internet tools. For example, Netscape and Microsoft Web browsers are used as open-viewing interfaces to global Internet sites. In this vast arena, anyone can find a multitude of methods to accomplish electronic banking, electronic payment, multimedia enhancements, buying and selling, and much more. For the first time, business policies, local laws, and other previously controlled environments are being challenged. Many governments around the world are taking advantages of this incredible global infrastructure and realizing the benefits of becoming a part of a larger, very powerful, global e-commerce society.

An incredible number of industrial and private-sector suppliers provide automated Internet tools. These tools include information services, increased bandwidth automation in telecommunication pipelines, improved security and encryption schemes, secure procedures and tools for monetary transactions, and, of course, the standard application development tools utilized to develop interactive applications for marketing and advertising strategies. This is true in every vertical market (for example, the insurance industry and the medical, manufacturing, legal, military, and government sectors). With the resolution of these key concerns, and by meeting the requirements of the global Internet user communities, the worldwide expansive growth trends of e-commerce on the Internet will significantly accelerate in both global industrial and social structures, to reach levels still to be defined. The emergence of the Internet and its effect on e-commerce are phenomenons that cannot be dismissed as passing trends. The Internet is one of the great agents of change that will affect all sectors of society and have a major impact on history.

This trend is all part of a larger, more global technological evolution. The many instruments of e-commerce, using the Internet as global transport mechanisms, will have unpredictable and unanticipated effects—effects that could lead to other, more profound changes in our global societies. In summary, the combination of Internet enablement technologies into large global network infrastructures, combined with faster telecommunication technologies available globally, and government regulations related to global Internet usage suggests that global communities (e-societies, of a sort) are enabled through many worldwide e-commerce infrastructures.

The Industrial Revolution introduced many important inventions that helped to improve the effectiveness, production levels, and quality of their Internet products. These technological innovations served not only to help businesses but also to improve our society. For example, the steam engine was invented by Thomas Savery in 1698. This technological breakthrough led to other innovations, like Richard Trevithick's steam locomotive (in 1804) and Robert Fulton's steamboat (in 1807), that revolutionized how people and goods were transported. Eli Whitney's cotton gin improved the quality of clothing and the speed at which yarns could be provided to clothing manufacturers. In 1908 Henry Ford introduced the Model "T" automobile, and in 1924 mass production, by means of the first component-based assembly plant, of the Model "T" was accomplished. In these few examples, the societal change agents that followed the innovation's became quite clear. As illustrated above, Society was introduced to several major advances in both lifestyles and business practices.

Today we live in a new era, in another form of the information age, where ubiquitous knowledge is ever changing, as are the ways in which our global societies can now interact electronically. For example, the Internet introduces a new way for people to communicate in not months, weeks, days, or hours, but in microseconds or even nanoseconds through cables, fiber optics, and the air. These communication capabilities are possible from our homes, our offices, or our automobiles—almost anywhere that we can imagine. The Internet has the fastest adoption rate of any new electronic medium. It's taken less than 5 years to get 50 million people connected. It took radio

38 years, television 13 years, and cable 10 years to reach an audience of 50 million people. The Internet phenomenon began as a military and academic tool, but it has now become one of the most fascinating technological shifts ever affecting the world.

The attractiveness of the Internet and Internet-based e-commerce is growing significantly across global business communities. A *business community,* generally speaking, comprises customers, suppliers, and organizations (such as banks, government agencies, and manufacturing and shipping companies) and is the environment where that enterprise does business, electronically, on a regular basis. The Internet, often referred to as the "information highway" or simply "the Web," is constructed for the networking transport and the mutual exchange of all kinds of electronic information, which includes (but is not necessarily limited to) the following:

- Order management information
- Invoices with accounting information
- Bill presentment and bill payment information
- Shipping instructions
- Shipment status information
- Material specifications
- Medical specifications
- Engineering drawings
- Product and services catalogs
- Supply-chain information
- Product manufacturing information
- Product movement data

The world of e-commerce has emerged into a new computing landscape for computer-savvy customers and suppliers, allowing them to monitor changes in their market space while facilitating more efficient and effective supply chains. Other very good reasons for the growth of e-commerce environments are its simplicity, its convenience, and its captivating variety. In the global marketplaces, e-commerce technology providers are now working to develop innovative applications and services to address the ever-changing requirements of almost all businesses, and definitely many of the key consumer needs, which include (but are not limited to) the following:

- Reducing time for simple transactions to complete
- Increasing availability of consumer and industrial goods, products, and services
- Faster reaction capabilities to meet current demands of the markets
- Forecasting future changes in the market, based on more information
- Continued improvements of slower telecommunication connections

The list is almost unbounded when one considers the various countries connecting to the Internet every day. What can these additional connections bring in the way of new technological solutions in e-commerce? Management of innovation has given us a colorful historical perspective on the Internet and its brief history to date.

2

The Internet Evolution and Social Changes

....

$\mathbf{M}$any companies have clearly positioned themselves as global leaders in the Internet e-commerce and e-business market spaces. Global chief executive officers describe the growth of the Internet in ways that suggest it impacts us economically, socially, and educationally—they describe it as an evolutionary agent of change. This phenomenon is happening now; it is not something predicted for the future. The Internet has the fastest adoption rate of any new technology-based medium. In fact, it has taken fewer than 5 years to get 50 million people connected around the world. It took radio 38 years, television 13 years, and cable 10 years to reach an audience of 50 million. The Internet phenomenon has now become one of the most fascinating technological shifts ever to affect the world. It has created a virtual community of global e-societies.

A FIFTH PARADIGM IN COMPUTING

In the 1950s, the world was first introduced to the paradigm of machine automation and computing. We refer to this as the first paradigm in computing. Next came the advent of mainframe computers and computing systems: the second paradigm in computing. Then, an incredible change came about through some clever concepts and management of innovation (and risk) in the introduction of the personal computer (PC): This we refer to as the third paradigm in computing. Then, just as the world began to understand the added value derived from innovative application programming techniques, we quickly discovered the need for client/server designs and more "open" architectures: the fourth paradigm in computing. The fifth paradigm is a new paradigm in social-economic thinking, now being realized by virtue of the Internet and global e-commerce. We explore what the fifth paradigm means for a vast number of global e-societies and global business enterprises as we progress through this (and other chapters) of this book.

It has taken fewer than five years after the birth of the Internet for it to grow to approximately 90 million people online, and heading toward hundreds of millions of people. CEOs assert (and rightfully so) that the Internet is a global medium that will transport knowledge in multiple languages. They describe the compelling phenomenon of "Internet leap-frog" as a competitive contest where the stakes are high. Those geographies with high concentrations of Internet participants will quickly surpass other regions in production, productivity, and profitable economic growth. It is common knowledge that at least one-fifth of the world's population lives in China and India; together well over 1 billion people live in those two countries. If just 4 percent of our global population was linked to the Internet, the worldwide number of end users would (at least) double in size. That is a profound thought. It is this line of "leadership" reasoning that continues to launch corporations as innovative global leaders in the industry of Internet e-commerce (see Figure 2.1).

Many global corporate philosophies introduce intriguing insights about societal transformation into global "networked societies." Based on this premise of a fifth paradigm, we could then easily imagine e-societies in a "highly networked economy."

INDUSTRIAL CHANGES WITH THE INTERNET

The changes introduced by the Internet are very quickly changing the way commercial and industry goods are purchased and sold. Even by the most conservative esti-

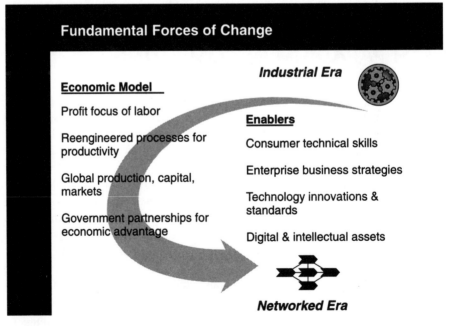

Figure 2.1
E-commerce solutions are effecting fundamental changes across all industries.

mates, e-commerce is currently estimated to be a $200 billion marketplace (all currency amounts throughout the book are expressed as U.S. dollars). The volume of network-based business transactions in financial services is expected to grow at least fourfold by the year 2001, to more than $5 billion (see Figure 2.2).

It will be during this same time period, 1999–2001, that both travel and entertainment will become multibillion dollar online market segments. Other e-commerce volume estimates for the same period are equally impressive. For example, in Japan e-commerce is estimated to grow to a $20 billion industry. It is, however, important to understand the nature of the transformation underway: Not only is what people think when they hear the term e-commerce, or Internet-based buying and selling, evolving, but we are active participants in an evolutionary societal transformation, one that may have an unpredictable social-economic result (see Figure 2.3). As an example, we are now able to help people medically by using the Internet as an information transport mechanism for highly skilled medical practitioners. That is, medical practitioners are able to view *live* imagery of a patient (for instance, via magnetic resonance imagery) while sitting at their desks, perhaps many miles from patient at the MRI site.

Therefore, it comes as no surprise that medical practitioners are able to perform robotic surgeries, using some of these same telecommunications technologies. These surgeons perform delicate procedures while miles away from the patient undergoing the surgical procedure. *Medical Miracles*, a feature on robotic surgeries, were described by

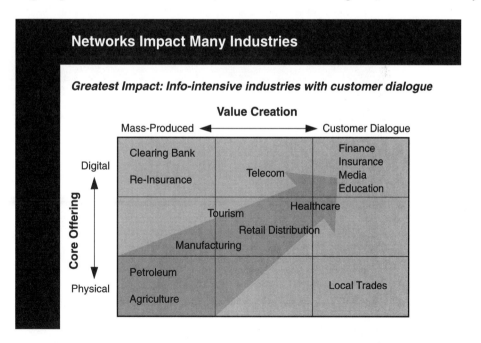

Figure 2.2

The Internet and its many e-commerce environments have introduced diverse changes across a wide variety of industrial segments.

a robotic heart surgeon, Dr. Didier de Canniere, in *Life Magazine*'s Fall 1998 issue. The article notes, *"The surgeon sounds more like a teenager playing a video game than a cardiac specialist performing one of the first robotic coronary bypass operations."* Will robotic surgeries too, one day become a long-distance procedure utilizing the Internet as a "backbone?" Will it become a medical-centric e-business?

Louis Gerstner, CEO of IBM, keenly distinguishes the definitions of e-commerce and e-business by defining e-business as the ways people and industrial enterprises realize the value of important *virtual* computer-based interactions and transactions. This includes (but is not limited to) many global enterprise personnel, global trading partners in a supply chain, teachers and students, doctors and patients, governments and public sectors, just to name a few. Mr. Gerstner stated quite candidly that "everything will change." Bill Gates, CEO of Microsoft, also states that we, as a diverse society, have not yet even started to realize the changes that are evolving— changes that are due, in part, to powerful technology mediums such as the Internet and e-commerce (see Figure 2.4). Both Mr. Gerstner and Mr. Gates are considered world leaders in the areas of Internet commerce.

Airlines are using online auctions to drive down ticket costs for last-minute travelers. Many daycare centers are using Internet-based "kiddie cams" to provide instant images on the parents' computer screens (at work or at home) of their children engaged in various child-care activities, at that moment, in the technologically enabled daycare center. Dr. Bob Ballard of the Jason Project is able to network together, with the assis-

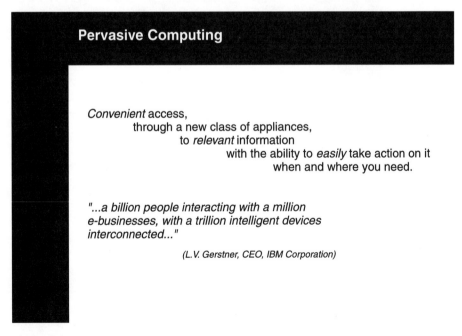

Pervasive Computing

Convenient access,
 through a new class of appliances,
  to *relevant* information
   with the ability to *easily* take action on it
    when and where you need.

"...a billion people interacting with a million e-businesses, with a trillion intelligent devices interconnected..."

(L.V. Gerstner, CEO, IBM Corporation)

Figure 2.3
Lou Gerstner summarizes his company's strategy for global e-commerce solutions.

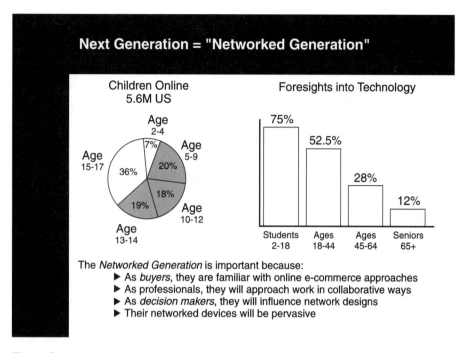

Figure 2.4

The Internet, and all of its subnetworks, are major change agents toward our future state.

tance of EDS, many children around the world; while participating from their own class-rooms, the children drive the Jason Robot down into the Old Faithful Geyser, in Yellowstone National Park, via the network. The transmissions and communications between all the children, in their classrooms around the world, and the Jason Robot were provided by the Internet. A simple joystick is all that the children need to drive the Jason Robot down into the geyser. All of Jason's imagery is delivered to the children in real-time, on large screens, and it is fascinating to watch as each selected global student drives the robot. What a fantastic accomplishment; our congratulations to Dr. Ballard for this magnificent milestone performance in using Internet-based technologies.

The global stock and bond markets are another interesting phenomenon. Financial experts have hypothesized that one of the reasons for our highly volatile stock market today, which has been realized worldwide, may be the ability of casual investors to buy and sell stocks and bonds, simply and quickly from home and online. Individual online participation in the stock market has, in some cases, offset the need for a "face to face" relationship with a stock broker. This development has both positive and negative effects—overall, it represents an incredible leap for technology and industry.

A decade ago this "Internet Brokerage" would have been unheard of; then again, so was the Internet (for the most part). The Internet enables this new Investment Brokerage capability by allowing immediate views into the financial stock and bond markets. It is hard to believe that it was only during the mid-to-late 1970s that the notion of a desktop, nonnetworked, personal computer was first conceived. Then the personal computer was described as a instrument that could automate the processes of writing a simple letter or perhaps managing a budget through use of crude financial spreadsheet programs. The PC was a great milestone in the computing industry (see Figure 2.5).

Today, every major religious denomination in the world is on the Internet. As an example, the Pope started conducting live Web broadcasts of many religious services for a worldwide audience.

This year, approximately 4.5 million people in the United States will use the Internet to shop for an automobile. In 1997, approximately 135,000 people who made a purchase, representing approximately 1 percent of all U.S. sales of new automobile, did so. Some forecasts suggest that these estimates could grow much higher in the future.

The U.S. Air Force has started putting the first of nearly $30 billion in annual requests for bids on the Internet—requesting responses from suppliers for everything from erasers to jet engines to warfare agents. The USAF belives that it can reduce its operational costs by millions of dollars by using Internet technologies.

Monterrey Tech, a school in Mexico, has approximately 70,000 students connected to the Internet and accessing more than 2500 course offerings. The Sloan

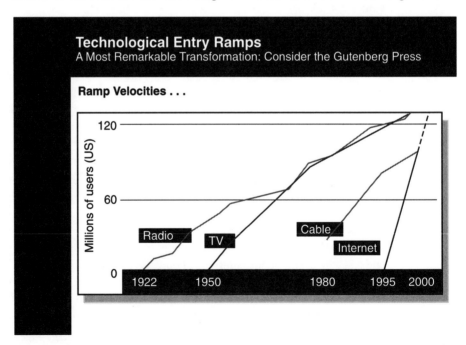

Figure 2.5

Most industry segments maintain a positive and aggressive rate of e-commerce adaptation.

School of Management at the Massachusetts Institute of Technology (MIT) used to print and mail approximately 30,000 enrollment applications annually; now the school will not accept any enrollment application unless it is submitted on the Internet. Many universities around the world now accept online registrations and encourage e-mail as a medium for course-work exchanges between professors and students.

The fifth paradigm suggests this: "One could easily imagine e-societies in a highly networked economy." Does this exist yet? We seem to be well on our way. It is fairly clear, though, that the Internet and all of its subnetworks, in one form or another, will remain a part of that fantastic future.

3

The Distinction: E-commerce and E-business

....

The e-commerce marketplace has been defined in a number of ways. For example, we might consider e-commerce as a set of electronic, networked transactions, including those pretransaction and posttransaction activities performed by buyers and sellers. Another e-commerce viewpoint might best be described as an evolving utility of packaged software applications that link multiple enterprises, and consumers, for the purpose of conducting electronic business (presales, sales, and postsales). No matter what the definition, e-commerce requires business strategies focused on optimizing the relationships between businesses, as well as between businesses and consumers, making sure each is capable of using information technologies.

The topic of electronic business (or e-business) will often include business-to-business process automation (like buying and selling). Ensuring that e-business solutions are effective at performing what they were designed to perform can get very complicated in several areas. Some examples are these: procurement (auction, bidding, and sourcing), selling (manufacturing and supply chain management), order status checking (shipping and logistics), bill presentment and payment. These processes, by definition, almost always cross external enterprise boundaries and potentially many other e-business service environments where e-commerce technologies are being utilized by end users, business enterprises, and other parties that wish to do business across the Internet. Most e-business environments require one (or more) e-commerce technologies to complete (in a safe and secure manner) that specific business transaction. Internet technologies like security, data encryption, e-billing, and e-payment methods are always good examples of the types of technology sets that enable opportunities. This holds true around the world. Each of these technology sets, however, possesses its own difficult and challenging ideas as to exactly *how* e-business practitioners might choose to implement it into e-commerce solutions (see Figure 3.1).

The issues surrounding e-business operations can become complicated across several dimensions. There are many innovative approaches to adequately ensure integrity of the e-business transaction: This integrity is paramount. Facing global e-business challenges may involve resolving any foreign language issues, resolving

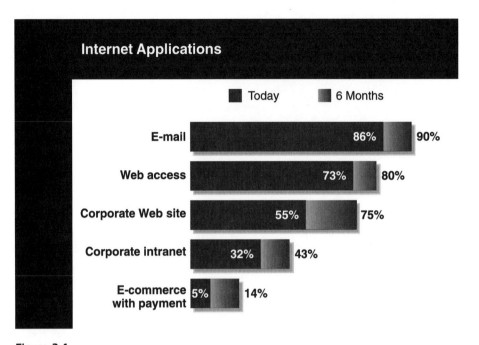

Figure 3.1

Internet e-commerce solutions are progressing quickly throughout several different areas.

technological incompatibilities, dealing with taxation issues, and reconciling mone-tary conversion issues. This is just a simple example of what is involved in establish-ing e-businesses that are capable of maintaining a global presence. The actual *content-hosting* of e-business information—e-catalogs, imagery, pricing information, terms and conditions, and rights—requires complicated schemes for end-user identification, registration, authentication, catalog updates, on-demand product pricing changes, security, billing and rights, and other complicated, lower-level topics.

Some have stressed that e-commerce is nothing more than a fundamental way of processing business transactions between buyers, sellers, and suppliers. This thought represents another straightforward approach in reasoning.

One interesting observation is that the evolution of e-commerce is an almost new business operations environment, one that is changing the dynamics of other related business environments. This idea becomes more obvious when we consider the requirements of global e-business enterprises for improved communications networks from both their suppliers and customers. This suggests that the current global business environment is extremely competitive, requiring faster responses to its customers and resulting in a more timely delivery of goods and services.

Internet e-commerce transactions satisfy the need for businesses to manage trade while leveraging (across the Internet) many specific Internet e-commerce technologies. This requires solution sets of e-commerce with the exchange of business-specific data.

Some examples of these types of data elements could be related to the following: purchase orders, manufacturing, invoicing, shipping documentation, billing, and other accounts receivable information. Basically, they include any forms of information required by other business trading partners. These forms are often e-documents, and they are electronically exchanged using the Internet. In this specific example, we see some newer versions of older technologies like Electronic Data Interchange (EDI). This particular example is interesting because even though the technologies have changed, the underlying information has not. The EDI data formats are very specific, and in many areas of the corporate world these EDI practices are deeply engrained into the corporation's business processes.

One observation is that e-commerce introduces an automated replacement for manual and labor-intensive processes. So, what's new about that? Exchanging electronic transaction documentation helps reduce business cycles, accounts for consistency and fewer errors, and generally lowers costs to the business. This helps any business enterprise to excel and continue to remain competitive in a global (or local) environment.

Some might say that e-commerce is an evolutionary set of technological solutions, enabling virtual applications and networked business processes to be joined in harmony. These application connections enable the electronic transfer of procurement, order entry, transaction processing, payment, production, inventory, and fulfillment information, and even the exchange of customer support information, between business trading partners and consumers (see Figure 3.2).

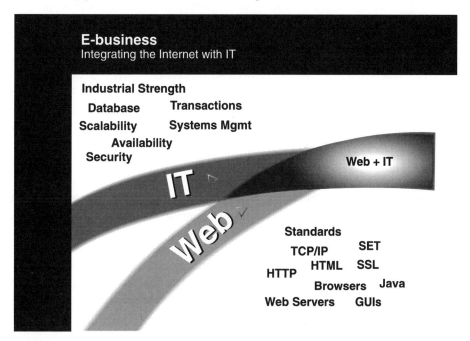

Figure 3.2

Integrating e-commerce technologies with daily business activities is challenging, but the rewards are quite remarkable.

E-commerce, according to Dr. Reinhold Büescher of the European Commission, is simply conducting commerce electronically. Dr. Büescher suggests that the main technologies for processing business transactions electronically, today, are often executed by means of electronic data interchange (EDI). Currently, only about 120,000 of the 2 million companies in the United States are EDI trading partners; about 6 percent of the companies that could be using EDI are actually using EDI. Aside from the traditional systems that utilize EDI, Internet EDI technologies are now highly standardized and capable of performing these types of transactions. We can find, in areas of advanced Internet-enabled technologies, a multitude of networking protocols and sometimes dedicated lines or value-added networks (VANS). Notable areas of progress in this environment are tailored industry-specific IT software services, combined with Internet-enabled designs. It is now common to observe corporate enterprises beginning to integrate the use of e-commerce technologies into their business infrastructures and subnetworks. This will emerge as an electronic interaction between businesses, with their own suppliers and consumers, using the Internet. This should be, if it is not already, a part of every business enterprises strategy.

Another definition of e-commerce, suggested by the United Nations, is "doing business electronically." This general definition (again) includes the sharing of various forms of business information by any electronic means. These ideas were originally considered in December 1997 by the United Nations' CEFACT (Centre for Facilitation of Procedures and Practices for Acquisition, Commerce and Transport).

These premises allow us to bring forth technologies such as e-mail, universal messaging services, electronic bulletin boards, pervasive computing concepts, and, of course, electronic funds transfers and Internet-EDI. All of these concepts (and probably many more) are commonly found among suppliers, customers, governmental agencies, and many business environments found throughout Internet e-commerce solutions. It is by virtue of combining these types of e-commerce conceptual approaches that an enterprise is able to perform extremely efficient e-business administrative and support activities, related to important consumer-specific activities.

Some enterprises portray e-commerce as an evolutionary (not revolutionary) set of technology applications that will turn the Internet into a transformational engine for global economic growth. This can be true. Other enterprises see e-commerce as a highly optimized channel for interacting with their suppliers, business partners, and customers. This can also be true. In-practice, both viewpoints are very necessary and correct; simply ask those who have ordained the transformation.

These suppositions assert that e-commerce is changing the nature of *how* we perform business transactions. For example, today we use online payment systems to purchase goods and services, over the phone and on the Internet with a practical, minimum transaction cost that averages some 20 cents. Basically, what this means is that the process of transferring, verifying, authorizing, and debiting the payment takes at least 20 cents from the margin of any given product or service. In many cases, the current, more traditional systems and networking protocols used for payments can raise total transaction costs to as much as one dollar. The result: improved overall economics.

Continuous management of innovations in e-commerce solution development brings forth new and diverse sets of technologies on a frequent basis (like Internet telephones for a penny per minute). Many of these technology sets assist now in bringing online transaction costs to well under one cent by early in the next century. These e-commerce technologies will make it possible for a business to charge, let's say, one-quarter of a cent (or perhaps even less) for services, while still providing an attractive profit margin. This causes the keen individual to realize newer and faster ways for his or her enterprise to interact with its global customers. In turn, the realization provides the stimuli for newer, more innovative approaches in Internet e-commerce solutions development. The ubiquity of global networks using e-commerce technologies can quickly turn a continual stream of opportunity into a river of gold. Although faster machines and more advanced e-commerce technologies will do their part to lower transaction costs, the impact may be relatively small if some form of *Design Quality* of the overall solution is not established from the very beginning. This is true because even though technology can increase the speed and rate of many Internet transactions, the original issue was whether it will lower the cost, thereby making the transaction profitable. An important consideration for e-business practitioners is what is the level of *Design Quality* of this solution? Design Quality allows practitioners to qualify reasons for certain design concepts, and track those concepts in a qualitative manner.

Many e-commerce practices use diverse online facilities for *doing business*. These online facilities include the Internet, intranets, extranets, and private networks; for that matter they may include any networking facility that enables buyers to communicate with sellers or partners with partners. "Doing business" is a set of buying and selling activities of goods and/or services. This set is usually an e-business transaction design set, using the Internet as its transport medium. It can yield an immediate cost savings, if applied properly.

The actual communication between buyers and sellers then implements the e-commerce business processes of shopping, buying, and customer service (just to name a few). It is by this interaction that e-commerce can support transactions between businesses or between business and consumers—for almost any type of goods, including digital goods like streaming audio or streaming video.

The recurring theme (as it relates to the definition of e-commerce) is this: *Trading electronically* in business-to-business, business-to-consumer, and government-to-business contexts. As a point of distinction, note that this was not the original intent of the "inventors" of the Internet.

E-BUSINESS WITHIN A WORLD OF E-COMMERCE

There are many ways to consider e-commerce. Some think of e-commerce as an evolutionary set of technological solutions, virtual applications, and networked business processes. These connections enable the electronic transfer of procurement, order entry, transaction processing, payment, production, inventory, fulfillment, and customer support information between trading partners. Socrates claimed this: There are two answers which are both correct; however, the answers were determined by two diverse solutions. This statement applies to innovation, which is realized through many e-businesses environments on the Internet. Look at two similar Internet e-business sites, Barnes & Noble and Amazon.com. Both have been designed to market books, but they are very different in their strategy and deployment as an e-business (see Figure 3.3).

It is possible to highlight the different views of e-commerce pundits. This suggests that some sources portray e-commerce as an evolutionary set of technology applications that will turn the Internet into a transformational engine for global economic growth. Others see e-commerce as a highly optimized channel for interacting with suppliers, business partners, and customers. It is true that both views are correct.

E-commerce: What is it?

E-commerce is defined by business processes that support selling and buying of goods... and services over a network.

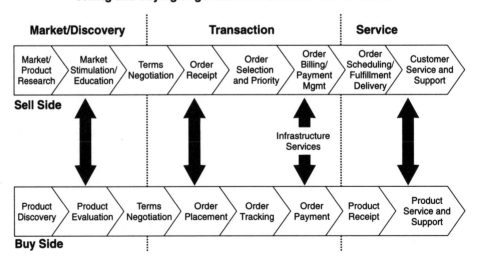

Figure 3.3

In general, e-commerce enables both the buying and selling of goods and/or services, while utilizing the Internet global infrastructure.

This supposition asserts that e-commerce is changing the nature of transactions. For example, today we use online payment systems to buy goods in a store, over the phone, and on the Internet with a practical, minimal transaction cost that averages 20 cents. Basically what this means is that the process of transfering, verifying, authorizing, and debiting the payment takes at least 20 cents (or 20% of one dollar) from the margin of a given product or service. In many cases, the current computer systems and protocols used for payments can raise total transaction costs to as much as one dollar, or even higher. Primarily, because the technologies are perhaps over a decade old, they may involve high maintenance and supports costs, and so become more difficult to justify as a cost-effective solution within the enterprise.

The technologies of e-commerce introduce a newer set of technologies that will bring online transaction costs to well under one cent (possibly as low as one-tenth or one-hundredth of a cent) by early in the next century. As an example, let's look at telephonic Internet protocols. The large telecom companies are carefully considering exactly *how* and *when* to enter this marketplace. It is purported that an individual will be able to make a call, anywhere in the world, for a penny a minute.

These e-commerce technological approaches will make it possible for a business to charge, let's say, one-quarter of a cent (or less) for services while still realizing a profit margin. This opens the door for newer and faster ways for an enterprise to interact with its customers over the Internet. The ubiquity of the global network using e-commerce technologies can quickly turn a continual stream of nickels and pence into a river of dollars and pounds. While faster machines and more advanced e-commerce technologies will do their part to lower transaction costs, their impact may be relatively small. And as we mentioned before, technology will increase the speed and rate of transactions, but the issue raised by some is whether it will really lower the overall costs—making the transaction more profitable. Exactly what will be the value-proposition during the second half of the next century?

As people all around the world become more involved in determining exactly what is an Internet server and selecting an e-commerce server that provides a comprehensive definition of e-commerce, they will quickly realize the intensity of any e-commerce solution. This can become complicated across several dimensions, depending on the e-business solution one is attempting to deliver. For example, consider the difference between world government bidding and auctioning systems and a local sporting goods store's system. The complexities as suggested by these two very different e-commerce solutions present both very simple and difficult technological challenges in the final e-commerce solution.

Consider the telecom companies around the world: MCI, WorldNet, AT&T, Italia Telecom, Global Crossing, New Zealand Telecom, Telephonica (in Spain), Britain's Cable & Wireless, and many others. These companies are quickly realizing the benefit of providing their own forms of Internet online support to their newly acquired Internet end-user customer population. Why? It is fairly simple and straightforward. The telecom companies stand to benefit (significantly) from the enhanced network traffic volumes of their global telecommunications infrastructures (their network pipes); however, this is not to say that Internet telephonic services are viewed as an advance that is welcomed with open-arms. Instead, it is an enormous challenge that does not come without a high amount of risk. Because of the impact to a given telecom company's revenue, contrasted by the increase in bandwidth of the IP networking infrastructures and costs, there will continue to be a gentle balance that is just now evolving. Fiber-optic lines and satellite communications will become business as usual during the next century. This, too, presents tremendous complexities to a telecom company's strategies. During the next few years, our globe will be laced (and is now) with expensive fiber-optic lines running across the ocean floor. These advanced telecommunication lines will continue to be laced from continent to continent. Satellites will continue to be deployed that are capable of supporting mobile telecommunication devices, at a cost-effective rate, for the casual end user. This is just the beginning.

Electronic commerce, simply speaking, is the use of online facilities for doing business. Online facilities include the Internet, intranets, extranets, private networks, and any other networking facility that enables buyers to communicate with sellers (or suppliers). "Doing business" is then simply a set of buying and selling activities of goods and services that make up a business transaction.

The communication between buyers and sellers influences the commerce: Business processes of shopping, buying, and customer service are often dramatically changed. For example, a consumer can buy an Oxford shirt from the Lands End Internet site, where that consumer can design his own shirt by pointing and clicking the computer mouse. In seconds, the consumer can view an image of the exact shirt that he is considering buying. Electronic commerce can support transactions between businesses and between businesses and consumers for almost any type of goods—hard, soft, and digital.

The recurring theme here is e-commerce as the act of trading electronically in the context of business-to-business, business-to-consumer, government-to-citizen, and government-to-business interactions. Although this may not have been the intent of the Internet's founding fathers, it is very clear that Internet e-commerce will change, in significant ways, our global societies.

E-BUSINESS DESIGN QUALITY ASPECTS

One way to define e-business is as the utilization of electronically enabled communication networks that allow enterprises to transmit and receive information in a variety of mediums, for a variety of purposes. The *Design Quality* aspects in exactly *how* this information is presented are paramount. The information can be used in numerous ways, including the transaction of business agreements, to conduct online auctions and to provide news updates, bond information, government securities information, weather conditions, airline traffic information, power grid tracking, and stock trade updates—and much more.

The e-business communications networks generally consist of intranets (networks within an enterprise), extranets (networks outside of but connected into the enterprise with controlled access to data repositories), and the Internet, which is the global network that is interconnected through numerous nodes managed by a multitude of Internet Service Providers (ISPs). The aspects of quality that tie all of these diverse networks together can be qualified from a *Design Quality* point of view.

Public and private-sector enterprises will require an increasing amount of support from external service providers as they are driven to reduce their costs. Because enterprises that become e-businesses will be enabled to operate globally, it will be important that the external services providers also have global support resources, utilizing the same guidelines of *Design Quality*. This will be very important to businesses and governmental agencies as they grow into the future. Businesses especially will be driven to adopt the global e-business model to improve customer service, attract (and retain) new customers, retain current customers, and reduce internal costs by redesigning older business processes into new e-business processes. To achieve this single, most effective state of e-business, enterprises will require an e-commerce vision, a high-quality vision. This vision must incorporate well-thought-out strategies, clear and succinct objectives, reasonable milestones, flexible tactical plans, and solid operational plans.

An e-business *Design Quality* model helps enterprises establish stable business environments that provide new e-business values, environments that are secure, well protected, well designed, available 24 hours a day, 7 days a week (on 24x7) the entire year, and highly scalable. Internet e-business sites with a high degree of *Design Quality* are well-tuned systems/environments that provide performance and capacity, on an as-needed basis, utilizing systems proven to be reliable.

Design Quality of any Internet site can be measured in terms of usability, scalability, interoperability, and maintainability, among other metrics. Think of the *quality* of any given design as an enabler that carries with it some very key objectives. Conversely, think of design *flaws* as patterns that travel in "herds." Where you find one flaw, you will find many. Remember, the quality of any design is a forethought, not an afterthought.

Some areas of consideration that are focused on high-quality aspects of any highly effective e-business design are as follows:

- Designs for custom options
- Designs for open-ended applications
- Designs that consider diverse customer requirements
- Designs that are intended for continuous operations and high-availability applications
- Designs which are tightly-integrated into seamless core business processes;
- Designs that leverage interchangeable application components
- Designs that demonstrate consistency
- Designs that recognize an appropriate form of *"just-right security"*

The *Design Quality* of an Internet site is the entire interface between the business enterprise and the customer. This interface is very important to both market share and profitability. If the design of the e-business site is difficult to use or frustrating in any way to the end user, the odds are high that this Internet customer will find competitive products or services elsewhere, on a simpler-to-use e-business site. Remember, end users are always just one click away from leaving your site, perhaps forever.

Design Quality *factors* all play a key role in the composition of an effective Internet e-business site design. The precise quality of any design needs to be assessed up front, at midcycle, and again postdesign. The intention here is to determine metrics (measurable metrics) that are key to the design excellence of the site, and to carefully monitor the progression of these metrics as the design approaches completion. These design metrics must be a forethought in every design—and many times this sequence gets reversed. There are 10 Design Quality *factors*:

1. *Correctness*: The extent to which a design component of an e-business system satisfies its functional specification and, most importantly, fulfills the end user's objectives.
2. *Efficiency*: The requirement that the program or functional module uses the optimal amount of computing to perform the specification it was designed to satisfy.
3. *Flexibility*: The effort required to modify an operational program or hardware environment.
4. *Integrity*: The extent to which a program satisfies its specification and fulfills the user's objectives.
5. *Interoperability*: The ability of heterogeneous computer systems, or programmatic modules, to communicate and cooperate in problem-solving objectives.
6. *Maintainability*: The effort required to locate and repair an error in an operational program or hardware component.
7. *Portability*: The ability of a programmatic unit or hardware component to operate on multiple hardware and software platforms, without having to be reworked.
8. *Reliability*: The extent to which a programmatic unit or hardware component can be expected to perform according to its intended function, with required precision.
9. *Reusability*: The extent to which a programmatic unit (or program module) or hardware component can be reused in other software or hardware design solutions.
10. Testability: The effort required to test a programmatic unit or hardware component to ensure that it performs according to its specification or anticipated load level.

Finally, the operation and support of such an enterprise entity are critical. The services, and the manner in which these services are delivered and supported, should be the primary objective for the lasting success of any Internet e-business site. The operational support of a managed operations facility required to support any e-business environments is complicated. Involved in these overall e-business support environments are complex processes, such as backup and recovery mechanisms, testing facilities, security and intrusion detection software, system performance monitoring software, telecommunication transmissions monitoring software and hardware, transcontinental fail-over software, high-availability schemes, and much more.

BUILDING E-BUSINESS, INCREASING BUSINESS VALUES

In the beginning of this chapter, we defined e-business as the "use of electronically enabled communication networks that allow business enterprises to transmit and receive information" in a variety of mediums. We discussed how the information can be used in numerous ways, including various business applications (for instance, to conduct online auctions), to provide news updates, current and forecasted weather conditions, airline traffic information, power-grid tracking information, and stocks/securities trades and updates.

The communication networks generally consist of intranets (networks within a business enterprise), extranets (networks outside of, but connected into, other enterprise network segments), and the Internet (the global network that is interconnected through numerous nodes), which is managed by Internet Service Providers, or ISPs.

Public and private enterprises will require an increasing amount of support from their external services providers, as they are compelled to reduce their costs. Business enterprises that become e-business enabled will now be able to operate globally. It will become increasingly important that external service providers also have global support resources. This will be critical to both businesses and governmental agencies, as they continue to conduct business on a global scale.

An e-business Design Quality model helps enterprises to establish stable business environments that provide added business values, secure e-business operating environments, Internet sites that are available 24x7 the entire year, scalable and well-tuned systems, a design blueprint, and a method for continuous improvements of their e-business enterprise. All of these combined will help to provide optimum performance and capacity (on an as-needed basis) and an Internet e-business environment that is reliable and simple to use.

In our next topic we begin to explore aspects to consider while building an e-business environment.

BUILDING AN E-BUSINESS

As organizations begin to think of creating e-businesses, their senior managers must give serious thoughts to some important, yet fundamental questions. These business leaders should ask themselves these questions:

- Where are we as a business today?
- Where are we heading tomorrow, and what is our strategy?
- What tactical plans must we create to help us adhere to our strategies?
- What gaps need to be filled?
- Where can external partnerships play well, and where can they not play well?
- Who is the competition?
- What is the build-out cost versus the initial payback in terms of revenue stream?
- What is the three-to-five-year plan?
- What services do we offer that can evolve into other industry segments or channels?

Some enterprises that have embarked on e-business ventures have regretted that they did not have well-thought-out strategies and a complete analysis of *how* they would successfully achieve their e-business goals. For example, how many times have we read about companies underestimating the number of customers that visit their Internet sites, not only to browse their catalogs but to actually order products. Or an even bigger disaster, a visitor comes to your site and waits a rather long time, only to click on the next site because yours was unavailable at the moment of need.

Solutions involving Internet e-commerce that are not scalable to high-performance goals are potential disasters. The design has to be based on a "single-point of failure" approach, so support teams can be ready if a disaster ever strikes. This requires a rigorous analysis of the entire design, up front, prior to deployment, and after the deployment. Establish a process that monitors the Design Quality aspects of the e-business site, and review the site's effectiveness on a regular basis. Change design aspects of the Design Quality model as the business warrants: Keep the Design Quality model *evergreen*.

Senior executives (in both public and private sectors) face serious challenges as our global economies become more of a "virtual reality." As new digital markets evolve, they will supplant older, outdated forms of trade. The entire economic infrastructure could (and most likely will) change forever. If enterprises' do not keep up with this evolutionary change, the danger that they will become, as businesses, much less potent is growing. Senior leaders must consider these emerging, new, and increasingly complex environments of Internet e-commerce to compete on a global (or domestic) level. Executives must also think about (and plan for) the significant cost pressures, the new critical skills and resources that will be required to manage the new e-economy, and e-societal challenges. This form of professional evolution is not new to industry. It is essential that business enterprises develop new strategies (evergreen strategies) that will leverage e-business technologies and e-commerce applications for strategic objectives—not just common-place applications, but business-critical applications. Enterprises must provide e-business solutions that bring added business-values to their organizations and, more importantly, to the global consumer audience.

Executives responsible for managing these new challenging environments will need to maintain careful control of their assets, understand the dynamics of their enterprise(s), and quickly realign their key resources into the strategic initiatives that provide enhanced business values to their organizations' objectives.

To become an e-business with enhanced business values, business leaders will need to leverage both in-house resources and resources from external service providers. Critical partnerships should provide support to help them reengineer their core business processes, reengineer their network architectures, and enhance security. All of this is crucial. Business leaders must also strive to standardize their IT infrastructures, extend their enterprise networks, integrate e-commerce applications, and link these e-commerce applications into their legacy systems (as required). This will all be a normal part of becoming an e-business.

This new e-business leadership support entity must span across the entire IT infrastructure and provide meaningful solutions over the entire "*model*" of the solutions suite. Some of the key achievements should include efficiency improvements, the removal of redundant tasks, and an enhanced quality of service for customers. An important place to start is the network and its deployment strategies because it will be the backbone of the e-business extended enterprise.

NETWORK PLANNING

When it comes to managing the growing complexity of an e-business network infrastructure, mistakes can be extremely costly, even devastating, to the business. Frankly, senior executives must take the position that failure is not acceptable. For companies like Schwab and Cisco, which do most of their business electronically, network failures would be costly and disastrous. Banking environments also face the same challenges. When you contemplate decisions about networking strategies, it is better to err on the side of caution. Recent surveys of IT managers, however, still show that over 90 percent of e-business participants have experienced total (or partial) network failures at least once a year. The consequences of network failure can range from trivial losses to the loss of tremendous amounts of revenues, to the loss of customers, and even to life-threatening situations in certain medical or aviation-related situations.

Senior executives of enterprises that have successfully become e-businesses recognized the following factors as they developed their business strategies and key objectives. An e-business will include an intranet component, an extranet component, and an Internet component. All of thse components have relative performance metrics, including availability, reliability, and timely customer enablement(s). These are not just options, but "*bet your business*" imperatives.

Savvy business executives now recognize the key importance of their IT infrastructure, and they understand the importance of having experts assess their networks' health and readiness to respond. It is important that the right amount of bandwidth is in place (or readily available) to support unanticipated peak volumes of network traffic. It is equally important that the e-business system servers are scalable with sufficient backup and recovery capabilities in the event of disaster or unanticipated outages. In addition, there will be situations where high availability is a mandatory requirement (for example, international banking environments and transcontinental fail-over capabilities).

A healthy network infrastructure is only one of several factors involved in supporting a successful e-business; you will also require systems management controls that align with your business objectives.

SYSTEMS MANAGEMENT PLANNING

During the last decade, IT infrastructures have become more distributed and more complex. In many cases, firms have a mix of mainframe, client/server, and remote computing environments. These environments need to be strategically linked to exchange relevant data and information. These systems are often disparate, not interoperable, and not standardized.

To successfully launch e-business initiatives, enterprises must transform into common computing environments, with systems that can communicate via standardized networking telecommunication protocols. Proper network planning and system management controls will help to minimize this problem.

As the e-business begins to mature and emerge, it is important for businesses to continue to grade themselves on factors like these: remaining a relevant player in that marketplace, competitive profiles of other like e-businesses, profitability, and business efficiencies.

Significant business transformations have occurred in the way enterprises conduct e-business. The requirements of both private and public enterprises have changed as a result of rapid and significant changes in the world marketplace and in trading practices. More and more, there is a growing reliance on conducting business and trade electronically. Business rivals recognize the need to transform themselves into electronic trading entities that are global. Enterprises are also leveraging e-business technologies to help them in the reengineering of their core business processes; the reengineering, in turn, is used to improve the value of the actual services rendered to their customers.

All of this has triggered major changes in the way Information Technology (IT) organizations operate. It has also changed many elements of our social lives, and how we used to interact with each other is not how we are now able to electronically interact with each other. WebMD is one example of how our social structures are beginning to change. Being able to obtain medical advice and information via the Internet, from professional doctors and nurses, is a dramatic change for many of us. Classroom education, via the Internet, is another example. Grocery shopping from home and having the orders delivered is a nice change from having to travel to the store, pick up the items, pack them, and carry them home. These are only a few of the many social aspects we may see in the very near future. And, yes, there are many more examples.

Standards for systems and network management began to be developed more than 30 years ago, and they have continued to evolve as computing technologies improved and matured. This is not a fad or trend, but an evolution brought on by many innovative researchers, business leaders, and highly skilled technicians.

Successful systems management processes, procedures, tools, and techniques are being established, with industry standards, that are used by public and private enterprises worldwide to implement e-business environments. As enterprises develop e-business strategies and goals, it is a good idea for business leaders to include systems management strategy and planning. This will help IT executives to develop a long-term systems management approach that is appropriate for their businesses.

An important consideration here would be the entire continuum and end-to-end framework of the IT infrastructure. The continuum is based on a series of systems management measurements, which are adapted to help identify and resolve e-business support issues. This provides a structured and logical approach that brings forth optimum service delivery solutions. The continuum provides the design and execution architecture for building the enterprise's e-business solution(s); it defines *how* the solution is designed, constructed, and deployed: This helps to ensure that the environment can deliver real values to the business enterprise and the consumers.

PERFORMANCE AND CAPACITY ON DEMAND

One of the more significant challenges for companies that are transforming themselves into e-businesses is predicting traffic volume. Volume has direct effects on the global telecommunication commercial grade carriers, as they are the pipeline for e-commerce. Telecom carriers are working feverishly to expand their telecommunication capabilities and capacities: This is not a trivial problem, but it is directly related to the timing of a global e-business world.

A number of widely known enterprises have made analyst press headlines for failing to plan for potential high-volume network traffic. Establishing an Internet presence is one thing, but processing real business transactions quickly is another challenge. The capabilities and tools for predicting the performance of the enterprise e-business infrastructure do exist. The topic of "performance" is viewed (and rightfully so) as mission-critical for many firms.

The success of an enterprise in many cases rests on its ability to be scalable. It is important for firms to source either internally or externally the skills, tools, and critical resources needed to provide capacity and performance planning. This will enable them to develop predictable models that simulate various types of transaction and messaging traffic. The key here is recognizing the importance of planning predictable e-business network traffic volumes.

The performance management and capacity planning services for any enterprise will vary in complexity. Important factors include various e-business and IT technologies, telecommunication protocols, computer hardware platforms, e-commerce technologies, and numerous other forms of software. Consideration must also be given to the actual servers, mainframes, local area networks, and wide area networks, as this set composes the e-business solution (that is, the Internet, business intranets, and business-to-business extranets). In addition, there are many types of data repositories, enterprise resource planning software, collaboration software, and e-mail software environments. This is just a short list of the various components that make up a potential e-business infrastructure. At a lower level, there are computerized global Internet gateways, routing devices, and specialized computing languages designed to support the success of any e-business solution.

It is important for business executives know that there are consultative resources that have heavy experience in performing the detailed analysis involved in capacity and performance planning. There are also a number of tools that provide modeling and discrete simulation to accurately predict and plan for future capacity requirements.

HACKER-PROOF E-BUSINESSES

Let's start out by saying that there is no such thing as a "hacker-proof" environment. Computer hackers are extremely talented individuals who are able to penetrate even the most secure sites on the Internet today. Consequently, once hackers have penetrated security, the back-end systems can become exposed—presenting some rather dangerous potential situations. The odd part about all of this is that even the best e-business environments probably are aware of only a small portion of the intrusions that have occurred in their environments. It is said that a really good hacker is able to breach security, enter a restricted area, find whatever was the target, and exit without any trace. Tools, instrumentation, policies, and outstanding computer scientists have all made themselves available to improve on this unfortunate situation; however, the problem is not going away. Given that, there are still many excellent ways to implement intrusion-detection capabilities. This is critical and must not be discounted during the development phases of any e-business environment.

Perhaps some of the most significant barriers to engaging in e-business (or the Internet, for that matter) are fear, doubt, and uncertainty. Recent surveys highlight that substantial numbers of Internet sites are easy targets for Internet hackers. According to some authorities, some 200–300 new computer network viruses are unleashed every month, and a significant number of public and private enterprises report electronic break-ins. In many cases, the enterprise has a firewall installed, and this helps to minimize the problem. The FBI reports that a different Internet-connected computer is broken into every 20 seconds. Even more disturbing is knowing that some of the world's most renowned hackers are out there deliberately trying to breach your system's firewalls and the other forms of security installed to protect your company's electronic assets.

Let's not overlook the malicious registered end user. The people also have the means to breach e-business environments if they are capable of reverse-engineering either the application or the infrastructure elements. There have been cases where hackers have simply wanted to show off their capabilities, so they may decide to trigger a shutdown in regional power grids supplying large cities with power. The FBI actually had an instance where hackers penetrated its site and altered many screens with obscene gestures. This is a sad state of affairs, but it is a reality that will continue to be a challenge. Be absolutely sure that, before an enterprise deploys its e-business environment, every precaution has been taken to protect that environment. IBM actually provides a service to its customers that executes what it describes as "Ethical Hackers." This highly skilled team of computer scientists is able to assess the vulnerability of any Internet environment and suggest where attention needs to given to potential breach points. Carnegie-Mellon University has an organization called CERT (Computer Emergency Response Team) that organizations can consult if they believe their Internet environments may have been compromised. And finally, many software programs and hardware devices can assist in this area. Nothing is totally secure—remember that.

To combat hackers, enterprises are obtaining help from e-business security consultants (for example, IBM and CERT, among others), who assess an enterprise's current security infrastructure, recommend improvements, and (if desired) help implement and test these improvements. In some cases, security consulting firms provide SWAT teams to respond to emergency situations where companies are in real danger and have experienced substantial infiltration (the SWAT team can be engaged even as infiltration is happening). Some enterprises will decide to leverage security consultants to conduct *ethical hacking* to expose, under friendly fire, security breach points. This is an investment well worth making when we consider the causal impact of a security intrusion.

SCALABLE, RELIABLE, AND SECURE E-BUSINESS SITES

Public and private enterprises are beginning to recognize that Internet-enabled businesses run 24 hours a day, 7 days a week, 365 days a year—with no vacations or holidays. It does not matter what industry your firm is a part of, nor does it matter if you are a school, government, or privately held company—downtime on an e-business system can be disastrous. It could mean the loss of large sums of money and, in some cases, even lives. E-business is beginning to emerge as a key factor in the bottom line of a number of enterprises.

One senior executive of a major successful e-business enterprise in the financial trading industry stressed that several years ago system availability was not important to their business, and now it is their business. Senior executives must adopt a high-level understanding of the key importance of availability as they become an e-business. They also must have a keen understanding of what is the specific "bounded" environment that is mission-critical to the firm. Let's explore the following important items as they relate to e-business:

- End-to-end system components
- System management processes
- Data redundancy
- Backup and recovery
- High availability

Attention in these areas will render enhanced availability and optimal performance. This, in turn, translates to customer satisfaction and increased revenue. In an e-business these factors are the key metrics that will have a positive or negative impact on the bottom line.

CUSTOMER RETENTION

To retain customers in the e-business enterprise, the provider must build e-businesses that are available on demand, scalable on demand, reliable, and secure. Early e-business enterprises will tell you that their experience is that designing and putting an Internet site up is easy. The harder part is transforming the Internet presence into some form of e-business values for an enterprise, one that causes return visits by end users. Will they return?

Successfully engaging in e-business is not so easy. For example, to process transactions you must tie into the back-end systems and data. The varying complexities of IT infrastructures—how current they are, how disparate they are, and how incompatible they are—point out just some of the many complexities of design points that system architects must resolve.

The challenge associated with the transaction and interactive traffic volumes is predicting their volume. Furthermore, even if you could accurately forecast these volumes, testing the e-business applications that your enterprise requires is not an easy assignment.

The bottom line here is this: Trades never made, orders not processed, suppliers not providing needed parts all have disastrous effects on profit and revenue. To avoid these problems, enterprises must take advantage of stress-testing capabilities that emulate the highest expected traffic volumes in their environments The developers must also look at the variety of potential transaction traffic as they test their e-business applications. Then, when the developers think that they understand the limits, they should "*kick it up a notch*" to see what happens when the unexpected happens.

The reasons for doing exhaustive testing are quite clear. For one thing, stress testing before implementation will help discover, diagnose, and solve potential problems with a client's e-commerce applications well before they occur. Customized testing, utilizing industry standards and stress-evaluation tools for both server and end-to-end response time tests, will also help to ensure that the proposed environment can handle average transaction rates, as well as peak-period transaction rates.

Potential bottlenecks in networks, server capacity problems, application integrity problems, or compatibility issues are all revealed and addressed during stress-testing phases. Rigorous stress testing is done to help determine the network's hardware and software requirements to support the predicted daily transaction volumes. This will also help avoid costly scalability issues and response time degradation as future transaction volumes dramatically increase.

CUSTOMER CARE IN E-BUSINESS ENVIRONMENTS

As business enterprises begin their migration to an e-business environment, they may find that they are challenged with the management of applications that run in disparate IT environments, usually with multiple databases and nonstandardized IT infrastructures. As they plan for standard IT infrastructures, common database repositories, and distributed e-business network environments that all work together in a harmonious manner, their customer care processes and systems support practices become equally critical.

What is required are operational e-business support frameworks that provide streamlined support for customers. It is not only technology that enables e-business (in fact, technology has been said to be the easy part); it is the surrounding business functions that are critical to the overall success. There are several areas for consideration, including the following:

- End-user registration
- Billing
- Service delivery
- Customer care and helpdesk functions
- Global issues, like follow-the-sun support
- Global currency and taxation issues
- National languages
- Federal trade regulations

To provide for this wide range of support for their e-businesses, enterprises need to address these (and other) areas adequately. Successful e-business enterprises provide customer care support that improves quality and offers rapid problem determination and resolution. Some of these areas can be addressed, while allowing reduced service costs, by using automated problem-solving tools. This can result in customers obtaining the immediate support they require, in a timely, effective manner—wherever and whenever they need it.

BUSINESS CONTINUITY REQUIREMENTS: AN IMPERATIVE FOR E-BUSINESSES

What happens to my e-business if we are hit with a natural disaster? That is the question that causes senior enterprise executives to lose sleep. They need to adequately prepare their businesses for the unexpected. What if my data repositories are destroyed? What if I lose linkages to my legacy systems where the data required for transactions resides? There are many *what ifs* to haunt executives.

After all of the planning and implementation is complete, and once you are running a successful e-business site, you begin to think about what would happen if the enterprise's key e-business components become unrecoverable. Well, in some cases, e-business sites have been constructed to mimic each other, yet operate on multiple continents. Therefore, if a natural disaster strikes, and if the enterprise has planned for *high availability* and *automatic fail-over*, then the remote possibility of a disaster is less concerning. This approach does not come without added costs and complexities, but it may be a requirement depending on the nature of the e-business environment. *Design Quality* factors are the key quantification points at this stage. In other words, exactly what design points have been implemented to relieve us of any liabilities, should a natural disaster or unexpected event occur? Test them and ensure that they work according to plan.

To be a truly successful e-business, an enterprise must leverage its business and technological expertise to keep its e-businesses running, despite disasters. The fact of the matter is that in today's distributed, multivendor, networked world, disruptions in business flows can be long-lasting. To meet this challenge an e-business strategy must include a variety of recovery services. Whether the service is sourced internally, externally, or in some cases both, it is a safety margin worth investing in, and it will help to keep an enterprise from incurring any devastating losses. The continuity of an e-business environment is a mission-critical imperative. Do not overlook the possibility of disasters happening—because they do happen.

One tactic to solve this problem could be for a firm to put in place a backup recovery center, while maintaining the same Internet address for its customers. Another aspect is rapid recovery for your businesses-critical applications. It is also important to have a customer call center ready to back up the primary call center, in case a natural disaster hits. What is required is a fail-safe business continuity plan, and a final implementation to whatever degree of completeness required, in order to keep your e-business fueled with the information required to keep your customers operational.

4

The Importance of Advanced Research

....

$\mathbf{A}$ primary mission of advanced research in the field of e-commerce, is to be able to actually measure results, trials, and deployment scenarios. To do this thoroughly, in-depth research and a team of good e-business practitioners are key. In the United States, the Organization for Economic Cooperation and Development recently requested that more research related to e-commerce be acquired in both commercial and private sectors, to evaluate its tremendous potentials. The organization recognizes that e-commerce is accelerating in growth and that e-commerce is enhancing the dynamics of worldwide trade. Compared to the current global, more traditional commerce cultures, the potential for e-commerce growth as it replaces more traditional means of processing business transactions appears to be substantial. The Organization for Economic Cooperation and Development in the United States predicts an explosion in electronic commerce.

This e-commerce growth prediction by the Organization for Economic Cooperation and Development specifically states the following: Spending by businesses in information technology to build an online presence will hit approximately $954 billion in 2002, up from $211 billion in 1998. Internet users worldwide are expected to reach 320 million by 2002, compared with 97 million in 1998. Furthermore, e-commerce on the Internet is expected to reach approximately $425 billion by 2002, up from $32 billion in 1998. Although many estimates of the projected costs and revenues for e-commerce growth may differ, it remains clear that each of the suppositions indicates an incredible growth rate during the next few years. All of this growth is directly related to combining advanced research topics across various e-commerce areas.

The Organization for Economic Cooperation and Development defines e-commerce as a form of shorthand for the massive amount of economic activities that will become available to business and mass-market consumers over the Internet. Consumers will be able to bank, buy cars, read newspapers, listen to music, and watch movies, all at the click of a computer mouse in the convenience of their homes. On the other hand, businesses will be able to reduce costs and attract new customers, electronically, while retaining old customers. Small and local businesses will now have a global presence. Mergers of complimentary inter-corporate objectives (for example, http://www.stamp.com with Microsoft product technologies) are brilliant. This is an excellent (and undisputed) description of e-commerce.

The growth of the Internet and e-commerce presents challenges for many global governments, as they continue to determine new, innovative ways to govern the ubiquitous global networks. The Governments of the world are especially challenged, because each is expected to be able to respond to change and provide improved services to its public—while on the other hand reduce costs. An interesting challenge. Some of the areas of focus are these: general services, taxation, legal jurisdiction, legal practices, security, military operations, and there are other areas. A key question that needs to be addressed is this: What are the analytic and statistical measures associated with e-commerce growth, in government? How are these advanced e-commerce research results introduced to various world governments and societies? What cultural impacts have we seen, to date, and what remains to be seen from the introduction advanced research topics in e-commerce?

Recall that earlier in this book, we stated that the U.S. government, in fact, commissioned the team who originally invented the Internet. So, it comes as no surprise that the government still maintains a high interest in exactly *how* many societies can (and will) benefit from this new global environment of e-commerce. By virtue of the government-initiated research (1969), we now have the global Internet, with all of its many subnetworks. New and more innovative versions of the Internet (for example, Internet/2 pervasive devices), and all of its global subnetworks are now appearing on the year 2000 horizon. New and improved telecommunications, satellite, and switching technologies will allow the Internet to become somewhat of a passive means for each of us to communicate and operate each day.

Advanced forms of research, probably (or ironically) utilizing the Internet, will help us, as a global online community, to better understand exactly *how* to regulate the global Internet. Or, advanced research may perhaps cause us to realize that we do not want to be in a position to regulate the global Internet. This conclusion brings us back to the point that advanced forms of research are, indeed, imperative.

EXPERIMENTAL EPISTEMOLOGY

In a world where many operational aspects are changing at a rapid rate, we must be comfortable with reading tremendous volumes of information. It is then useful to be able to apply what we have read, in order to determine the relevance of the test. Should the results be worthy of publication, it then makes sense for the individual to publish the findings, thus enabling another person with similar interests to apply and build on those findings.

THE PRACTITIONER'S VIEWPOINT

This e-business practitioner understands the inner workings of the server farms hosting the e-business application designs, and the application design itself, from a performance perspective. Routing within the Internet can become very complicated very quickly; thus it is important to keep a view of the practitioner in any formative research being performed.

Language issues, security issues, human factors, pervasive computing—all of these are easy to describe, but they play a very different role in their application. Trial and error affords some practitioners the luxury of learning, but in most cases, the trial-and-error approach can be detrimental to the overall strategy of the e-business deployment.

As advanced research is being performed, involve the practitioners responsible for the deployment of these other global e-business environments (if possible). Resist the urge to recreate something that already exists; instead, engage the practitioners of e-commerce in your study of successful e-business application deployments. Areas such as Design Quality, security, telecommunications, and infrastructure support can be leveraged from other environments that have proven to be successful. The practitioners viewpoints, and research of the successful and not successful events encountered (lessons-learned) in any e-business environments, can pay off in the end of creating the e-business solution.

In the global sense of the word *e-commerce*, many practitioners, researchers, academicians, and business executives are all open and willing to share ideas as they relate to the overall success of their e-business interests. Intellectual property, which is often the results of advanced research, needs to be carefully (and appropriately) safeguarded; this is a distinction that goes well beyond the scope of this book. However, this distinction is the catalyst (in many cases) for large corporate mergers to occur.

(Additional reference materials of significant research topics on e-commerce may be found in Appendix A, "Further Reading.")

5
Businesses That Leverage E-commerce

....

$\mathbf{A}$ccording to some, sizing intercompany e-commerce predicts that the total value of goods and services traded between companies over the Internet will jump to $327 billion by 2002. Companies have started to use the Internet as a fourth channel for processing online business transactions. The size of this fourth channel is growing rapidly and has the potential to dramatically affect business processes. In addition to this, three dynamic business trading processes will emerge by virtue of e-commerce: electronic auctions, electronic bidding, and electronic catalogs. These areas of focus will render dynamic industrial e-commerce trading, which will demand faster, less expensive telecommunications; at the same time, they will force highly scalable technical and business processes.

SIGNIFICANT RESEARCH OF E-COMMERCE CONTENDERS

Studies have been conducted that analyzed the e-commerce plans of approximately 150 companies, across several major industrial categories in 1999. These studies included conducting in-depth interviews with several corporate executives. Approximately two-thirds of those businesses indicated they were now actively involved in trading goods and services over the Internet, and on a daily basis. These companies consisted of durable and nondurable goods manufacturers, wholesalers, retailers, utilities, package and freight shippers, paper goods producers, and computer makers.

In addition, this research included 25 suppliers of Internet e-commerce software, services, and systems integration services relative to their experience with companies building electronic commerce. This research describes insights from corporate executives who perceive tremendous value in Internet business trade practices. The companies that actively participated in this research were engaged in e-commerce. These companies will sell an estimated $5 billion in business-to-business goods and services, using the Internet, in 2001, an increase of 10 times more than that sold in 2000. Approximately two-thirds of these companies expressed a desire to establish themselves as leaders in e-commerce. The key reason for their aggressive approach to e-commerce is the perceived value of multiple cost savings, reduced order-processing times, and better information flow.

THE COSTS OF INTERNET TRADING

By utilizing e-commerce trading techniques, transaction costs are approximately two-thirds less expensive than those associated with telephone-based salespeople. Through creative approaches in e-commerce solutions, many enterprises are demonstrating a high degree of *Design Quality*. It is possible to launch corporate profit margins nearly four points higher, simply because a customer is able to place orders online.

A large beverage company realized significant improvements in revenue by simply providing an extranet (essentially, a business-to-business network) environment for their top 100 distributors. This approach demonstrated that by applying various e-commerce methods internally, the company has cut the time between order placement and order delivery from months to weeks. As a direct result of applying some simple, Internet-based trading methods, orders reached approximately $100 million during 1998. Distributors are now able to provide this beverage company five months of sales and inventory numbers at their e-commerce Internet site.

A large, global aerospace company successfully added more than 150 Internet-based customers in eight months, reaching an impressive $1 million, per day, in spare parts sales—utilizing its e-commerce Internet sites. It is apparent from this significant increase in sales that many buyers prefer electronic methods of downloading complicated blueprints, online viewing and analysis, and instantaneous product comparisons—as opposed to the more traditional paper-handling methods of the past. This same aerospace company essentially eliminated the overhead costs of printing and sending paper by implementing these creative e-commerce solutions.

During the past several years, implementations utilizing various methods of e-commerce far surpass those of more traditional telephone and fax machine methods. Corporate executives are rapidly moving to e-commerce methods to leverage the Internet with a clear objective: to reduce costs of operations and improve the effectiveness of their salesforce. Here the end result is to capture more business orders, which, in turn, yield more corporate revenues.

By taking advantage of the creative solutions of e-commerce, many companies are shifting the bulk of their incoming phone calls (approximately 70 percent of all calls) that request product data into electronic visits to their electronic catalogs, accessible through their e-commerce Internet sites. These Internet sites have many hidden benefits; for example, they are available 24 hours a day, 7 days a week. A noted benefit related to career path growth is that many corporate salespeople are now able to advance to customer account managers (a displacement with retention of critical skills), relieving them of the more traditional employment positions as telephone "order takers" and information providers.

INDUSTRIAL E-COMMERCE MARKET SHARE INCREASES

Many industries are rapidly gaining market share as incoming orders for products and services shift from the phone to the Internet. An e-commerce Internet site (*well designed*) does not slow down when large numbers of distributors frequently visit to place orders. Industries utilizing e-commerce methods do not need to be concerned about their business partners being placed on hold on the phone, and then hanging up after waiting too long. The equivalent situation will not occur with a properly designed Internet site.

A primary reason why industries are doing business on the Internet is their desire to demonstrate (to other businesses) their own leadership capabilities in using e-commerce. This endorses the idea "we should use what we sell." The second key reason is that their customers are already using the Internet.

There is a clear shift in the results of the second premise: using the Internet as a key channel to generate revenues. Companies have collectively recognized the technological shift from the use of phones and fax machines, to the use of e-commerce utilities. The stock markets worldwide have also noted the introduction of Internet technologies. These technology stocks seem to present a pattern that might indicate a global demand for faster telecommunications service providers, advanced media-related industries, and other Internet-related business entities. Pay close attention to these types of stocks across all global stock markets. For example, the telecommunication industry is especially challenged to increase speeds and services, on a global scale, for optimal Internet end-user operations. Companies such as AT&T, MCI, WorldCom, Global Crossing, British Cable & Wireless, Telstra, New Zealand Telecom, Italia Telecom, and many more commercial grade carriers, all want to be the "best of practices" for their industry. Timing is prudent to watch these types of technology and other more general infrastructure stocks (for example, routers, switching, and so on). Volatility is anticipated in these markets, but then again, return on investments is likely to be widespread.

Confirmation of orders placed online is perhaps lagging. Business executives have pointed out in public interviews that completing transactions end-to-end, from order to payment, delivery, and continuous support, means added-value beyond simply completing a single part of the order process. It is often very expensive and very time-consuming to integrate front-end customer systems with back-end order-entry systems.

Many global customers can order, and then follow and check their order status, online. It becomes painfully obvious that to perform this, enterprises need connections to back-end systems, in order to support the distribution channel that ships to customers. To provide this form of instant data on products, pricing, manufacturing, shipping, and quantities, many industries and companies were quick to build electronic catalogs, hosted by their e-commerce Internet site.

There is tremendous value in business-to-business e-commerce environments. Business enterprises are becoming more engaged in the electronic trading of tens, hundreds, even millions of dollars of goods and services, through this fourth channel. These business enterprises are the fortunate ones that have recognized the value of building effective Internet e-commerce sites.

6

E-commerce, Management, and Organizations

....

$\mathbf{T}$he introduction of e-commerce technologies and practices has reinforced on many large industries how they need to craft their internal business processes to meet those of their competition. This chapter describes some of realignments and other organizational issues associated with managing e-commerce organizations. In some cases, incredible corporate turnaround scenarios have occurred as a result of e-commerce and its worldwide competition for desktop dominance.

Some companies around the world will be able to create enormous competitive advantages, and others will not be able to meet this challenge. Many regions and countries around the world will be able to excel, and some, such as Indonesia, Thailand, and Korea, will find it more difficult to excel.

In a CNBC U.S. News interview, the CEO and President of IBM, Lou Gerstner, said, "Information technology is actually the science of institutional restructuring." This premise is fundamental to the success of all business leaders and corporate management individuals. Restructuring applies directly to many concepts and practices of e-commerce.

Mr. Gerstner also asserts that Japan has probably realized that it has to change many of its own business practices, in order to better operate and thrive in a global economy. Likewise, he recognized that Latin America has been experiencing a slowdown during the last few years. This is most likely a consequence (in part) of what is happening in Asia. There is a high probability that if we can help to stabilize the underlying financial communities in Latin America, it would help to strengthen their worldwide e-commerce opportunities.

On a worldwide basis, e-commerce is a new business model that will drive enterprises to transform their core business processes to remain profitable, competitive, and efficient. This new business model is an integral part of the e-business cycle. The transformation starts with solving business problems by modifying core businesses. The transformation then proceeds to leveraging knowledge and information, as intellectual capital. Very important at this stage are the customers' needs; contrast these needs with the solution being proposed. Finally, the tactical stage of the transformation occurs, building e-commerce applications while operating available and scalable network computing infrastructures: This model addresses a wide range of elements—for example, the need for knowledge to help enterprises select markets in which to compete in or changing core businesses processes to create added customer value. Well-designed e-commerce solutions (in part) help to enable the linkages required for businesses to connect to their customers and business partners, using existing network-centric infrastructures (see Figure 6.1).

TRANSFORMING BUSINESS

The adoption of e-commerce may very well come in three phases. The first phase is already manifesting itself in that global business enterprises are working to improve

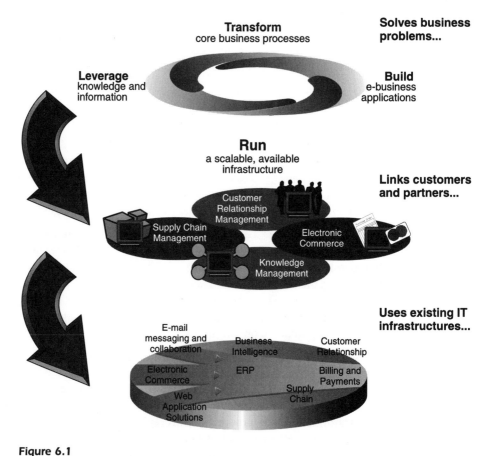

Figure 6.1

The transformation of a business to an e-business requires an in-depth inspection of almost every aspect of a company's business practices.

their core business processes. The next is core business process reengineering, focused on where businesses seem to be threatened by new competitive pressures driven by e-commerce. It is indeed time that these threatened businesses reinvent themselves, discovering new ways to go to market and new ways of linking their business partners. A third phase is the actual crafting of the "new ways" of doing Internet e-business; also very important in this final phase is the invention of new products and services leading to other new e-businesses. This third phase is heavily driven by the Internet e-commerce marketplace.

To achieve the three phases of e-commerce efficiently and cost-effectively, the enterprise's legacy systems must be leveraged while new e-commerce technologies are integrated. The legacy systems include business processes, organization structures, information technology infrastructures, application functionalitiss, application development environments, and system data. To gain significant economies of scale, policies for dealing with legacy code should be an integral part of the business transformation: Reengineering business processes and integrating e-commerce technologies will become a key focal point. Business transformation must be a continual process of reinventing both the business process and the e-commerce enabling technologies.

MANAGING AND LEVERAGING KNOWLEDGE

Knowledge management technologies focus on information access. They provide business enterprises with knowledge repositories and advanced search capabilities. Thus, they enable "knowledge workers" to share intellectual capital by utilizing online collaborative computing environments.

There appears to be an increase in the number of organizations that recognize the importance of knowledge that is electronically stored. For example, important legal issues must be considered as e-commerce becomes the status quo mode of conducting trade and processing business transactions. This will need to be resolved in a manner that complements the needs of e-commerce, globally, while using some form of e-commerce automation in its approach.

There is a growing trend toward a paperless environment among public and private enterprises. As e-commerce solutions rapidly proliferate, more and more businesses will move their legacy records that are paper-based to electronic storage. In fact, some predictions say that 75 percent of all document-based information would be stored electronically during 1999. During the first half of 1999, we have been introduced to the first online pharmacy, online liquor sales, and online gambling Internet e-business sites. What legal questions come to mind when we consider the diversity of each of these new e-business domains and the global Internet?

Consider legal domains. Public and private business enterprises have embraced an increasing awareness of legal trends and court cases, and a legal process known as *discovery*. Utilizing the Internet to access vast amounts of information has proved valuable in the discovery phases of litigation. In the litigation process of U.S. law, the discovery phase is a legal process that allows the parties involved in litigation to provide each other with all records that are relevant to the disputed facts. Under discovery, if a relevant item exists, it must be produced even if it could have and should have been destroyed. Organizations may not claim undue burden as an excuse not to produce relevant records.

In 1993, the U.S. Federal Rules of Civil Procedures 26 (a)(1) stipulated that documents and things relevant to disputed facts in court cases must be made available, without waiting for discovery requests, within 85 days after the defendant's first appearance. FRCP Section 34 (a) specifically states records that are stored electronically are discoverable, and since then several states have enacted laws related to information stored electronically; for example, California Senate Bill 1034, Texas Proposed Rule 11, and in Canada, the Uniform Electronic Evidence Act. What is the correlation, you ask? In this example of Internet e-commerce, the Internet serves as a legal search and discovery instrument for a formal legal process. This was probably not a consideration when the original Internet design team (ARPA) decided to engage.

As e-commerce becomes a more widely embraced fashion of conducting business, government and business enterprises must be concerned about knowledge management and its legal implications. Using our previous example, *discovery*, consider what is meant by the term as it relates to records stored electronically. *Discovery*, in the case of electronic records, includes documents stored in host computer databases, on personal computer hard drives, network computer drives, portable diskettes, jukeboxes with multiple disks, backup tapes, and probably many other areas. Electronic records are great for lawyers because they often include more information than their paper counterparts, including annotations and hidden text that do not appear when the documents are printed. Audit trails showing creation dates, revision dates, e-mail transmissions, electronic routing slips, and delivery confirmations could arguably show who knew what and when, and what was done (or not done) about it.

Some recent examples of these types of cases include an insurance company facing fines of $35 million and settlements expected to tally between $410 million and $2 billion, based on documents stored electronically showing that the company knew of illegal practices by its sales agents. Another case where an e-mail message, uncovered as part of a $160 million damages suit, showed that an automobile manufacturing company knew of defects in one of its model's doors. E-mail clearly showed that nicotine's addictive properties were known and fostered, and its disclosure has publicly shamed tobacco companies. Another car company was legally damaged by an internal document stored electronically that showed one of its cars had a major safety problem that could have been prevented with a part that cost a dollar. Then, a U.S. court charged a CEO of a large software manufacturing company with evidence in an e-mail, where he might have been suggesting less-than-desirable business practices.

The implications of this appear to be quite clear in that most businesses would rather settle out of court, even if they could have won, rather than attempt to comply with a discovery order and risk allowing their legal opponent access to their electronic records. They would probably consider the risk of not knowing the full content or extent of their digitized records and documents, and they would prefer not to be forced to give an adversary broad access. In the context of this discussion as it relates to e-commerce, records are "documents" used to maintain information related to an enterprise's business or organizational activities. These documents are stored electronically, online, in some capacity. Examples include e-mail, word processing files, spreadsheets, business presentations, and graphics files; they can also be items captured and converted to digital form like document images, voice mail, and video clips. This category also includes several variations, revisions, versions, and formats (for example, Adobe PDF, HTML, and so forth). Any or all of these documents are discoverable.

As e-commerce usage grows, it is quite clear that various enterprises and organizations, representing all segments of our society, will have to deal with sensitive issues of knowledge management. With the continued influence of the Internet, extranets, and intranets, electronically stored records are becoming pieces of information based on linked objects. Records will be harder to classify and save according to standard retention schedules, which presume that a document's content is stable and does not change for each reader. Future e-commerce technologies will require ways to place retention periods on documents, linked objects, and components; later, destruction will be enforced by dissolving links and overwriting outdated component objects.

INFRASTRUCTURE MANAGEMENT

The Internet has had significant effect on Information Technology organizations. The Internet was initially deployed as an external extension of the information technology infrastructure first for government, education, and research, and then for corporate organizations, and it has become prominent within organizations' systems architectures (see Figure 6.2).

The Internet provides a ubiquitous linkage for consumers, businesses, and government users. They use the Internet and e-commerce solutions to support communications, collaboration, and e-business applications within an organization. This has proved beneficial for employees and, in some cases, it has limited inclusion of business partners such as suppliers and contractors. Extranets are designed to give the trading partners of businesses limited (and secure) access to their intranets, while using their chosen Internet browser as personal gateway to the Internet. Extranets provide support for communications, collaboration, and the use of specific applications between organizations for business-to-business information sharing and commerce. The consumer Internet uses technologies for business-to-consumer communication

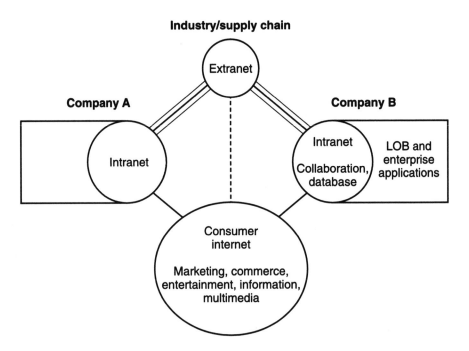

Figure 6.2

Supply chain integration with e-business practices often becomes complicated, due to the nature of the complexities of supply and demand.

and commerce. In addition to these segments, the Internet has spawned three notable changes to user interactions with technology: push technologies, lower-entry-cost thin-clients or network computers, and Java and ActiveX language environments.

Netcasting is synonymous with push technologies that are a means of automatically pushing downloads onto an organization's servers or even the user's desktops. While most users still experience the Internet as a downloaded HTML or multimedia file from a local or remote Internet site, netcasting is the way many suppliers of Internet services are partnering with media, entertainment, and consumer products companies to deliver "channels" to market(s). Information Technology (IT) organizations are also finding push technologies as a powerful means for software distribution, updates, monitoring, and maintenance.

Network computers are thin-client devices that are network-, server-, or host-centric forms of computing. The Internet, or intranets, allows the majority of information, applications, and logic about computing to be placed on a server (or host) to be downloaded, in whole or in part, at discrete intervals to meet user needs. This server-centered approach enables lightweight, low-storage computers that replace terminals and personal computers (or fat-clients with application software stored on the device) within organizations. This may clearly, and quite simply, extend the penetration of personal computers into the home.

One challenge to overcome regarding this thought of a thin-client is related to the need for enhanced telecommunication speeds. This is forced by the application processing components of the application, residing remotely on the server (as opposed to being installed on the device itself). Internet connectivity speeds, in general, lack consistent, affordable bandwidth capabilities for transportation of networking information. New telecommunication endeavors are replacing the slower transmission lines of the past with faster fiber-optic lines and laser lines. One aggressive leader in this industry, Global Crossing Ltd. is a provider of global Internet and long distance telecommunications facilities. This includes services utilizing a network of undersea, transcontinental digital fiber-optic cable systems and associated networking backhaul capabilities.

The Java language is significantly affecting the software and application development activities being performed by enterprises: This, too, is occurring on a global scale. Java is a ubiquitous, multiplatform language, and it provides a widely accepted open-standard set of programming methods designed for Internet, intranet, and extranet e-commerce solutions. Java is aligned with object technologies and ActiveX computing components. Java is purported to be (by a large community) the new programming metric by which Internet e-business application development is measured.

Many enterprises are utilizing extranets to provide linkages for their trading partners into their intranet infrastructures. There are some key reasons for supporting the extranet solution. Deployment costs are reduced because extranets are usually added to existing intranet or Internet configuration(s). Telecommunication costs decrease due to the dynamic allocations of backbone resources, rather than dedicated, expensive leased lines. Furthermore, long distance (dial-up telephone) costs are lower because the Internet and most private networks offer local dial-up access hubs. Training costs are generally minimal because the personnel in most enterprises are familiar with using Internet browsers. The things that must be carefully managed when implementing extranet solutions are network performance, reliability, and security.

Various types of enterprises will use extranets. In addition to finding business-to-business solutions of tremendous value, other groups will implement extranets as a way to control and reduce online distribution costs. The U.S. federal government, for instance, is evaluating different methods and techniques that can be used to distribute welfare checks and food stamps through controlled extranet solutions. In one scenario, recipients will obtain their food stamps from kiosk walk-up stations, situated in government buildings or supermarkets.

Healthcare providers and insurance companies continue to investigate extranets as a fast and efficient way to distribute prescriptions and centralize the storage and retrieval of vital medical information. Using the Internet as a transport vehicle would make these records universally accessible. Despite the attractive cost savings and efficiencies, health maintenance organizations are proceeding with caution due to concerns related to the potential for abuse and loss of confidentiality.

Intranets are used by enterprises to facilitate collaborative internal communication environments. Extranets also help enterprises communicate more effectively with their preferred business or trading partners. Extranets are virtual private networks that physically exist within the global Internet, and they are linked to private networks or intranets, combined with the programmed rules for firewall access. They leverage security technologies to manage integrity. Intranets function inside an internally defined physical and logical space, whereas extranets extend secure communication links to a geographically diverse set (for example, city-to-city, state-to-state, country-to-country) of remote access points. Those remote points can be customers, sales agents in the field, other servers, buyers, or suppliers.

The primary rationale for this remote access point solution is to allow trading partners controlled access to a company's data, based on a need-to-know. Secondary benefits include enhanced communication among customers, suppliers, and business partners. Most organizations stand ready to give these selected, trusted sources access to their intranets (thereby transforming them into extranets) to improve working relationships with these trading partners, improve efficiency, and reduce costs in the supply chain.

Both intranets and extranets are designed to move complex technologies off the desktop machines and onto the network and servers, where the technologies (or applications) can be centrally managed by IT professionals. An extranet that is built on an enterprise's intranet has two primary elements: establishing high-priority access capabilities via ISDN, T1, fractional T1, E1, DS3, leased-lines, or dial-up through Internet service providers, and connecting through the firewall or placing a dedicated server outside the firewall that is then linked to the internal network.

In an extranet solution, the data must pass through the company's firewalls to reach the intranet and then be routed to the company information server(s). This means that user authentication and validation are mandatory. Through the use of SSL (Secured Socket Layers), SET (Secured Electronic Transactions), and/or smart cards, extranets give trusted parties (employees, suppliers, business partners, or selected customers) high-level access to the corporation's product pricing, inventory, selected financials, and other vital information in their e-commerce environments.

Extranets are both complementary and competitive technologies to collaborative computing, electronic data interchange, enabling technologies for e-commerce, and supply chain management. The primary focus of extranets is to reduce the costs inherent in complex processes and large, expensive network computing frameworks. Extranets improve on electronic data interchange (EDI) standards in four critical areas: Extranets allow business partners to communicate in real time as opposed to batch processing. Extranets are interactive; they allow callers to browse, which could result in an increase in the number of new orders and improve overall accuracy. The extranet's access is through the Internet instead of private or leased lines. Extranets cost 20 percent to 40 percent less to operate than traditional EDI technologies, and they cost about 80 percent less in training efforts. The bulk of the operational savings result from the reduced cost of software acquisition and configuration.

There are some very important differences between EDI and extranets. EDI is a tool used primarily in financial exchanges, record keeping, inventory operations, shipping, ordering, and more. Although extranets can provide that same functionality, EDI's focus is on machine-to-machine communications; extranets emphasize human-to-human communications. The user friendliness of extranet browsers is another critical difference. The character-based screens of EDI are highly structured and quite intimidating, whereas extranets encourage staff with even limited technical experience to participate.

Even though extranet adoptions are still in the early deployment stages, another benefit this technology will offer (over EDI) is ease of technology turnover. Customers do not invest as heavily in hardware and software for their extranets (especially if they have existing intranets). Utilizing extranets, they will afford mutual benefits and greater flexibility in migrating to e-commerce technologies.

EDI will most certainly continue to grow. The current growth rates of EDI are 20 to 30 percent per year. For many enterprises, EDI investments have long been amortized. Although extranets have many advantages and attractions, EDI will still remain a key commerce technology. In addition, eliminating EDI involves a costly structural change to a business automation processes. Furthermore, even though operating an extranet may cost 20 to 40 percent less per year, the potential saving is more likely to capture the interest of customers considering a new installation than those eliminating an existing system. This may especially be true in the small to medium-sized companies. The heightened and growing interest on the part of businesses and public sector enterprises, and the advantages of e-commerce, are clear driving forces toward the adoption of extranets.

One key factor worthy of consideration is the GET ON & GET OFF end-user scenario. This scenario is largely driven by a new mindset on the part of intranet and extranet site users. For example, on an Internet site, there is a desire to encourage people to linger and browse. The longer the e-business site captures a visitor's interest, the more banner ads the visitor will see; brand recognition increases, as does the likelihood that the visitor will respond to these product offerings. On the other hand, with intranets and extranets, the goal is to help staff members or business partners exchange information quickly so that they can get back to work.

Another very critical issue for every e-business to comprehend is scalability. As a single factor of Design Quality, the term scalability implies that the performance of any network environment should remain as fast and efficient as it is with three concurrent end-users even when peak loads present 2000–3000 concurrent users.

BUILDING INTERNET COMMERCE APPLICATIONS

Global solutions of e-commerce are becoming one of the major forces driving the global economy as we enter the new century. A key economic area that is driving this growth is the business-to-business market segment. This segment can be classified into three categories:

- Online wholesaling, which is businesses selling goods and services to other businesses on the Internet
- Internet corporate purchasing, which represents various public- and private-sector enterprises making online purchases of office materials, manufacturing supplies, and more using the corporate intranet
- Supply chain trading over the Internet, which involves businesses working closely together using the Internet to automate the transfer of goods for production and distribution

Some of the key areas of growth appear in the business-to-business sellers, with many of their customers and suppliers already using the Internet. Companies that use online catalogs to sell goods or services are generally in a business-to-business distributor situation. Businesses that distribute products over the Internet discover quickly that selling products requiring dynamic updates (for example, airline tickets, financial instruments, product pricing changes, and imagery) is a huge challenge. All of the these factors are clearly the driving forces requiring businesses to automate how they will conduct trade, today and in the future, with other businesses and consumers.

One of the important considerations for public- and private-sector enterprises is whether to customize the electronic application or to purchase it off the shelf. This decision appears to depend on the customer's flexibility. Most enterprises want the convenience of a product that can function immediately. The reality is that in most business-to-business situations, a certain amount of customization is required. Many e-commerce software companies are delivering solutions that include what the customer wants through automated features such as *wizards* and *templates*. This approach most often requires the least amount of custom coding. This is generally is the key to win over new business. Another important factor for businesses to consider is the responsibility and complexity of maintaining a site, in addition to the relative ease of implementation of the site.

From a technical perspective, public and private enterprises planning to build an e-commerce site must consider the following technical factors: an end-to-end and complete business-to-business solution, legacy back-end integration of e-commerce applications, a flexible architecture, scalability, open standards, interoperability, and reliable performance. *Design Quality* is key throughout the entire life cycle. An Internet e-commerce site can be measured in terms of *Design Quality*, and it should be. The critical quality aspects of the design must be monitored throughout the entire life cycle development.

Legacy back-end integration provides seamless linkages to inventory and accounting records, with real-time updates and reporting considerations. A flexible architecture is required to provide either a high, medium, or low e-commerce capability. *High* is defined as both Internet- and EDI-enabled, with plug-and-play capability along with multiplatform integration with other applications. *Medium* includes both using the open-standards of the Internet and value-added networks (VANs) for EDI connectivity with suppliers or trading partners. *Low* means that only proprietary EDI is used in connecting selected partners. Open standards means support for open API communications. Interoperability is defined as the capability to operate across various platforms and languages. Scalability is the accommodation for future growth in business volumes, multiple customer transactions, and additional services. Reliable performance means just what it says: The system works all the time, exactly as it is expected to work.

What are the key requirements for businesses and other forms of enterprises wishing to engage in e-commerce? Basically the general objective of enterprise computing using e-commerce technologies from a business-to-business point of view is to build customized online markets for multiple customers who use the Internet. Some of the key factors driving these requirements are the ability to link the front-end buying process to the legacy back-end systems that generally include accounting and inventory management; the use of Electronic Data Interchange (EDI) to process purchase orders, invoices, and other online type transactions over the Internet with a multiplicity of trading partners; e-commerce applications that are integrated with the variety of trading partners using their individualized business rules, ease of installation features, user friendliness, and simple interfaces; a payments processing system, with cross-selling capabilities; outstanding customer care and support functions; and the desire to reduce the total cost of ownership of the end-to-end e-commerce solution. These requirements are a monumental challenge.

An important objective for enterprises using an Internet EDI capability is to provide the same offering to a multiplicity of customers, suppliers, and trading partners. In this case, one catalog can be used. In the consumer-to-business scenario, the general transaction model is that of one consumer or business purchasing from a standard catalog and paying with a credit card. Another important goal is the handling of customers or trading partners under varying business rules. These rules are necessary to provide approvals for a varying customer set with different spending limits and approval cycles. These business rules enable the selection of preferred vendors and shippers, differentiating product and pricing of packages for specific trading partners. There are also cost savings associated with the partners, by means of setting purchasing limits.

One effective way that e-commerce companies market their Internet commerce applications and platforms is through integrated strategic alliances. This gives these enterprises another way to differentiate themselves and provide complete solutions for their customers. An alliance has the added advantage of tapping into the channel partner's customer base and shifting some of the marketing efforts to the channel partner. The channel partner can then bundle e-commerce products as complete packaged solutions for their customer base, and it can earn more profits through the transactions. This creates stable relationships with the channel partner's customers and a greater opportunity for customer retention. Everyone in the value chain, including the e-commerce enterprise, benefits. In the channel partner's strategies, there are systems integrators, Internet service providers, and Internet hosting companies, to name just a few.

Second- and third-tier businesses that access and use e-commerce technologies are doing so to be competitive and cost-effective, and because it is affordable. It also provides them with a significant new reach into the markets in which they choose to compete. The e-commerce service(s) and technology providers are offering to small and medium-sized business (SMB) customers a service bureau solution allowing SMBs access to e-commerce technologies for a monthly charge, without having to deploy these complex systems for themselves. The business utilizes an Internet browser provided by the e-commerce company to customize the software for creating a site and building its own brand presence on the Internet. The customer benefits include the technical support that the e-commerce company provides. The service bureau model allows SMBs the ability to outsource the complexity of online commerce, maintenance, support—and easily start up an e-commerce-enabled Internet site.

7

New Channels That Intensify Competition

························

Businesses are working feverishly to find ways to generate profits by using e-commerce solutions. Some of the problems they are encountering involve finding innovative ways to bring buyers and sellers together, despite the fact that there are millions of users and thousands of companies connected to the Internet. They are placing high values on Internet search tools; conversely, there is a lack of trusted content and trusted (authenticated) payment systems throughout the global Internet. Tremendous progress has been made, yet e-commerce is still viewed as an underdeveloped business medium. A vast number of buyers are using the Internet for e-commerce purchasing transactions. They often require help finding the right products, responding to the right bids, and protecting their rights as individuals. The Internet is a huge warehouse of information. For example, if a buyer searches for a new personal computer or a promising mutual fund or stock, by simply browsing through the results of a search engine's query, a tremendous amount of information can be acquired. Likewise, sellers always need innovative ways to attract customers to their Internet sites. Simply hanging a shingle out on the Internet does not mean that they will receive site visits by millions of potential customers.

CONDUCTING E-BUSINESS AND E-COMMERCE

It is important to explore *how* e-business and e-commerce will be conducted in a virtual, highly automated world. In contrast, it is also important to ensure that we understand exactly *how* it is conducted in the physical world. There are the functional middle-people who are compensated for their piece of the respective transaction chain that joins buyers with sellers. This transaction chain can be divided into four categories: customer acquisition, shipping and delivery, payment and credit, and support and services.

In the physical world, customers are often attracted by suppliers who invest heavily in advertising and direct-marketing practices. At the consumer retail level, the product lines from competing suppliers are aggregated and sold to interested customers.

65

The orders are processed by shippers and then prepared for delivery. Shippers are expected to deliver the products to the customers while providing these customers with a way to track their goods, to make sure the product arrives at the delivery point undamaged and on time. Financial institutions (like banks and credit card processors) authorize credit, offer investment opportunities, offer loans, and transfer monies to appropriate parties to conclude the transaction.

What appears to be emerging is the requirement for professional e-commerce middle-people, or intermediaries. These intermediaries are called *Internet Transaction Brokers* (ITBs). Furthermore, it appears that Internet buyers and sellers will not be able simply to collaborate in great numbers, without significant help from the *middle*, or intermediaries. What is envisioned is a whole new class of online intermediaries, Internet transaction brokers. One definition of an ITB is a fee-based firm that facilitates Internet transactions, end to end, without assuming ownership of the product. The most obvious characteristics of an ITB are that they appear to be facilitators of complete Internet transactions: think of Online banking firms and stock brokerages, like E*Trade, TradingDirect, and Net.B@nk. These ITBs must offer electronic services that combine and take responsibility for all services that are provided by the functional middle-people of the physical world.

Customer acquisitions represent one of the primary success factors for profitable ITBs. This is in part assisted by placing a strong emphasis on the things that customers value the most. The best ITBs will be positioned as independent voices representing their customers and building Internet sites that are based on vertical product categories like personal finance, car buying, or computer peripherals. Another important area where ITBs offer customers value is related to the integration of payment presentment and bill payment systems. A number of Internet sites fax orders to suppliers and key credit card information into secured terminals for the processing of orders behind the scenes—the back-office. This approach results in a lack of real intersystem connectivity and communications, forcing customers to be personally responsible for following up on their orders status, if necessary. The value proposition for ITBs will be their capability to be directly linked from the Internet to the corporate intranets, the back-end legacy systems of major shippers, the payment processors, the clearinghouses and settlement organizations, and more e-commerce types of service offerings. Thus, the ITBs provide value-added services to the consumer.

Global ITBs offer another important value proposition by providing personalized customer support services at reduced costs. Customer support organizations leverage their internal expertise capabilities by using e-mail technologies to answer customer queries. This helps to reduce costs, and it lowers the need for highly skilled people who are always available to answer difficult and complex questions. When end users touch the ITB's Internet page, they will be provided with customized information that contains all the details of their latest orders or transactions—ITBs are a sort of customer care robot.

The ITBs provide four functions, which in-turn bring added values to customer support situations. First, there is *trust*. Today, buyers have little guarantee that the information presented on the Internet is valid or that the payment and delivery systems being used are reliable. Also of great concern, the novice end user cannot distinguish the insecure Internet environments from the secure Internet environments. The most successful ITBs will ensure that every aspect of the transaction maintains the highest degree of integrity required to safely complete any transaction. The second important function is match-making. The ITBs will provide product-based clearinghouses (for example, stock brokerages, car buying brokerages, and office supply brokerages). They will use computer-based *content-hosting* methods for their promotional materials while conducting Internet promotions online. This may include Internet accesses to many databases, in many locations. This approach attracts buyers to sellers: This is a fundamental principle of e-commerce, which continues to help many societies become electronically linked, as e-societies. Although some customers will have the patience to suffer through the do-it-yourself approach, most will leverage the advantages offered by the ITBs. A third and equally important function is the attraction and *convenience* factor. Many of the ITB transactions will have to possess all the necessary personal, financial, and product-services-related information—at each step in the e-business cycle. The ITBs will eliminate the need to make inquiries about an order or to authorize payments that need to be completed as a part of the e-business online buying transaction. Finally, the fourth function (which is actually a benefit) is the relief that is provided by the ITBs because they (for the most part) own and manage many systems in the middle, relieving the sellers from independently having to build and manage similar types of systems.

The ITBs are beginning to emerge with early forays in two areas: e-procurement, basically focused on electronic superstores, and electronic auctions. For example, consider the area of procurement where GE's *Trading Process Network* (TPN) is brokering business-to-business purchasing. GE is currently in the process of Internet-enabling its installed base of 44,000 EDI-based suppliers. TPN will give them bidding capabilities online through private-offer negotiations, EDI ordering applications, billing and payment functions, electronic tracking functions, and advanced shipment tracking and notification. Several corporations are providing both bidding and sourcing opportunities through e-procurement types of Internet solutions to many governments. This enables global end users to view opportunities for the sourcing of various types of government opportunities. These opportunities are addressed by interested parties as e-bids, resubmitted to the sourcing government, and electronically evaluated; the winners of the bidding process are subsequently notified.

The focused superstores are firms like InsInternet that have designed and delivered a service that matches insurance buyers with a wide range of potential insurers. Customers place their requirements out for bid, and insurance companies respond with their best offers through an online application form. Once the buyer selects a product, the buyer and the seller are then electronically linked, and the ITB is no longer involved.

The auction and bidding areas of e-commerce are in their infancy. Transaction brokers like FastParts, e-Bid, OnSale, and others have created Internet-based (anonymous) bidding/auction environments. Settlements and shipments are handled offline, but posting, bidding, and pricing are completed on the Internet. Profit margins have risen dramatically for firms that operate in this area. For example, without the cost of warehousing, shipping, cardboard, shrink-wrap, floppy disks, fork lifts, and CDs, Netscape is enjoying profit margins of 90 percent (or higher). The Internet plays a major role in this success story for Netscape and the distribution of its products. In trucking and shipping areas, some shippers like UPS and FedEx have already linked their back-end systems to the Internet, and telecommunication practices that transmit information (via the Internet) give their global customers real-time access to package delivery information and their highly accurate tracking systems.

ITBs in the payment and credit areas are beginning to demonstrate a strong presence. Card processors like First Data, FirstUSA, CitiBank, and more are currently processing credit card authorizations, where the original request was generated from within the Internet infrastructure: an endpoint, of a sort. These payment and credit ITBs like First Data are using the Internet as another point-of-sale channel. There is tremendous room for growth in this area because today's volumes are very small because relatively few merchants are connected to the Internet and prepared to process transactions online. Telecommunications speeds, while improving day by day, still are prohibitive to some areas for timely processing. Banks and insurance firms are developing an Internet presence. Banks recognize the importance of the Internet banking, and many financial firms are in the process of reeengineering, or have already reengineered, their current business processes and applications. Insurers are in the process of reengineering their processes and applications so that they can begin to issue loans and insurance policies using the Internet, as their capabilities for connections into various diverse social structures continue to grow.

In the area of customer acquisition, ITBs are showing a presence. A number of Internet sites are beginning to assert their presence online in many communities. For example, the ITB *OnSale's* site creates an auction environment for computer equipment; still another ITB, *Auto-By-Tel*, provides linkages between auto dealers and customers who are using the Internet to look for the "best" automobile deals. Other somewhat larger ITB players are thinking about supermarkets, retail foods, and home shopping. These examples cross many industry segments. One example in the financial industry segment is Intuit; it is working to offer its customers basic Internet banking services, generalized investments services, and insurance services on the Internet. This is evident by its Quicken Deluxe 99™ product offering, and by its tight-integration with the company's Internet financial services site(s). Another important area of e-commerce is customer support, also referred to as customer care. Because most customer service databases are not directly linked to the Internet, this area often presents a challenge to potential ITBs. Sometimes, Internet sites (seemingly missing certain *Design Quality* characteristics) are perceived as crude for answering customer's questions. Furthermore, the most frequently asked questions (FAQs) are often not presented well, nor are they organized well. Sometimes these FAQs can be valuable, but more often than not, the FAQs are too general and out of date. Response times of e-mail to support customers with problems or questions are very slow (response times are reportedly measured in days, not minutes or hours). Timing is key. There will always be the case when people just need to speak with another human being, especially when difficult system troubles are at hand and time is of the essence. In this case, no e-commerce or Internet technology available (that is, in general use today) will satisfy that requirement. Internet telephony technologies and multimedia telecommunications technologies are progressing at aggressive rates. One day, in the not too distant future, the Internet will provide real-time viewing and real-time speech transmissions as simple-to-accomplish tasks. This form of personal interaction, a virtual-reality Internet interaction (if you will), will one day be a standard means of interpersonal and interbusiness communications throughout many global societies. Virtual-reality technologies, which extend beyond the scope of this book, have made tremendous advances in this area, with the incorporation of "Pervasive Computing" instruments and techniques.

To successfully develop ITBs today, several key challenges have been identified that require an in-depth treatment: the reluctance of sellers to significantly develop an Internet e-commerce presence; the difficulty and complexity involved in developing Internet-based channels that safely link and securely communicate with legacy systems and databases; and the fact that broader types of e-commerce technologies are still, in some cases, under development, such as telecommunications. The speed of Internet-hosted sessions seems to be slightly less than desirable. As telecommunication corporations and other commercial-grade telecommunication carriers improve their consumer services, with ISDN, cable, fiber-optics, and laser optics, then so will transmissions speeds improve. That is why the evolution of Internet e-commerce has been slow (and actually limited by telecom speeds, in some areas). The results for most of the pioneers in establishing ITBs have been traffic that is minuscule, with promises of higher demands through the evolution of the Internet itself. On the impressive side of the telecommunication problems, many telecomm carriers are finding wealth in becoming a "portal" to the Internet. To name a few, AT&T, WorldCom, New Zealand Telephone, and many more entrepreneurial solutions are coming forth from this sector of industry. Growth in this sector will render many benefits, yet unrealized by the Internet and Internet-2.

E-BUSINESS FACTORS TO CONSIDER

A factor for consideration when contemplating e-business is that many industry contenders, such as banks, insurance companies, investment companies, health care providers, and entertainment firms, believe that they control their customers and, furthermore, that their customer *brand* loyalty remains a strong metric. This is not always the case. Business enterprises do not believe that loyal customers, and loyal government-sector consumers, might simply leave their trusted brand for the convenience of one-stop shopping from another Internet-based broker. This, though, is a reality.

Inadequate services from any Internet solution provider is very simply resolved by the end user or consumer—in one simple click of the mouse: no problem.

Another equally important factor is that developing a transaction-based or e-commerce-focused Internet presence is both challenging and difficult, to say the least. The back-end integration is often the most difficult, costly, complex, and time-consuming of all the transition efforts. Technology is fine, as everyday it only improves, along with the practitioners' experiences with the application of any technology in the particular set. The general lack of *standard* interfaces for any of these "back-end" transactions forces internal developers (or consulting firms) to work on custom code to complete interfaces with each other's shipping and payment systems (for example). These particular processes could be enhanced by ITBs that outsource payment and delivery applications and services.

Finally, innovative e-commerce applications and massive amounts of Internet-based development continue to emerge almost daily. We can imagine the challenge in achieving the following goals:

- Building a context-sensitive graphical user interface and set of appropriate screens
- Provide multilingual support for end users so that they can view their most recent business transactions online
- Dealing with monetary and taxation issues
- Managing security and privacy issues
- Deploying personalized direct marketing Internet schemes that show product suggestions and usage patterns, for example, that are based on the last six buys a consumer may have executed online

These goals—and all of the ease and simplicity that they suggest—presents major challenges for e-commerce solution providers.

These problems introduced by e-commerce are not insurmountable obstacles; in fact, the opposite is true—they are, in many ways, being resolved each day. Many enterprises challenge these obstacles and overcome them with the determining factor as to *who* will play and *who* will lose in the ITB race to market. IBM, Microsoft, CitiBank, Netscape, America OnLine, just to name only a few, are leading contenders. The ITBs will be required to address a number of issues—for example, leveraging many types of established brand names, or branded types of services. An example of this occurs in the banking and finance industry where banks (for example, CitiBank) are using their brand to establish an ITB, believing that their *trusted* brand will attract both customers and suppliers such as insurance companies, mutual fund investment companies, and other interested corporate entities.

Another excellent example involves those companies with established and very large customer bases. Consider Intuit, which is quietly establishing a large customer base via the Internet and emerging as a major clearinghouse for personal finances. This, by some, is considered a major threat to financial institutions that have not yet gained their own competitive advantage in the banking and finance industries by using Internet e-commerce and e-business practices. Another good example of this is "portfolio management" that is secure and integral in all ways. Some public research groups believe that e-commerce technology adoptions represent a major opportunity for firms seeking to establish themselves in the global commerce space. An important entry barrier that acts as a hurdle for competitors is how long it takes to get established on the Internet, and how effective is that establishment. Generally, it takes several months before Internet development tools, and Internet developers, are able to deliver dynamic content-hosting environments, and then perhaps another several months to fine-tune the site. This elapsed time gives anyone with an existing Internet-based customer acquisition and support system a tremendous lead over its competition.

GLOBAL E-COMMERCE COMMUNITIES

The introduction of ITBs suggests a new global community of Internet intermediaries, one that includes competition in industry channels, banking sectors, finance sectors, and investment and insurance segments. Consider the intense competition across these channels of the various industries. In retailing, some enterprises will potentially face serious disadvantages. For example, ITBs avoid the overhead of inventory and can therefore provide significantly lower prices to consumers. To compensate and compete, some retailers must, in turn, establish closer relationships with their distributors so that they can handle direct drop-shipments, even split-shipments, to individual customers. This could prove less cost-effective in the long-term.

In the distribution industry, for example, companies that assume the role of "distributor" must leverage ITBs, rather than just compete with them. In essence, the distribution industries might consider leveraging a variety of ways of competing. Competition will not necessarily be just from manufacturers executing direct channels; rather, it will come from the ITBs. Distributors should not make the assumption that existing resellers or new online retailers will carry them through to their desired position. Distribution companies (that is, entities like Ingram and Merisel) could work with ITBs, such as pcOrder, to provide the appropriate consumer coverage. Shipping companies are beginning to lock in relationships with ITBs. Shipping firms such as FedEx and the United Parcel Service (UPS) are starting to engage in intercorporate relationships by integrating their package tracking systems deep into the fabric of the new intermediaries' Internet systems. This approach is a very smart strategy.

In the finance industry, banks, insurance companies, investment firms, and their respective processors will have to develop strategic methods to collaborate and to work with the ITBs. A good example of this approach is the third-party processors of credit card applications.

Some of these third-party processors (for example, First Data, FirstUSA, Total Systems, Net.B@nk, and CheckFree) are positioned well in this market place. ITBs will use these processors to create much higher volumes of electronic transactions to be processed. Interestingly, some new corporate entities (for example, CyberCash and First Virtual) may still be on a learning curve in the area of secure payment systems. Nonetheless, these Internet-based corporate entities are quickly finding that they can effect some of the largest changes in the New York Stock Exchange. Many areas in e-commerce, for instance, e-bidding (http://www.ebay.com), are allowing massive amounts of end-user Internet traffic, capable of gaining access to and using many of their e-business services.

New industrial channels will become a strategic imperative for banks, insurance companies, and brokers. These finance players will need to create their own Internet sites and transactional capabilities. These entities continue to perform this realignment, recognizing fully that their customers will also use other channels online—perhaps other, simpler, more attractive, and more efficient Internet sites. Credit and payment providers must be able to provide secured services for ITB partners across many sites. Certain ITBs (for example, Auto-By-Tel) will require some assistance in basic banking processes to complete the specific automobile purchasing transaction in a safe, electronic, and secure way. Global financial enterprises like banks, investment firms, certificate authority firms, and credit issuers can leverage their existing clearing and settlement processes—if they can provide these services in a simple-to-use, Internet-based service, again using the ITBs.

The notion of ITBs is beginning to grow significantly and is appearing in some rather fascinating areas. Internet *search engines* are one such area. Many vendors have already found lucrative markets in this consumer marketplace. The major vendors in these areas (Lycos, Yahoo!, Excite, InkTomi, Genesis Direct) must create or incorporate vertically focused search tools that can determine the difference between *research papers* and *paper products*.

Another group that could benefit from the emergence of ITBs is the digital certificate authorities (like Verisign) because some of the new intermediaries will require digital certificates for personal site financial customization, secured transaction designation, and final negotiations of sales contracts. Finally, there are the content-hosting providers. These entities may typically want to seek out business partnerships. One example of how these partnerships render value, is promised by those content providers that sell publications (Borders Books, Amazon.com, and so on), those that sell specific products (OfficeMax, Staples, and so forth), those that evaluate different products (Consumers Reports), or even those that provide specific types of reports.

Computer resellers, news periodical distributors, various financial magazines, and many different types of "Advisory" reports have all found a home on the Internet. The number of enterprises is large, and they all play a role in the world of e-commerce. These types of e-commerce companies will continue to appear, in numerous and innovative ways, with a variety of valuable content-providers of third-party information. This is occurring on a global scale and at an hourly rate.

IBM claims that *"servers are the computer engines of e-business. Furthermore, that every month there are 53,000 new servers that are connected to the Internet. That is 1.2 servers being connected per minute. And most important, this is only the beginning."* This claim makes an interesting discussion topic, which helps to establish the scope of the vast growth elements surrounding the world of e-commerce. Present the following assertions to an audience sometime:

- There are X number of servers connected to the Internet each month. Determine X *{answer 53,000 per month}*.
- There are Y number of servers being connected to the Internet each minute. Determine Y *{answer 1.2 per minute}*.

The audience responses will be varied with a wide range of answers, but this set of assertions (by IBM in late 1999) is guaranteed to generate some interesting discussions.

Part 2
E-commerce Channels to Generate Profitable Revenues

Electronic commerce has introduced new operating environments for business-to-business and business-to-consumers. The introduction of e-commerce raises new, innovative possibilities for global commerce and trade. What is beginning to emerge is the tip of an iceberg, which very much resembles that of an electronic global economy, using a common worldwide network where trade will be viewed as virtual. Internet commerce (or e-commerce) is ushering in a new way to help buyers find products and sellers to find buyers.

This part of the book includes several subjects related to marketing and distribution channels, information such as new channels that enhance competitive positioning and other important information related to electronic business environments, or e-business.

There will be several aspects of e-business explored in this part of the book. Many of the challenges surrounding specific industry solution sets are explored in this part of the book, including the "enablers" important in an e-commerce environment.

8

E-business Life-cycle Patterns

....

The practice of e-business is now the single fastest-growing area of e-commerce, especially in the business-to-consumer segment. The business-to-business segment is also aggressively advancing. Areas of key concern for businesses that are currently competing for business on the Internet are how to successfully reach consumers who use the Internet (especially for commerce or trade) and how to attract new consumers to engage in e-business. To address this issue, a good starting point would be an analysis of why consumers choose this medium of commerce over other, more traditional means. Why are online services and cell phones so popular? Some recent research provides interesting insights.

The identification of *target groups* and the characterization of these groups are important. Many e-commerce technology providers have already provided basic networking frameworks. The next challenge is *how* to build value into their products and services, the same value-added services the consumers are indicating they desire.

Key factors worthy of consideration look beyond demographics. Techno-graphics is a term based on a new segmentation that considers consumer motivations, spending, and attitudes as they relate to technology. This concept, *techno-graphics,* defines several market segments based on four technology motivators: family, career, entertainment, and status. For example, one of the larger segments is composed of technology lovers who are inclined to stay at home or are too busy in their careers to have the time to shop in malls. To attract these consumers, e-commerce firms should deliver efficiencies that appeal to nesters and careerists. Discount shopping for the home is made easy by e-business catalogs; these are very popular and growing across the consumer segment.

LIFE-CYCLE STRATEGIES WILL BE CHALLENGED

One hurdle that businesses must overcome is the question of *how* to successfully market their e-commerce technologies. Currently, one strategy is to ride all the media attention regarding the Internet and new technologies that link to the "information highway." This strategy anticipates some motivation based on mass understanding of the value these technologies bring to the target markets. Three things are occurring that will cause technology marketers to rethink their strategies: innovation overload, recession-related resistance, and technology backlash. In the area of innovation overload, consumers are being lambasted with media messages related to e-commerce technology hype.

The economy in the early 1990s was in a recession, and this had an effect on consumer attitudes on buying. The general consumer will not buy without proof of value. Furthermore, a significant number of consumers are struggling to balance career and family life with increased workloads due to downsizing. They do not always have the time to evaluate and possibly buy complex technologies that provide no immediate benefit. A good example of this is the recent advertising campaign of Honda with the theme, "*Simplify.*" Effective.

E-commerce companies marketing to consumer segments are finding that traditional demographic targeting falls short of expectations. Early users' experiences of e-commerce technologies vary from product to product (or service to service) and customer results are sometimes uncertain. There is a major dependency on the *quality* of the questions we as consumers are able to ask and, likewise, on the *correctness* of the information in the answer we consumers receive in turn. Simplification and accuracy are two key elements.

The techno-graphic segments of consumers are separated into three categories: primary technology motivation, attitude toward technology, and disposable income. The primary technology motivation category focuses on the primary reasons for the purchase of technology. For example, is it family, self-improvement, career, entertainment, business-related, or something else? The consumer attitude toward technology generally measures whether we as consumers believe that the technology solutions will enhance our lives. This is a key determining factor as to whether consumers embrace technologies that require high investments of time, like personal computers, or limit themselves to cheaper technologies like fax machines or answering machines. The last category is disposable income, which is simply stated: "What is affordable, based on the need?"

As business-to-business e-commerce trade continues to emerge, traditional boundaries will pale to insignificance. The Internet is rapidly transforming business-to-business marketing functions like advertising, sales support, and service delivery. Using the Internet, buyers are able to communicate directly with sellers and industry communities of interest. New forms of e-business marketing on the Internet are rapidly changing the rules of strategy.

Another manifestation of how e-commerce changes the way business is conducted is trade publishing. Trade publishers have traditionally used forms of "print" business models. Many publishers are now faced with the complex challenges associated with transforming their print models to the Internet e-commerce model. New business enterprises are entering the Internet trade publishing arena, with significantly lower costs, by using e-commerce models. These Internet-based trade publishers are gaining significant ground as they are earning as much as six times more in revenues than the traditional "print" trade publishers. These new enterprises utilize an e-commerce model that, in turn, helps to significantly reduce advertising budgets. Internet access for large and medium-sized businesses will be pervasive by the year 2001, and business-to business Internet commerce will rocket to $327 billion by the year 2002. Advertising will follow this e-commerce shift to the Internet. With the imminent growth of e-commerce and revenues surpassing $300 billion by the year 2002, it is projected that business advertising will top $2.5 billion by this same year, 2002. This will force traditional publishers to change their business processes from the business "print" model to the online e-business model.

VIRTUAL COMMERCE

Internet e-commerce indicates an incredible growth rate of 75 percent per year. The Internet will evolve into a *virtual commerce* transport platform during the next decade. Everyone will have access to the Internet. Enterprises of all sizes will link their remote sites via the Internet, thus making Internet e-commerce sites as indispensable as today's telephones.

Contact with customers and new prospects will be more frequent, providing a company's marketing wing with the increased responsibility of managing these new relationships. This means that traditional marketing vehicles are being challenged. As companies gain skills at managing customers and prospects, low-cost e-commerce marketing applications will yield high returns on investments. Companies will quickly recognize this new opportunity.

The challenge facing traditional publishers will be to find a niche in market space, using their industry savvy, their experience in offline promotions, and their contacts, to make an Internet portal pay. This will require that these companies acquire new skills. The ability to electronically collaborate will be very important. The old paradigm of traditional publishing must give way to collaboration and the forming of partnerships to create transcendant Internet experience for their consumers. These companies will need to invest in e-commerce solutions, and instead of seeking short-term profits, secure idea shares in the valuable vertical markets. The days of the paper directories are not what they were 10 years ago. Instead, online directories are being used as highly efficient e-commerce tools that attract interested consumers. Traditional publishers need to move their data online and add new e-commerce interactive capabilities while mixing in advertising and fee-based online models.

BUSINESS CHANGE

Internet startups have the opportunity to be competitive in this "content-hosting" market space, by taking on the challenge of building sufficient network traffic and loyalty to provide a formidable entry barrier to trade publishers who decide to move into this market space. They will do this, if for no other reason, to protect their online franchises. They should leverage their independent status to pursue traffic-sharing deals with multiple partners, especially when these partners have some form of industry influence.

By sharing traffic with trade publishers that have content, Internet start-ups that have transaction features can negotiate nonexclusive deals with the two or three key publications in an industry to become the premier "portal" with the broadest variety of content. Internet start-ups can provide Internet site hosting services to industry associations that have been slow in putting up Internet sites and infrastructure. They can also even help construct Internet sites in exchange for exposure to the association's membership, thereby giving the Internet start-up instant credibility (and good will) in a large community of interested consumers.

Business-to-business marketers can begin to prepare for the Internet's central role in marketing. What they need to do is explore ways in which they can provide more value to their customers. One way they can do this is to evaluate their existing sites to see *how* much increased value they can offer customers; they can also begin to develop and offer a stream of features that draw customers back frequently. The Internet then becomes the hub of their marketing efforts (see Figure 8.1). Using various incentives and online ads, portal sites tend to lure customers to their sites, frequently offering online surveys and promotions, allowing them to better understand the buying patterns of their customers.

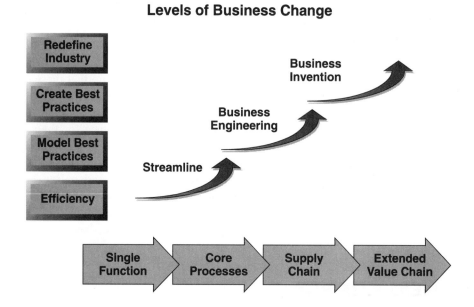

Levels of Business Change

Figure 8.1

Businesses must evaluate their existing sites and determine how to offer increased value to their customers.

With this market intelligence they can apply this knowledge, determining the timing and context of future contacts. This will enable them to provide more value to their customers and reach them at key decision points.

The online marketing opportunities are available now, and they can be very profitable for creative e-business specialists. Using relatively small investments, e-business enterprises can render significant customer values, with significant corresponding returns on the initial e-commerce investments.

9
Challenges Surrounding E-banking

....

$\mathbf{T}$he state of banking (including investment banking) on the Internet is progressing at a rapid pace, with routine services including balances, account transfers, and bill presentment and payment being delivered daily. Securities brokerage solutions on the Internet are also growing at a rapid pace, and conversely, banks are being challenged by aggressive online competitors, like E*Trade, TradingDirect, Net.B@nk, Schwab, Ameritrade, Intuit, and many more. Many financial firms are being forced to respond to this global, electronic need—or, they may find themselves facing a potential for corporate restructuring. What banks are attempting to do by going online is primarily to retain customers.

Strategically, banks will be continually challenged for distribution to retain their customers and market share. Today, many of the leading banking enterprises distribute their presence (pervasively) over the Internet, opening financial distribution chains that include (but are not necessarily limited to) content hosting gateways, open financing portals, and investment sites. It will be difficult for many SMB (small-to-medium business) banks to succeed as open-finance providers. These SMB banks will need to specialize, using larger financial enterprises that act as consolidators to distribute their products online—throughout the world. There are many examples of commercial banking institutions today that leverage e-commerce for their own competitive advantages.

Many banking institutions currently offer online banking via proprietary platforms and personal financial management packages (for example, Quicken) using the Internet. Some examples of such institutions are Net.B@nk, CyberCash, FirstUSA, Ameritrade, Art Technology Group, Broadvision, CheckFree, Destiny, Edify, Excite, Home Account Network, Home Financial Network, IBM, Integrion, Intelidata, Intuit, mbanx, MECA, Merrill Lynch, Microsoft, Prudential, Quadravision, Security First, Vanguard, Vertigo, Swiss Bank, Women's Connection Online, and Yahoo!—and this is only a partial list. The results of these different e-business enterprises are more than remarkable.

E-BANKING LEVERAGES E-COMMERCE

Banking institutions are countering their competitors by leveraging e-commerce technologies and various service offerings online (see Figure 9.1). They recognize that cus-

Banks and Online Banking Strategies

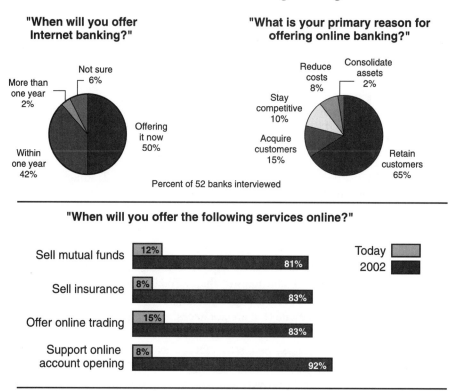

"When will you offer Internet banking?"

Not sure 6%
More than one year 2%
Offering it now 50%
Within one year 42%

"What is your primary reason for offering online banking?"

Reduce costs 8%
Consolidate assets 2%
Stay competitive 10%
Acquire customers 15%
Retain customers 65%

Percent of 52 banks interviewed

"When will you offer the following services online?"

Today / 2002

Sell mutual funds 12% / 81%
Sell insurance 8% / 83%
Offer online trading 15% / 83%
Support online account opening 8% / 92%

"Will you allow consumer data to be passed through third-party sites?"

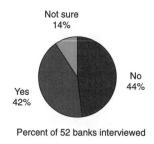

Not sure 14%
No 44%
Yes 42%

Percent of 52 banks interviewed

Source: Forrester Research, February 1998

Figure 9.1

Banking e-commerce strategies are very aggressive and yield many added values for consumers.

tomer retention is key to their corporate strategies. The biggest threat to banks from a competitive perspective is coming from the nonbanking business community. Typically these competitors are online brokerages and software companies (for example, Microsoft, Intuit). Brokerages appear to be the greatest threat to banks. Banks generally agree that, when their members go to another bank, there's the potential that they'll come back because the services are comparable. But, once money runs into those brokerages, those customers are never coming back.

Banks (in general) agree that some of their top competitors are the software companies that wear a cloak. Microsoft and Intuit pretend they are aggregators; few see them as enterprises that might want to get into the banking business. The term "aggregators" is derived from the fact that various IT companies can serve as enablers for other types of industries that are working to create an e-business brand image.

Another important tactic that banks are using to compete for e-commerce business opportunities is adding online investment services and various insurance products to their portfolios of offerings. This aggressive expansion into nonbank products like investments and insurance planned for the next five years demonstrates the determination of the banking community to diversify by offering other companies' products or developing their own. For example, banks contend they have to build their own brokerage and insurance services onto their own *xyzNet* product, as soon as possible, so their customers will not go looking around. Banks also contend that when they already have a product—like a brokerage service—it is hard to make the argument for offering someone else's brokerage services.

NOTION OF MASS-MARKET AND E-BANKING

The notion of mass-market is quite specific. The customer does not want an internet stock broker type of service—instead, the intent is that a bank can migrate customers to invest with their own commercial investment products. The reality is that many consumers, as investors, choose to utilize many banking and investment management sites for specific content related to specific types of products. As for the banking Internet sites, very few (perhaps none) of them possess the capability to manage a diversified investment portfolio. The answer for many people is to use third-party Internet stock exchange brokerages, which allow the customer to buy diverse products and manage many different investments in an objective environment.

An important strategy for the banking community will be retaining aggregated customer data. Some banks contend their customers do not want to see the banks providing consumer data through third parties. Banks generally try to hold on to what is theirs (so to speak). Financial institutions still get nervous sending information to CheckFree. They do not want to relinquish control because they will then be like a lot of other organizations, passing consumer data through third parties. Banks may try to resist until the last minute, but ultimately almost all banks will have to join the e-commerce environment in an open, more objective, and customer-centric role.

E-BANKING COMPETITION

It seems clear that to remain competitive banks must do three things: go online to retain their customers, engage in nonroutine banking online, and maintain customer controls. Banks, however, will face enormous pressure to significantly change their processes, changes that include strong biases toward in-house proprietary products and tightly held data. There are three key driving forces that support this premise: consumer requirements, market pressures, and e-commerce technology innovations.

What banks have to recognize is that consumers want convenience. For consumers, simplification is the key. The financial lives of today's consumers have become more complex than anyone could even imagine a decade ago. Therefore, asset ownership is an important question that needs to be addressed on a daily basis, and some might say on an hourly (or per-minute) basis.

The point here is that consumers require easy-to-access information about their financial account(s). They require the capability to query their account balances and transaction histories electronically in a user-friendly manner. Simply stated, consumers want online data whenever and wherever they have to retrieve it. Consumers also require consolidated account reports because many consumers maintain multiple financial relationships. Another very important requirement is universal access to account information. This requirement has led to banks creating shared financial services networks on the Internet. One example of this is a large banking consortium that is emerging as a backbone of an online banking network. Another excellent example is how Quicken™ allows the end user to publish his or her portfolio on the Internet, for viewing while away from his or her normal workstation location(s).

The e-commerce market forces financial institutions to open up. The current barriers that prevent financial institutions from sharing account data and products will topple. A compelling force driving this change (or paradigm shift) is from financial institutions that do not fear breaking with the status quo. These include firms like Schwab's Mutual Fund OneSource and BankOne's HomeByNet mortgage marketplace(s), which have enough confidence in their own brands to form partnerships with competitors.

Furthermore, there are the financial content aggregators who are developing new models for e-commerce. As an example, these financial content aggregators (for example, sites like InsInternet, Intuit's Quicken.com, Microsoft's Investor, and others) are establishing themselves as virtual hubs by offering other financial institutions the capability to leverage their online financial services.

CONTENT AGGREGATORS

The content aggregators charge participation fees and advertising dollars. They attract consumers by offering many diverse choices. Typically these sites provide a variety of financial educational materials, news, and financial planning tools. The offerings at these sites are from a wide range of global financial services providers. Furthermore, there are communities of interest that provide their members with content-hosting environments, financial product information, and adhoc investing opinions. For example, there is "Women's Connection Online." This site provides services for professional women, including a value-added service center for personal finances, discount brokerage information, insurance, and other banking services. This is a very innovative environment.

E-BANKING DEPENDENCIES ON TECHNOLOGIES

The emerging technologies that are being developed to accommodate the growth of e-commerce make account consolidations simpler. These e-commerce technologies include security, intrusion detection, firewall filtering, messaging protocols, data warehousing, and protection from competitive sniffing or intrusion technologies. An example of messaging protocols is the Open Financial Exchange (OFX). The OFX technology is a portal for data retrieval from e-commerce financial management applications (for example, Quicken, Money). Other examples include very complicated encryption schemes for the protection and integrity of data in transit. Integrity depends on technologies, and e-banking depends on integrity.

An important capability is moving sensitive data to and from Internet-based financial e-business sites. Data warehouses will (and do now) serve as large data repositories. The data contained in these data warehouses may be from different sources. Enterprises that act as consolidators will make it possible to share data from different companies using technologies from data warehousing vendors (for example, IBM, Microsoft, Informatica, Red Brick, Oracle, and Sybase). Other companies will act as "outsourcers" that will provide easy-to-use front-end applications that consumers can use to manage their own financial and investment accounts. One clear requirement for this consolidation approach will be the development of technologies that protect detailed account data from being observed by competitors: This is an ongoing challenge.

As mentioned in the beginning of this book, there are many definitions of e-commerce. It is therefore useful to continue to explore yet another e-commerce model for the banking and finance industry, one called the *Open-finance Distribution Chain* (see Figure 9.2). This model represents a movement away from the individual bank ownership paradigm of financial data, to an *open and sharing* environment among finance companies—resulting in a new online distribution hierarchy. Some industry participants predict that three primary distribution layers will evolve during the next five years:

1. Portals
2. Open-finance providers
3. Proprietary sites

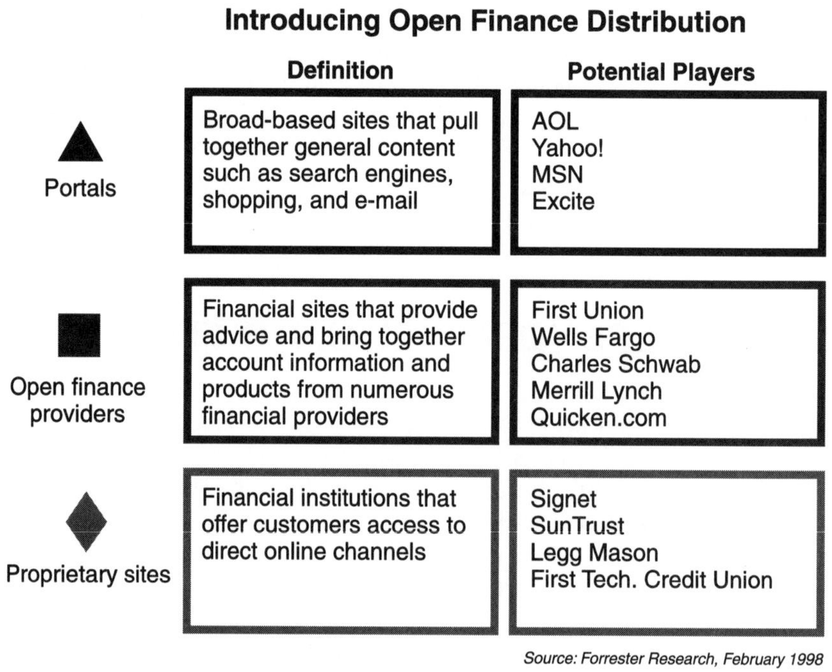

Introducing Open Finance Distribution

	Definition	Potential Players
▲ Portals	Broad-based sites that pull together general content such as search engines, shopping, and e-mail	AOL Yahoo! MSN Excite
■ Open finance providers	Financial sites that provide advice and bring together account information and products from numerous financial providers	First Union Wells Fargo Charles Schwab Merrill Lynch Quicken.com
◆ Proprietary sites	Financial institutions that offer customers access to direct online channels	Signet SunTrust Legg Mason First Tech. Credit Union

Source: Forrester Research, February 1998

Figure 9.2

The Open Finance Distribution Model illustrates how many diverse companies can work together to appear as a seamless e-business solution.

In this model, portals will deliver an audience to finance providers by providing content that consumers want (for example, search capabilities, news, purchasing, and e-mail) (see Figure 9.3). In turn they provide fee-based access to companies that wish to advertise goods or services.

This model is attractive to banking and finance industry critics for a variety of reasons. One key reason is to gain attention from potential customers. One way these firms will achieve this is through personalization of the financial account information. Furthermore, those sites demonstrating excellence in *Design Quality* will attract millions of loyal users. The attraction will result from compelling content and site competence (for example, Yahoo! reportedly dedicates nearly 75 percent of its staff to content management and technology development). Another factor to consider is the potential to become one of a few players in this market space, as their value grows very significantly through the addition of millions of users (for example, AOL has more than 10 million subscribers and Yahoo! has over 26 million site visits per month).

Open-finance providers represent a new type of enterprise that attracts consumers by aggregating account information and by selling financial service packages from many finance companies and banks. Some estimate that one-fifth of the banking and financial

Open Finance Distribution Hierarchy

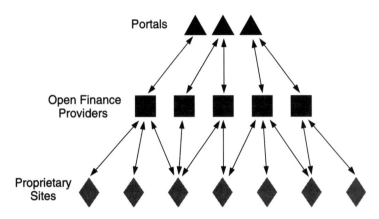

Portals

Open Finance
Providers

Proprietary
Sites

Source: Forrester Research, February 1998

Figure 9.3

The Open Finance Distribution Model implies a hierarchy. This figure simply illustrates a directed graph (of a sort) to other relevant services in the e-business environment.

industry customers will enter business relationships through interactions with open-finance providers. What are some of the key characteristics of open finance providers?

Destination sites aim to gain customers by analyzing account data to provide the best financial guidance to their customers. They accomplish this by combining analytical research from consolidated account summaries and products from multiple finance and banking institutions. Another outflanking ploy these companies will use is to purchase distribution from portals, thereby controlling finance channels (for example, Intuit spends more than $70 million to retain control of the finance channels at AOL and Excite). These companies are also investing in the building of transitive content, which integrates financial transactions with account interactivity.

ESTABLISHED BRANDS

Some larger companies with well-established brands will always prevail in the e-commerce market space. The reasons for this appear to be threefold:

- Well-established brands inspire trust (for example, First Union, Wells Fargo, Bank of Switzerland and other brands consumers might trust)
- Larger companies can afford the entrepreneurial spirit to market and sell other products (brokers like Merrill Lynch, Schwab, and Fidelity Investments aggregate the financial products of other firms)

- Larger companies foster early adoptions of e-commerce and therefore will (for some period) control distribution (for example, Citibank, Schwab, Fidelity, and Net.B@nk, which display the importance of leadership in Internet distribution channels)

To provide support for their existing customers, banks and other financial institutions will provide channel linkages to serve their customers. They will accomplish this by using proprietary sites. One characteristic of the proprietary sites is the basic services that banks and financial institutions can provide their customers. This includes services like searching transaction histories, investing in CDs, bonds, and mutual funds, or correcting a bank error or client discrepancy. Another distinction is the linkages to other open-finance providers.

These e-banking linkages will give customers access to other accounts or the options to buy products from other open-finance providers. These financial services companies and banks will tend to gravitate toward emerging technical standards (for example, Microsoft's Distributed Internet Architecture for Financial Services) that enable banks to rapidly develop new customer-focused applications, using special e-commerce tools to connect to legacy transaction systems.

E-BANKING WITHIN THE COMMUNITY INTEREST SITE

Finally, there is the syndication of sales through Internet community interest sites. Banking enterprises are beginning to multiply their points of presence as a means to increase sales of their products. As an example, Chase and KeyCorp sell auto loans at the Auto-By-Tel Internet e-business site. This collaborative approach makes very good sense in the e-commerce environment: Simply speaking, only one click of the mouse through a "hot-link" and the customer is there. This process needs to be as seamless as possible; this is a *Design Quality* issue.

Open-finance distribution and e-commerce technology innovations will act as catalysts for the growth of online banking. This growth will not appear very dramatic during the next few years, probably because many banks may be competing to begin providing banking services on the Internet. During the first few years of the next millennium, open-finance distribution will make significant progress and consumers will find it much easier to do business with banks online. By the year 2003, a significant percentage of U.S. households will bank online (see Figure 9.4).

The emergence of new e-commerce technologies will make it easier for consumers to engage in online banking. Ultimately private dialup systems will become obsolete. Key Internet financial service providers offer fee-based services to banks and financial institutions for the use of their e-commerce banking and finance applications. Furthermore, bill presentment and payment innovations will continue to accelerate

Households Banking and Investing Online By Income

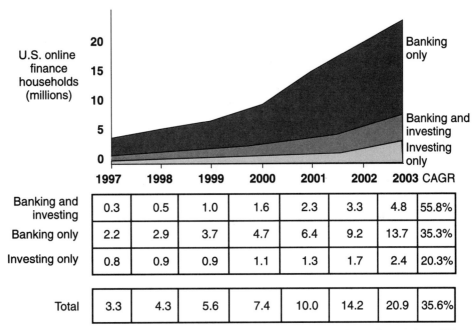

	1997	1998	1999	2000	2001	2002	2003	CAGR
Banking and investing	0.3	0.5	1.0	1.6	2.3	3.3	4.8	55.8%
Banking only	2.2	2.9	3.7	4.7	6.4	9.2	13.7	35.3%
Investing only	0.8	0.9	0.9	1.1	1.3	1.7	2.4	20.3%
Total	3.3	4.3	5.6	7.4	10.0	14.2	20.9	35.6%

Source: Forrester Research, August 1998

Figure 9.4

Open-finance distribution and e-commerce technology innovations will act as catalysts for the growth of online banking.

during the next few years. This is all occurring as a direct result of the introduction of new e-commerce applications.

What are the banks and other financial firms doing, from a business and strategic perspective, to position themselves so they can effectively leverage open-finance distribution? One clear tactic appears to be to place a *lock* on portals. These financial enterprises (for example, First Union, Wells Fargo, Merrill Lynch, and Schwab) will move with lightning speed to gain control of these financial portals making, three key moves:

- Differentiate themselves by their market segments
- Dichotomize product development and its distribution channels to keep competitors at bay
- Unload content hosting and associated support functions to portal partners that are not related to their industry

Another tactic will be for e-banking enterprises competing in this market space to engage in ubiquitous distribution tactics. As an example, many small-to-medium companies do not have the resources (or brand recognition) to compete as open-finance providers. These companies must flood the available distribution channels, open-finance providers, and special-interest sites. This will make it difficult for competitors that are not early adopters of e-commerce, who may insist on traditional processes and products. There is right now, and there will continue to be, a long and steady stream of existing customers who insist on easy-access and user-friendly banking or financial e-business sites.

Then, of course, there is always the case where the early adopters are well rewarded. As an example, Internet upstart Amazon.com has a market capitalization (from time to time) that is two to three times that as book retailing giant Barnes & Noble. Amazon's secret? It is quite simple: Amazon.com entered the Internet e-business market first and made it easy for end users to reach its site through thousands of affiliates that distribute its products. Furthermore, many universities are now beginning to attach Amazon.com's link to their own Web pages, to encourage students to purchase helpful reading materials for their coursework. This example should be an impetus for financial institutions and banks to move swiftly. Speed to market (or to Internet) is the strategic thrust.

What are the effects of solutions like *open-finance distribution*? The Internet and e-commerce will drive the open distribution finance model toward the development of a new market space that will expose the commodity nature of most financial products.

This will greatly reward early e-commerce finance adapters of e-commerce: the first movers like Net.B@nk (stock NTBK:NYSE). This e-banking growth segment will potentially result in a huge chasm in the market. Large enterprises that are early e-commerce contenders in the open-finance distribution space will continue to grow. The Internet seems to exemplify the advantages of brand and scale.

Simply stated, larger banks have millions of customers that interact with them on a daily basis while other financial institutions do not share the same interaction. Therefore, these larger banking enterprises will acquire smaller but effective open-finance distributors (for example, Merrill, E*Trade, Direct Trading) and capture open-finance leadership. Meanwhile, medium-sized financial companies will find themselves deep in the market chasm. Remember that smaller banks (between $10 billion and $100 billion in assets) do not have the assets or resources to wage battle on all e-banking fronts, as do some of their larger counterparts. A fundamental means of survival may be specialization. Examples of *specialization* would be in areas like the sale of best-of-breed products (for example, manufacturing mortgages for a few basis points less) that can be sold through open-finance providers. Some others will specialize in niche markets, like community-oriented banks.

Internet banking is an exciting area of e-commerce progress. The possibilities may be more than what we already understand of the banking industry. Day traders have purportedly caused the U.S. stock markets to fluctuate on certain days (still for unknown reasons), and many traditional financial experts criticize the objectives of day traders as reckless and potentially dangerous to a financial portfolio.

It is amazing that these types of financial securities trading transactions are now daily activities for many people on the Internet (both novices and experts). And most amazing of all, a person requires only a PC, a modem, and time to execute the trade. Personal financial wealth is now simpler to self-manage for many, by virtue of innovative Internet e-banking solutions. This paradigm shift is welcomed by many.

10

E-business Enablers

....

$\mathbf{T}$he growth in the number of businesses moving toward enabling e-commerce technologies to conduct e-businesses on the Internet will accelerate exponentially during the next few years. Research firms are predicting that business-to-businesses e-commerce growth will skyrocket. As seen in Figure 10.1, during 1998 only $43 billion of online e-commerce was conducted by businesses. Recent forecasts from some of these same research firms predict that in the United States alone business-to-business e-commerce will reach unprecedented levels: $1.3 trillion by 2003. That figure represents about 9.4 percent of the total business sales projected for that year. The migration of other industries toward e-commerce will vary, with the computing industry reaching 20 percent and other industries (like heavy-duty equipment) reaching less than 2 percent. The results of applying e-commerce solutions will change the tactics of many companies, especially in terms of supply chain management. This startling e-commerce growth will accelerate to high speed between 2002 and 2003, growing at a projected annual rate of 99 percent.

E-BUSINESS CATALYST

What is the catalyst behind this astounding e-commerce and e-business growth rate? In fact, many industries are moving toward the e-business life-cycle continuum at an alarming rate. Industries are crossing over business *chasms* by linking their customers, business partners, suppliers, decision makers, and other key employees together to conduct various forms of collaboration and e-business (see Figure 10.2). This is being achieved through the utilization of Internet, intranet, and extranet technologies.

During the coming years, more industrial and business enterprises will move toward e-commerce solutions, primarily because of the enhanced business value they will yield, once carefully crafted into one or more innovative e-business solutions. What once was more suggestive of a corporate strategy will become a key component of their core business operations management. This is a catalyst. Global networking

95

U.S. Business iCommerce Revenue

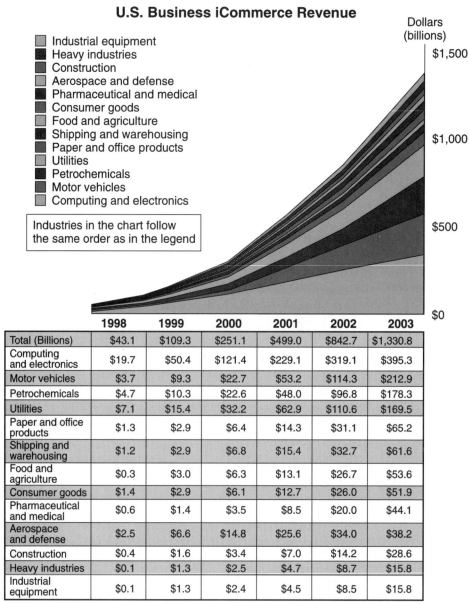

Legend:
- Industrial equipment
- Heavy industries
- Construction
- Aerospace and defense
- Pharmaceutical and medical
- Consumer goods
- Food and agriculture
- Shipping and warehousing
- Paper and office products
- Utilities
- Petrochemicals
- Motor vehicles
- Computing and electronics

Industries in the chart follow
the same order as in the legend

	1998	1999	2000	2001	2002	2003
Total (Billions)	$43.1	$109.3	$251.1	$499.0	$842.7	$1,330.8
Computing and electronics	$19.7	$50.4	$121.4	$229.1	$319.1	$395.3
Motor vehicles	$3.7	$9.3	$22.7	$53.2	$114.3	$212.9
Petrochemicals	$4.7	$10.3	$22.6	$48.0	$96.8	$178.3
Utilities	$7.1	$15.4	$32.2	$62.9	$110.6	$169.5
Paper and office products	$1.3	$2.9	$6.4	$14.3	$31.1	$65.2
Shipping and warehousing	$1.2	$2.9	$6.8	$15.4	$32.7	$61.6
Food and agriculture	$0.3	$3.0	$6.3	$13.1	$26.7	$53.6
Consumer goods	$1.4	$2.9	$6.1	$12.7	$26.0	$51.9
Pharmaceutical and medical	$0.6	$1.4	$3.5	$8.5	$20.0	$44.1
Aerospace and defense	$2.5	$6.6	$14.8	$25.6	$34.0	$38.2
Construction	$0.4	$1.6	$3.4	$7.0	$14.2	$28.6
Heavy industries	$0.1	$1.3	$2.5	$4.7	$8.7	$15.8
Industrial equipment	$0.1	$1.3	$2.4	$4.5	$8.5	$15.8

Source: Forrester Research, November 1998

Figure 10.1

Almost every industry has established some form of Internet e-business presence.

infrastructures now exist to support such advanced e-commerce models as auctions, bidding, contracting, service deliveries, product deliveries, hosting e-business content, and more. Solutions are really limited only by one's way of thinking: an *idea-share* of a sort. This of intellectual capital (for the moment), and not yet intellectual property.

The Movement Toward E-commerce

Informational   **Transactional**

Access	**Presence**	**Integration**	**E-commerce**
•WWW	•Establish home	•Leverage existing	•Networked
•Newsgroups	page	infrastructure,	applications and
•E-mail	•Marketing-	applications,	services
•FTP...	oriented	content...	•Virtual enterprise
	•Relatively static	•E-commerce	•Communities of
		•Security and privacy	interest
		•Customer service	

The CHASM

Simple   **Rapid**
Approach   **Growth**

Figure 10.2

The "chasm" seems to be the most difficult area for businesses to traverse in their movement toward a successful e-business transformation.

The enablement of e-business services is rapidly reaching the stage where information technology competitors are focused on supporting e-commerce, rather than the more traditional methods of computing technologies (see Figure 10.3). In line with

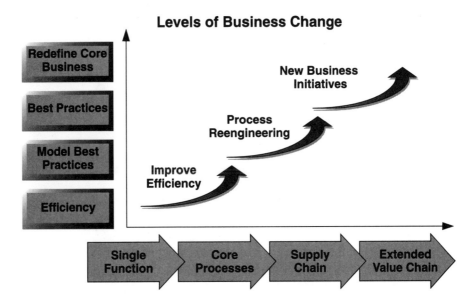

Levels of Business Change

Redefine Core Business

Best Practices

Model Best Practices

Efficiency

Improve Efficiency

Process Reengineering

New Business Initiatives

| Single Function | Core Processes | Supply Chain | Extended Value Chain |

Figure 10.3

The e-business transformation has very distinct levels of change that tend to result in improved revenue streams, new e-business service lines, and more effective business practices.

this, mainstream hardware and software suppliers (for example, Microsoft, IBM, Netscape, Oracle, Compaq, Dell, Cisco, Novell, and others) are developing and introducing advanced e-commerce application environments and machine platforms.

The e-business transformation effect will spark a hyper-growth catalyst that will lead to unprecedented levels of innovation in e-commerce solutions using the Internet. There is, perhaps, an e-commerce threshold that symbolizes the dynamics of e-business—that is, a radical change from rudimentary supply chain relationships, toward an environment with much broader and deeper market dynamics (see Figure 10.4). The effect of e-business is somewhat analogous to the chain reaction of a shock wave; it sets off what appears to be an endless chain reaction of businesses embracing e-commerce and adding their own innovative solutions to the chain. In a sense, e-businesses acts as a vortex staging other e-business opportunities that, in turn, leverage other e-business solutions.

LEAD FROM THE FRONT

E-business leaders, such as IBM, EDS, Cisco, L.L. Bean, Schwab, CitiBank, and Federal Express, provide excellent examples of the business values realized in applications of e-business solutions. These firms, along with other early leaders of innovation, are leading by example, acting as a catalyst sparking the excitement of other e-business effects. An e-business road rage, of a sort.

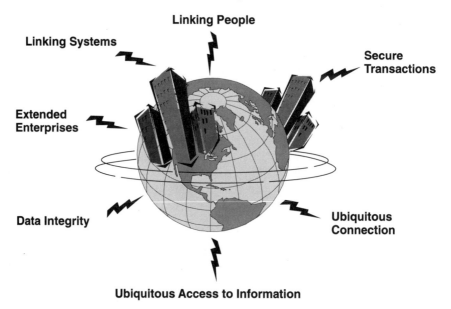

Figure 10.4

Corporations able to "lead from the front" will be those enterprises that can best manage their own innovations.

As larger enterprises create e-business environments and leverage e-commerce applications in their own core businesses, they will encourage *buy-in* from other supply chains. For example, Ford, GM, or GE strongly encourage their key suppliers to trade with them, online, as they seek to lower their own costs of doing business and improve their internal efficiencies. This means that meeting customer demands will supplant staying even with competitors.

Suppliers, in turn, will provide much of the stimuli for customers to buy over the Internet. They will also offer incentives to their own suppliers by means of various partnership or alliance programs, hoping that their customers will gradually embrace online channels instead of more costly channels like telephone and fax. Customer relationship management, which aims to leverage e-commerce solutions to manage enhanced customer relationships, looms large in the era of online trade. Enterprises are looking to gain economies of scale through the collaborative environments fostered by the Internet. There will clearly be (*and there are today*) outstanding leaders in e-business solutions. These corporate leaders will be the pace setters for other businesses and industries around the world. These business leaders will change the rules of many, if not all, of our industry practices. As illustrated in the text that follows, there is an e-business continuum that enterprises must traverse in becoming an e-business, with significant realized values as the result.

Typically the path starts out with simple and small initiatives, soon showing gradual growth toward reengineering their core business processes to achieve their strategy. This will then help them to realign themselves to be more profitable and to gain greater competitive advantages.

The travel industry is a leading e-business model; it has crossed the business chasm and reengineered its core business processes. Interestingly, the insurance industry is definitely challenged in the e-business continuum.

THE E-BUSINESS EFFECT

The e-business model will emerge as the new model for doing business (see Figure 10.5). This will represent a major shift in how global trade is conducted and will clearly force new economic models to emerge. Buyers and sellers will reengineer their core business processes to adapt to the new e-business economy.

Perhaps the most significant area that will act as a catalyst to online trade will be the supply chains that link trading partners as they develop and distribute products. Each industry will have varying rates of adoption. How quickly industries enable e-business in their respective markets will depend on the level of sophistication of the their current IT environments, their agility and their core skills, and their use of new e-business technologies and e-commerce applications and platforms.

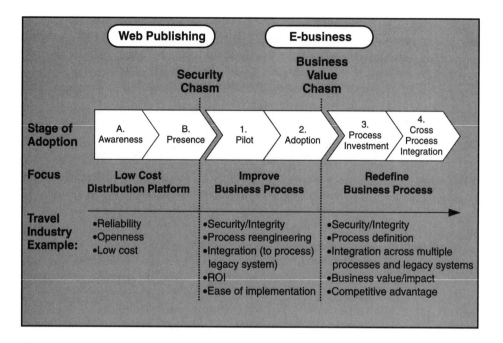

Figure 10.5

An example of the business transformation that can occur, depending on the industry segment and specific e-business objectives.

Some examples of early adopters of e-commerce representing various industries would include L.L. Bean, Boeing Aerospace, Moore Business Products, Cisco, Citibank, Schwab, IBM, Intuit, and Microsoft. Consider IBM, which began reengineering core business processes as early as 1993, gradually moving toward becoming an e-business company that offers many services (see Figure 10.6). No longer would the "*big blue*" company image make tremendous sense.

Companies like IBM began with their human resource and financial systems and moved rapidly to integrate e-business technologies into their supply chain; they ultimately have successfully linked their suppliers and business partners into their legacy systems. The results of these initiatives are nothing short of spectacular: hence the term *e-business*. For example, e-procurement e-business solutions have resulted in a tremendous savings for many global corporate enterprises. This area of business is often a starting point for many e-business transformations. The time it takes to process and fulfill purchase orders has dramatically been reduced, from days to minutes.

In the supply chain area, IBM has significantly improved its order-processing cycle-time, thereby dramatically improving customer satisfaction numbers. Now IBM has achieved an overall savings of about $1.7 billion annually. Cisco was able to double its annual revenues from $2 billion to $4 billion, in part by using e-business technologies. Cisco, with its many *router* products, is also considered by stock analysts to be a main infrastructure provider to the Internet industry. IBM is a main provider to the Internet

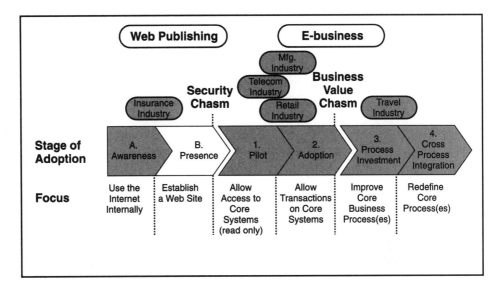

Figure 10.6

The e-business transformation enterprise needs to consider the various levels of e-commerce.

industries, with its innovative leadership in "e-business" and its diversified set of platforms that support and interact with the Internet in almost any way one could imagine.

Both IBM and Xerox Palo Alto Research Center (PARC) spend vast amounts
of money on research. It was PARC that in 1993 first began to research *ubiquitous
computing*. The Internet, at this early stage, was merely a topic being carefully introduced by the ARPA development team. Many creative scientists have contributed
to this e-commerce playing field over the years. Such individuals are key to the
overall success and direction of both Internet and Internet/2 practices; the future set of
e-commerce technologies.

Schwab created a whole new way of trading stocks and other securities using
e-business technologies to enable online trading capabilities for its customers. Schwab
grew rapidly from day 1, gaining more than 100,000 customers; in just three months,
Schwab found itself serving 1.5 million clients. There are many other excellent e-business
trading companies on the Internet; Schwab is merely one example. TradingDirect,
E*Trade, and many more e-business sites are definitely worth investigating for those
interested in placing closer (more personal) controls on their investments. Some trading
sites like E*Trade offer after-hours trading capabilities for the convenience of its customer
base. These "benefits" are attractive to the casual Internet end user.

Safeway, the grocery store chain, offers still another example of an enterprise
achieving new innovative business values through the integration of e-business technologies. Safeway currently manages point-of-sale profile data on 6 million customers, helping the company to determine which stock items to maintain on their
shelves to meet customer demands. Safeway is not the only supermarket performing

this. NCR (National Cash Register, Co.) is working on home-based virtual shopping. Chase Manhattan Bank delivered significant business values by using e-business technologies to develop a *big picture* view of its customers, greatly enhancing its customer relationship management capabilities and online banking facilities.

MARKET DYNAMICS

Market dynamics will drive industries through the e-business continuum. These powerful, rather unpredictable forces will also be a major factor in how quickly online trade will develop within any given industry segment. The speed of e-business adoption will vary from one industry to another. Market space structural factors and available e-business technology adoptions will be the ultimate determining factors. For instance, industries that are more innovative yet agile will forge new ways to accommodate customer demands for online buying.

Table 10.1 describes some examples of industrial supply chains and their gradual adoptions of e-commerce solutions.

Table 10.1　　Vertical Markets with Centralized Needs

Industry	What's Included	What Moves to E-commerce
Computers and electronics	Semiconductors, manufacturing, wholesale and business retail of hardware, software products	Wholesale, business retail, and manufacturer supply chains
Motor vehicles	Auto components, manufacturing, distribution	Vehicle wholesale, subassembly supply chain, spare parts wholesale
Petrochemicals	Equipment, extraction and refining, manufacturing, distribution	Wholesale and distribution of petroleum, chemicals, and plastics
Utilities	Gas and electric industry equipment, exploration, production, distribution	Transmission and wholesale distribution of gas and electricity, equipment, spare parts
Paper and office products	Paper and furniture manufacturing and supplies, distribution	Distribution and replenishment, manufacturing supply chains
Shipping and warehousing	All modes of transport, warehousing, and logistics	Load tendering commitments, contract bids, dead-load auctions
Food and agriculture	Farm equipment and supplies, farm products, food processing, distribution	Equipment supply chains, grocery and farm supplies distribution, machinery spare parts
Consumer and goods	Manufacture and distribution of appliances, home electronics, leisure goods, furniture, and apparel	Consumer goods wholesale, manufacturing supply chains
Pharmaceutical and medical	R&D, manufacture and wholesale of pharmaceuticals, medical equipment, and supplies	Pharmaceutical distribution, supplies replenishment, medical manufacturing supply chains

Table 10.1   Vertical Markets with Centralized Needs (Continued)

Industry	What's Included	What Moves to E-commerce
Aerospace and defense	Manufacture and wholesale of aircraft, space vehicles, and defense materials	Commercial aircraft spare parts, military replenishment, some manufacturing supply chains
Construction	Logging, construction materials and machinery, fixtures, engineers, contractors, and architects	Project and subcontractor bidding, materials wholesale, replenishment
Heavy industries	Mining, minerals, steel production and wholesale, infrastructure construction	Raw materials and steel wholesale spot markets, construction bidding
Industrial equipment	Industrial machinery and equipment, manufacture and wholesale, industrial supplies	Spare parts and supplies, some wholesale and some supply chain

Source: Forrester Research, November 1998

The current trends in technology, telecommunications, and media markets highlight an increasing interest in e-commerce solutions by supply chain enterprises across many industrial segments. This growth is beginning to gather a great deal of momentum. In fact, some investment analysts believe that the success rate will reach high speeds during the next few years. There are several reasons for this somewhat rapid growth; it is a technologically-focused change. Continuous management of innovation and evolutionary change are also very fundamental to fostering the growth.

INTERNET THOUGHT CONTINUUM

Internet years are currently introducing a new thought continuum for the computer industries, one that is challenging to companies that compete in this space. The challenge is to establish success criteria that embrace greatly reduced technology development life cycles.

The Internet has emerged as an effective and inexpensive means for new competitors, and well-established competitors, to quickly earn a "*brand*" presence. They can perform this "branding" while providing support for their customers, their business partners, their supply chain constituents, and especially their employees and any other prime influences. This is done in an environment where changes occur rapidly and where products and business relationships are in constant flux.

A WHITE-HEAT PACE

There is no doubt that the computing and electronics industries have entered an environment of exponential growth. Companies that are leaders in the online race, like

Cisco, IBM, AT&T, Dell, Microsoft, Amazon.com, Verisign, Excite, Yahoo!, and Lycos, continue to set a *white-heat* pace for their competitors. Other competitors like Microsoft, Intel, and Sun have quickly adopted e-commerce channels-to-market, as well as using e-commerce in their own logistics and supply chains. Other industries have entered the race and are now picking up speed as they begin to integrate online Internet technologies with their core business processes. Some key industry sectors that appear to be making significant progress in the adoption of e-commerce are telecommunications, computers and peripherals, networks, software services, and multimedia. Each of these sectors shares common but unique interests in e-commerce.

The aerospace industry is beginning to use extranets in its supply chains. An example of this is Boeing's sale of commercial aircraft spares, using e-commerce applications linked to its back-end systems. The utilities industry is being compelled by federal order to begin retooling. This forced innovation by the utilities industry is heavily influenced by significant wholesale trading of electricity and gas over the Internet. Pressures to reduce information technology costs while embracing new supply chain requirements are driving the automobile industry to leverage e-commerce and the Internet. For example, large automobile auctioneers are using the Internet to generate billions of dollars of sales. At the same time, the automobile industry supply chain is leveraging extranets to realize additional revenues from their production supplies.

In the strategic horizon years (beginning in the year 2001), cost pressures will drive most industries to leverage e-commerce applications and the Internet. The petrochemical industry trade will shift from traditional EDI and fax to extranets, and the shipping and warehousing industries will use the Internet for shipping, billing, and responding to requests for proposals from other enterprises that are interested in the competitive bid market. The consumables industry (paper and office products suppliers) will move distribution channels online to drive down costs; other online communities in the pharmaceutical and medical supplies industry will use e-commerce to move hospital requirements for new supplies to the Internet.

There will also be an impact on many supply chains as they go through a metamorphosis, reacting to the turbulence caused by the dynamic growth in Internet use by most industries. This will be most notable in the beginning years of the 21st century. This will affect supply chains from commodity supplies, production capabilities, and distribution services.

Another major industry affected will be the commodities markets. Linking the commodity exchanges (for instance, corn, pork bellies, and soybeans) to the Internet will enable buyers and sellers to price products—based on real-time supply and demand. Furthermore, these buyers and sellers are now able to operate from their own homes, using home computing devices to assist in their decision processes. This encourages market-clearing prices to avoid artificial price supports. The utilities industries will experience lower prices and new online trading services from new and emerging energy intermediaries that will, in-turn, have significant effects on the commodity supply chain.

Even raw materials businesses—for example, steel, mining, and minerals—will be realizing the effect of e-commerce as new online exchanges emerge. As the gap between the early contenders and the new beginners continues to grow, this progress will lead to significant shifts in market power and positioning across all competitive environments. Supply chains will also strive to become more efficient by working with partners in demand-driven production environments, for instance, in banking and financial markets. There will also be a drive by some industries (for instance, consumer products) to leverage the use of e-commerce solutions to reduce development cycles; this too will render some realizable competitive advantages.

What does all this mean? It means that industrial supply chains will potentially streamline themselves, causing the elimination of traditional approaches of suppliers. Conversely, this yields an increase in suppliers' revenues, which in turn provides improved services, simply by designing and integrating e-commerce solutions into core business competencies. Following the realization of this, managing inventories online and better controlling their own costs and efficiencies will become the next challenge.

Perhaps the most dramatic e-commerce changes will be realized in the distribution areas of many supply chains. Companies competing in this market space will strive to differentiate themselves by providing value-added services. These firms recognize that leveraging e-commerce solutions will be needed to stay competitive. Buyers will be better positioned to dictate, or perhaps they will be able to screen out (even programmatically) the suppliers that make their supplier short-list. This will encourage suppliers to leverage e-commerce procurement applications. Intermediaries in most industries will be forced to make investments to scale or to pursue other niche markets. Spare parts will be auctioned online as industries begin to leverage the Internet and take advantage of the convenience of online purchasing to sell spare parts. Major automobile suppliers will disintermediate traditional middlemen, just in order to sell direct to dealers.

The United States is anticipating market share representation of approximately 45 percent of worldwide e-commerce by 2003. This rate is influenced by the rest of the world's pursuit of aggressive entries into e-commerce areas.

In summary, e-commerce will absolutely change the ways that many company decision makers and business leaders think, as their companies compete in an online virtual world of business: a real-time, highly competitive marketplace. Companies will be required to rethink their core business processes and then create new strategies for performing e-businesses. Supply chain businesses that play in multiple industries will gain significant and substantial competitive advantages. Distributors that do not quickly adopt e-commerce solutions and leverage their own online e-business capabilities may face the volatility of disintermediation.

Enterprises are currently investing aggressively in *Year 2000* correction initiatives while, at the same time, recognizing the importance of investing in e-commerce solutions to resolve and offset the (known) Y2K problems. Competitive advantage is the primary intent in the "offset." They recognize that e-commerce is clearly the future and that they must find ways to finance e-commerce initiatives, strategic to their visions.

These aggressive businesses may choose to seek assistance from integrators, services providers, and hardware and software providers—with in-depth industry knowledge to apply in a short time. This is essential because their customers are linking e-commerce applications to the back-end systems; at the same time, they are reengineering their core business processes.

Finally, enterprises will gradually move from simple online services to e-commerce-based e-business distribution relationships. Support of customers across the value chain will drive collaboration with suppliers and their partners.

Part 3
Structured Transformations Through E-commerce

This part of the book explores several different dimensions in e-commerce. There are many interesting aspects to implementations of e-commerce Internet sites, which display obvious signs of Design Quality. Aspects surrounding factors of Design Quality are explored, in this part. Factors that will ultimately entice the overall experience of end users, and vertical markets wanting to extend their Internet reach, are discussed here.

The various aspects of e-commerce that are important to manufacturing are explored in this part of the book. Business intelligence models and growth factors are also discussed in the following chapters. These particular topics are critical to the Internet e-commerce enterprise.

Utilizing the Internet to extend market reach is then explored, as an important factor of success to any industry segment. Other aspects of some very divergent financial markets are explored—cross-channel selling and, most important, business change. All topics that are included in the overall life cycle of the e-commerce enterprise inspection process are discussed.

11
Manufacturing: E-commerce, E-societies, and E-governments

....

The governments of the world face an ever-changing challenge, no matter where they might be located. This is due to ongoing pressures to increase services to their citizens and businesses, despite the opposing tax revenue pressures and shrinking budgets. Governments around the world have been forced to do more with less. Many worldwide governments are now trying to reach out in attempts to provide single e-commerce gateways across other government sectors and to many of their worldwide suppliers. This collaboration (of a sort) is desirable as all governments seek to form healthy international relationships with allied countries, in hopes of reducing the costs of internal inefficiencies and increasing opportunities for citizens.

Several successful Internet service models provide for *buyer/supplier* relationships to be performed across both government and industrial sectors. These types of environments are typically referred to as electronic procurement (or e-procurement), and they are found in a variety of design solutions throughout the supply-chain. Today, governments seem to face two concurrent cost pressures: the actual reduction of prices that they pay for their goods and services, and the expenses associated with the administration of any particular Internet e-commerce procurement solution.

E-GOVERNMENTS AND E-COMMERCE

It is estimated that by 2000, governments worldwide will spend over $50 billion a year on goods and services (maintenance, repair, and operations). The associated costs to administer those purchases is estimated to be approximately $4 billion. This is just in the area of procurement solutions.

Related to general buying and selling worldwide are several examples of electronic trading environments, or e-trading Internet-based sites. Likewise, e-auction types of environments are becoming very popular (refer to http://www.ebay.com, http://www.onsale.com, Ubid, and many more) for buying and selling communities.

109

There are certain governments that have selected certain e-commerce technologies to create and place online opportunity bid presentment e-business sites. This is where a particular government may choose to place online, in public viewing, an opportunity for which it invites public and government enterprises to bid on the opportunity. Once bids are submitted, they are held in confidence until the final decision has been made as to exactly who is awarded the contract; then the decision is announced to all parties.

Applications of e-commerce in world governments and social groups will continue to explode, as will the future of domestic and international distribution channels. Enterprises are demonstrating many innovative strategies for buying and selling. Many industries are now electronically tied directly with their buyers and suppliers via the Internet. Manufacturers are beginning to leverage e-commerce to bypass distributors and resellers when doing so is convenient. Therefore, three points appear to be important:

1. Suppliers utilize e-commerce and the Internet to reach their customers.
2. Manufacturers utilize e-commerce and the Internet to reach customers.
3. In the near term, supply chain companies will be challenged.

Many government-supplier companies in the manufacturing industry are taking advantage of the opportunity to leverage e-commerce solutions to reach out to their customers. The e-commerce technologies provide excellent instruments or tools that many companies can use to extend their products and services. This is an intentional, tactical approach to reach both current customers and potential customers quickly (see Figure 11.1).

BUSINESS INTELLIGENCE MODELS

Many business enterprises are planning to use e-commerce on the Internet as a primary and direct link to potential buyers and suppliers. These same companies are beginning to build business intelligence knowledge models to study their customers' buying patterns. These modeling results help companies to validate and verify their own e-commerce strategies. For example, some companies are beginning to sell parts (and spare parts) online with Internet service offerings to potential buyers and other alternative channels in their distribution and supply chains.

Many companies are proceeding cautiously because they do not want to unnecessarily alter existing distribution partnerships, where Internet solutions of e-commerce may not yet be available. The use of e-commerce will cause many challenges in the distribution and supply channels. Consequently, what some companies worry about is the effect of cutting off a significant portion of their channels, which provide a formidable

Manufacturers Connect to Customers Online

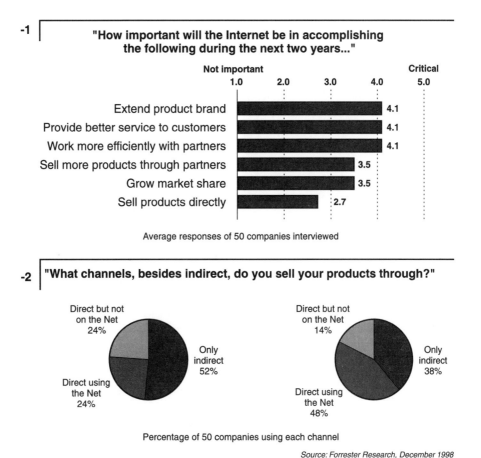

-1

"How important will the Internet be in accomplishing the following during the next two years..."

Not important   Critical
1.0   2.0   3.0   4.0   5.0

Extend product brand — 4.1
Provide better service to customers — 4.1
Work more efficiently with partners — 4.1
Sell more products through partners — 3.5
Grow market share — 3.5
Sell products directly — 2.7

Average responses of 50 companies interviewed

-2 **"What channels, besides indirect, do you sell your products through?"**

Direct but not on the Net 24%
Only indirect 52%
Direct using the Net 24%

Direct but not on the Net 14%
Only indirect 38%
Direct using the Net 48%

Percentage of 50 companies using each channel

Source: Forrester Research, December 1998

Figure 11.1

It is important for e-business end users to be connected through e-commerce channel strategies.

means of access to indirect buyers. These same channels may assert that the cost savings (or justification) for eliminating them may not yield the anticipated strategic business results.

Businesses that enter the direct-selling channel through the Internet have experienced some opposition in both public and government sectors. Companies will approach the use of e-commerce as a direct selling tool with caution, preferring to maintain sensitive partnerships with resellers that constitute the majority of their future business. The key for manufacturers is *trust* and interbusiness relationships. That is, they must continue to work closely with their established business partners, and to include their partners in their own e-business ventures. One way to do so is to move some products or services exclusively online, while maintaining their normal channel of distribution with existing public or government trading partners for other products or services.

Another approach taken by some manufacturers is to offer online ordering of products or services to their customers via their own sponsored dealers. If the customer orders any of these products or services directly from the manufacturer (for example), the manufacturer would then share revenue with its dealers. Determining the most effective means of customer fulfillment will be essential because most firms will have different pricing levels (or some other clip levels) for products they offer directly via the Internet and for other products they make available through their normal distribution channels (see Figure 11.2).

Manufacturers Assess Channel Roles

"What values or services can be disintermediated?"

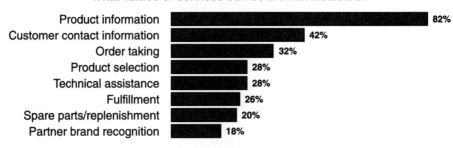

Product information — 82%
Customer contact information — 42%
Order taking — 32%
Product selection — 28%
Technical assistance — 28%
Fulfillment — 26%
Spare parts/replenishment — 20%
Partner brand recognition — 18%

Average of 50 companies interviewed
(multiple responses accepted)

"What values or services can be disintermediated?"

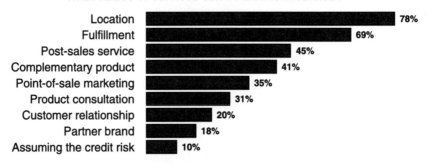

Location — 78%
Fulfillment — 69%
Post-sales service — 45%
Complementary product — 41%
Point-of-sale marketing — 35%
Product consultation — 31%
Customer relationship — 20%
Partner brand — 18%
Assuming the credit risk — 10%

Average of 50 companies interviewed
(multiple responses accepted)

Source: Forrester Research, December 1998

Figure 11.2

Channel roles will transform as e-businesses are deployed.

MANUFACTURING STRATEGIES LEVERAGE E-COMMERCE

It is clear that manufacturers are interested in using e-commerce and the Internet to reach their customers while harnessing the advantages of using the Internet. The entire strategy is, of course, to widen their customer base. Although the migration of the global (or even local) enterprise is to go online, it will most assuredly result in some form of a channel conflict. The majority of companies are not planning to completely bypass their channels. What this does mean, however, is that the current and established channel strategies of distribution (especially those not online) will be challenged.

The growing evolution of e-commerce applications over the Internet will have major effects on distribution and supply channels. Enterprises are noticeably beginning to retool their go-to-market strategies and their customer relationship management policies. This will change the methods and processes of *how* firms work with their trading partners. For example, many organizations may choose to compartmentalize their products and establish multiple brands. Resellers may want to maintain warehouse(s) of products and sell products from many different manufacturers. Some manufacturers will begin to sell directly (and also through resellers). A redundancy of inventories will occur.

In a number of cases, resellers in a serial relationship with manufacturers will be the only visible entity in the supply chain. This will, in turn, justify utilization of the Internet and e-commerce solutions to reach customers. Business intelligence via the use of e-commerce tools will help firms learn about customer buying patterns and behaviors. This can be accomplished by using the Internet as an instrument of information gathering. Companies can use the vast amounts of information (often subjective in form) accumulated in this way to gain and maintain competitive advantages.

INFORMATION AS A COMMODITY

Three interesting areas of concern for resellers who strive to improve their competitive posture are these: the proliferation of vast amounts of information available over the Internet, the lower cost and ease of acquisition of products or services via the Internet, and the platform for more comprehensive information gathering that the Internet provides over more traditional information gathering techniques. For example, customers' reliance on distribution channels for product specifications is dwindling.

Manufacturers are starting to go directly to customers online with this information, bypassing traditional channels. A cliché is relevant to information over the

Internet: "knowledge availability anytime and anywhere." Another thought-provoking cliché is "knowledge is a commodity." This means that online buyers can initiate purchases whenever (and wherever) they choose. This also might cause one to wonder if every end user is only a simple mouse-click away from another competitive provider.

Traditional channel players now face the pervasive use of multiple point-of-sales presences across a global network. These channel players will no longer (easily) dominate the market space where customers traditionally process their business transactions. The use of e-commerce over the Internet is forging a very dynamic knowledge exchange. Channel partners, in both public and government relationships, are being forced to leverage the Internet to share knowledge. This is a paradigm shift.

BUSINESS-TO-BUSINESS GROWTH

The growth of business-to-business e-commerce is purported to exceed $3.4 trillion by 2003. This will result in significant numbers of corporate enterprises reengineering their core business processes. Manufacturers, distributors, resellers, and other entities in the supply and distribution chains will compete vigorously to avoid disruption or loss of revenue and market share (see Figure 11.3).

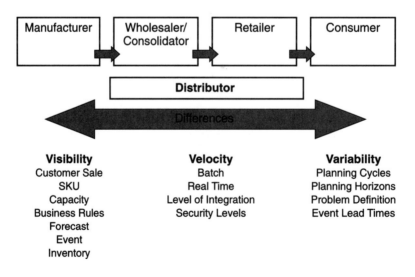

The supply chain problem presents challenges

Figure 11.3

The various complexities across the supply chain management environments.

These enterprises will have to consider the rising temptation for manufacturers to resort to leaving traditional channels, in order to interface with their key customers in a more direct manner (that is, via Internet e-commerce). These manufacturers will extend direct selling in three areas: customer enticement, proliferating knowledge of their products or services, and the provision of customer support after the initial sales engagements are completed. A new set of virtual intermediaries will become evident, entities that will not be burdened with the more traditional business models. Instead, they will operate within a set of *e-business utilities*, a highly integrated solution set related to Internet e-commerce environments.

These intermediaries will strive to fill a void between manufacturers and customers—using the Internet as an instrument of trade. Many mainstream resellers will face the pressures of quickly learning how to adopt e-commerce and Internet technologies into their core business practices.

There seems to be a limit that manufacturers will try to achieve while utilizing the Internet to reach customers. Rather than take the approach of revenue loss or corporate disruption, their channel partners and manufacturers will decide to beef up presale and post-sale customer interactions, while leveraging their e-commerce partners to facilitate mass sales. Another set of important factors has to do with the lack of skill that manufacturers may have in information management, marketing, and the operational details required for customer care. These critical skills need to be identified and effectively harvested as "*group gold.*"

One large interest area for leveraging e-commerce on behalf of manufacturers is found in spares and replacement parts. There are several reasons why parts manufacturers will make this shift and eliminate their resellers:

1. Spares do not require multiple manufacturer participants.
2. Manufacturers can improve their brands using spare and replacement parts services.
3. Manufacturers gain customer buying business intelligence about product usage.
4. Manufacturers are managing customer queries and orders via the Internet, through their channel partners.

VIRTUAL INTERMEDIARY COMMUNITIES

New virtual communities of intermediaries have formed, and they will continue to form as a result of the introduction of e-commerce—across all industry segments. These virtual intermediaries will appear in a variety of markets, including the apparel, automobile parts, education, and medicine markets. It is quite likely that these new intermediaries will have major effects on a variety of industries. There are a number of reasons for this, including the following:

1. The cost of doing business delivers lower margins and low overhead.
2. Their skilled workforce is generally higher than 25 percent as compared to traditional resellers who maintain a lower (or outdated) technology skilled workforce; therefore, the virtual intermediary needs to leverage e-commerce applications and technologies to gain competitive advantage.
3. The wholesale distribution firms will enable new virtual intermediaries, even hosting Web sites for new intermediaries.
4. These virtual intermediaries have access to Internet investment capital unlike their traditional counterparts, which might have very tightly managed capital investments.

Long-established, more traditional resellers will feel the competitive pressures of the rapidly growing number of virtual intermediaries. They will feel as if they are being increasingly pressured to face the threat of business disruption, by their key manufacturers going direct by using Internet e-commerce solutions. The obvious play for the traditional resellers would be to leverage the strength of their own brands while taking positive steps to reinvent themselves online. Compounding the problem that the traditional resellers might face may be potentially tight operational margins. Thus, creative instruments and highly skilled people are often commissioned to perform interim approaches to quickly, but effectively, build the requestor a successful presence on the Internet. Some examples of traditional resellers that have been somewhat successful in the online road-rage race are Office Depot, Office Max, and Black Box.

A mass consolidation of resellers may be on the horizon as these firms begin to retrench their strategies, partnerships, and alliances. Mature enterprises faced with a decline in prices and aggressive new virtual intermediaries going after "low-hanging fruit" both suggest that the established intermediaries will also feel great pressures. Firms that are resellers with restricted access to information and limited inventories may discover that the best strategic move is to reinvent their businesses by seeking ways to leverage e-commerce and Internet technologies. Established and larger distribution channels perhaps may have the luxury of waiting for some time period, allowing them to follow the trend of e-commerce in the distribution channels, essentially watching it take off. These "watchers" will buy their way into the e-commerce market by leveraging their brands (some of which may actually represent highly inflated stocks) to make huge e-commerce mergers and creative deals.

Sometimes watching stocks rise and fall for specific types of e-commerce-related enterprises is amazing. What these companies offer is power in innovative approaches to doing e-commerce business online. This means money. An interesting point to consider for the large contenders in the e-commerce space is this: Remember that to really have a well-established online presence one will have to immediately address creative solutions for overcoming issues in new technology introductions. This will involve inspecting the actual logistics of their own (or hired) design and development practices. This inspection process can be rather extensive but, more than likely, necessary.

The threats of corporate disruption throughout the distribution industry should be of concern to manufacturers, wholesale distributors, and business-to-business resellers. Strategic steps taken by each of these groups will position them to better deal with the very real threats caused by e-commerce and innovative time-saving Internet solutions.

Manufacturers should selectively choose direct tactics instead of engaging in all-out battles with channel partners over customer contract penetration rates. Timing may be prudent to nurture virtual intermediaries and foster incentives for traditional channel partners into innovative e-commerce solutions. Meanwhile, wholesale distributors should encourage online intermediaries, thus leveraging existing economic ecosystems, resulting in stronger ties with manufacturers.

Resellers should move aggressively to strengthen their consumer-based relationships, by encouraging and (if appropriate) helping to move their customers online. By electronically collaborating with the manufacturers and the distributors that are their channel partners, they can retard the growth of other virtual intermediaries. On the other hand, virtual intermediaries need to be able to respond to requests for changes very quickly and to scale their operations on demand, when called on to collaborate. They should waste no time in building a customer base and technology infrastructure, ensuring a high degree of *Design Quality* in the solution.

Virtual intermediaries must recognize that if they stay small, the larger players will potentially force them out of the market over time. Finally, retailers must take advantage of the hyper-growth of the business-to-consumer online retail market space by aggressively pursuing e-commerce strategies. If they do not do this they may face business disruption and brand erosion.

The impact of e-commerce and the Internet on distribution channels will be an enormous, compelling stimuli for businesses to radically reengineer their core processes. Customer relationships will change significantly as customer points of purchase will be ubiquitous. Customers will participate in single purchase scenarios that will cross multiple company domains. The rules of the "high-flyer" businesses will evolve to new heights, as real-time Internet data analysis emerges as a competitive tool and finely tuned instrument of e-business success. Once the knowledge base acquires marketing opportunities, sales patterns, and key forecasts, the information then matures for the enterprises that do the best job by leveraging the knowledge. These enterprises will prevail only to remain profitable.

In the distribution world of e-commerce, companies will no longer enjoy substantial and sustainable competitive advantages due to large on-hand inventories. Instead, what we will find is occurring now (and will continue to gain momentum)—that is, the movement to logistic analysts who will be able to deliver products to customers, without ever actually handling the products. Gone will be large investments in loading docks, fleets of trucks, transportation foremen, warehousing equipment, facilities space, and complicated logistics systems. Instead, out of necessity many of these functions will continue to exist online, affecting the consolidation of the physical entities. This, in-part, will leverage the economies of scale (as cost reductions) that come with e-commerce solutions and Internet use.

Manufacturers are beginning to develop business intelligence databases that capture key information about their customers; more important, though, are their buying behaviors and purchasing patterns. With enhanced forms of Internet technology, like data mining capabilities, the new knowledge in the manufacturing communities will serve as an enticement to be more proactive in determining distribution channel marketing priorities and product designs. This will result in the loss of revenues for trading partners that traditionally spearhead this activity. New types of partnerships are also emerging as forward-thinking players in the channel space begin to align themselves. For example, resellers are beginning to dovetail (or connect to) each other, thereby leveraging huge investments in logistics infrastructures, manufacturer relationships, and a convergence of service organizations. This is performed to nurture relationships with new players, rather than battle with them. Meanwhile, retailers can provide profitable installation, maintenance, and repair services that these new virtual intermediaries may try to avoid. Here is another paradigm shift.

The ubiquitous nature of newly formed customer relationships is that they seem to result from this causal effect of e-commerce solutions. Oddly enough, this could cause new ways of defining intercompany remuneration models. For example, a large software company may be compensated for providing leads to resellers, while a computer reseller may be compensated by a computer manufacturer for fulfillment of customer orders. This type of desegregation will compel channel players to reevaluate the business values associated with each activity, from customer buying through order taking, to fulfillment and service: requisition-to-check or, in corporate jargon, Req-to-Check.

In summary, as global Internet e-commerce growth explodes, the future of distribution and supply channels will continue to change dramatically. Enterprises are successfully engaged with selling directly to many types of *buyers* via the Internet. Manufacturers are beginning to leverage e-commerce, in some cases bypassing distributors and resellers. We have seen that three things appear to be most obvious:

1. Manufacturers utilize e-commerce via the Internet to reach customers.

2. In the tactical horizon, supply chain companies will strive to survive.

3. Some corporate disruption between corporate enterprises continues to occur.

Many supply chains will turn to firms to diversify and become new virtual intermediaries. There are also enterprises that use e-commerce on the Internet as a direct link to potential buyers. They too are building increased business intelligence by studying their customers' buying patterns. These results will help them to build a highly efficient strategic e-commerce strategy.

12
E-business Sites That Enhance the User Experience

....

A challenging situation is looming for businesses beginning to engage in e-commerce. A large number of Internet sites are not performing up to their "billing." There is a general lack of sites that address the requirements of site visitors; basically these poorer sites rate rather low on the Design Quality scale, at least from a usability viewpoint. The results have been painfully frustrating to potential customers and trading partners. The good news is that these sites continue to struggle to add meaningful content, user-friendly search methods, and other enhanced functions. Many of the sites failing the usability tests seem to illustrate a void in design and development methods that directly address the problems associated with usability: Design Quality of Internet e-commerce sites separates the highly frequented sites from the under-utilized sites. What constitutes Design Quality, and how does one know when they have achieved it? The quality of any design must be determined prior to developing any computerized environment. Design Quality, as an afterthought, will most assuredly cause havoc later, while many users are trying to become familiar with the site. Design flaws travel in herds. This general lack of high quality in the design phases of Internet site, causes measurable effects on revenue, the cost of doing business, customer retention, and brand recognition. Companies are trying to address these problems, knowing that the growth of Internet e-commerce is not slowing down. In line with the notion of "quality," many business enterprises are beginning to reengineer (or redesign) faulty business processes that are in-house or somewhere else in the supply chain. Simply creating an Internet site will never correct faulty business processes.

The key for enterprises interested in developing effective Internet sites will be to analyze the user experience in site visits and make appropriate adjustments to ensure that the user experience is satisfying.

The bottom line for most enterprises developing Internet sites is very simple: They want their customers to easily find information or areas of interest, and they want their customers to be able to execute transactions in a fast and easy manner. This means that companies developing Internet sites must have clear and concise Design Quality goals that are tied to business strategies and that have measurable business value and quantified design points that may be monitored for correctness.

FEW INTERNET SITE OWNERS MEASURE USABILITY

Still another important factor is the capability to measure the site's performance. Enterprises are finding that this is difficult to do because beauty is in the eyes of the beholder. This means that each user's experience is unique to that user, and what intrigues one user may very well have an opposite effect on another user. Some firms measure things like download time, logo use, graphics use, colors, patterns, screen time, and data manipulation. The ways to measure effective usage of an Internet site are limited.

There is a growing conflict between the strategic mission of many firms to establish their brands and good usability site designs. Some firms strive to achieve brand goals as the primary objective; others emphasize excellent Internet site navigational capabilities. Many enterprises deal with issues that involve the visibility of their brands (via graphic-intensive sites), while at the same time requiring that sites are quick, eye-catching, and simple to use.

Some impediments, however, prevent Internet site developers from simplifying their sites to make it easier for customers to find the information they seek. Internet developers are often overwhelmed with heavy workloads that include a number of projects. This type of schedule does not allow adequate time to maintain and improve already existing sites. Some executives complain that their customers have unmet requirements, and yet their sites present only a list of lines of business. This scant information leaves the customer guessing as to where to go next.

QUANTIFY YOUR INTERNET SITE'S DESIGN QUALITY

It appears that Internet site development teams have few Design Quality objectives, with the exception of speed and consistency. An area that is often overlooked is measuring ease-of-use. Basic human factors of computerized solutions remain the same, as they have for several decades. Other impediments to effective Internet site design are corporate politics, weak corporate development standards and processes, lack of skilled resources, and management's general inability to foster design creativity while managing innovation. Design *guidelines*, not standards, need to be inspected for effectiveness.

As shown in Figure 12.1, the following questions suggest revealing insights about four underlying design issues that enterprises must address as they commission Internet Site design projects:

- *Payoff*. Do content and function meet users' diverse needs and expectations?
- *Courtesy*. Does the interface respect the user's time and avoid wasting it?
- *Trust*. Does the site work consistently, or does it degrade under high-traffic loads?
- *Intelligence*. Does the site proactively aid users to achieve their goals quickly?

20 Tests Make up the User Experience Review

	Evaluation factor	Effect on visitor
Payoff: Do content and function meet needs and expectation?	1) Is information relevant and complete? 2) Can visitors conduct transactions? 3) Is the site organized by user goals?	Feels frustrated, can't complete mission Must use phone, mail or store to buy Can't tell if the site has value or is just hype
Courtesy: Does the interface respect time-not waste it?	4) Can users find content at the second level of the site? 5) Is the text legible, especially on buttons and menus? 6) Are color and position of controls consistent? 7) Are navigation elements clearly visible? 8) Can visitors find content at the third level of the site? 9) Is the site free of irrelevant content? 10) Are words on links and prompts consistent? 11) Is text in plain English not jargon? 12) Are pages uncluttered?	Additional levels make finding content take twice as long and cuts the chance of success in half Navigation slows down, causing aggravation and error Time spent hunting for links slows tasks by 5% to 10% Misses content and function Chance fo finding content drops even lower Gets in the way of user goals Visitors slowed by confusion by as much as 25% Can't tell if the site fits needs, newcomers leave Content gets lost in the clutter
Trust: Does the site work consistently— not break easily?	13) Is the site reliable? 14) Are basic functions always available? 15) Does the site give feedback? 16) Does the site perform consistently?	Can't count on the site for important tasks Wonders what happened Undermines confidence that site works Snail's pace is annoying
Intelligence: Does the site proactively aid users to achieve goals?	17) Does a search list retrievals in order of relevance? 18) Can users save preferences or personalize? 19) Does a search find most fo the relevant content? 20) Can visitors interact to achieve their goals?	Must slog through irrelevant content May need to reenter information for every visit Thinks content is no there Does the work for the computer, wonders why

Source: Forrester Research, September 1998

Figure 12.1

Focus on the actual end-user experience is key to any successful e-business solution.

It is clear that design problems exist in abundance: This problem remains the same as in previous computing eras, like client/server, structured programming, and other computer science areas. Some sites basically seem useless, lacking both content and function. Other sites struggle with having good navigational tools that can guide customers to the information they seek.

The area involving *customer fulfillment* appears to be a problem with some sites that have problems simply completing the customer transactions. For example, missing but vital information is a constant problem. This information is imperative, as it is required to help the customer make a purchasing decision. As an example, a firm that advertises heavily on affordability but lacks pricing information will frustrate customers, who may go to competitors' sites for more concise and hard-hitting information. Remember, customers are only one click away from a simpler-to-use site.

One major and very consistent problem is the lack of readability of a page. A site might have multiple interfaces on one page (many different links or a mix of user interface design metaphors), and each of these interfaces is unique. Another common example of poor Design Quality occurs when the tool bar on each page is partially covered, making it difficult for customers read or use the toolbar. Again, this results in one click of the mouse button, and that customer leaves the site. The second click of the mouse button occurs when the customer visits the other, easier-to-use, competitive Internet site. This translates into a loss of revenue for one company and a gain of revenue for the other.

DESIGN CHALLENGES FOR THE EFFECTIVE SITE

Important in any design are reliability and consistency. Examples can be seen in some sites that consistently neglect the placement of critical information on the Internet site page. Any lack of key information causes customers to develop negative attitudes toward using the Internet to do business. To net this out, some Internet sites are broken, possess unreliable functions, and host content that is often unreliable or incorrect.

Many sites lack good navigational features. Often Internet sites lack (as an example) reliable and easy-to-use search engines. Interestingly enough, in some cases information not meant for customers or other unsuspecting users was not hidden or deleted; thus, this can leave the company exposed to negative customer experiences.

These problems have clear effects on a company's brand image, and therefore they are one reason for caution on behalf of any enterprise establishing an Internet presence. A second and less obvious design flaw deals with site integrity. It is a fact that users have been known to be both trustworthy and malicious. Ethical hacking should always be applied to any Internet site, to ensure integrity prior to placing the site into production. One visible security or integrity flaw can very quickly decommission an entire Internet site (not to mention incurring liabilities for the hosting company). A decommissioned Internet site, due to a malicious hacker, can often endanger other sites being hosted in that environment. Intrusion detection business processes and software resources are helpful in determining immediate resolutions in these situations.

These problems are clearly something that must be resolved early in the Design Quality determination phases, or enterprises will lose tremendous amounts of money in wasted expenses or other unexpected complications. Several areas can be identified where organizations need to provide some special treatment. For instance, look at the costs associated with a redesign. The redesign efforts to address quality problems on Internet sites most likely will be very costly. Speed, consistent look and feel, and other functions will require unexpected enhancements or improvements as usability patterns are monitored and analyzed for aspects of design quality. Leveraging many commercially accepted aspects, involving the ease-of-use capabilities, is key. Staying with a previous example, search engines that are effective (and flawless) offer one form of excellent solution design by the Internet site designer(s).

If Internet sites are not designed and constructed in a way that makes it easy for potential customers to process buying transactions (as an example), then they won't buy—and this results in loss of revenues to the sponsor. Another challenge is that customers are sometimes unable to see all the products in a given catalog, and therefore they may not buy the products that they seek simply because they can't find them easily. Multilayering of Internet site pages presents still another problem, in that customers are sometimes distracted and may get redirected before they reach the second or third layers they originally sought. This too can result in a loss of potential sales. Slow performance also results in loss of sales, as frustrated customers visit other high-performing sites or resort to traditional means of searching for and purchasing products or services.

FOCUSING AND HOLDING THE CUSTOMER'S ATTENTION

Remember that in the Internet environment a potential customer is many times only one mouse click away (see Figure 12.2): This must be a serious consideration when designing the site. Some research studies suggest losses are as high as 50 percent of the Internet site's potential sales, following this notion of "one click away." Furthermore, some research purports that failing sites are losing as high as 40 percent

Problem Statement: E-commerce

At the portals of the 21st century, private and public sector enterprises find that in order to increase their effectiveness and profitability they must leverage e-commerce; it is a new and dynamic business trading model.

Profitability

- ✔ Personlization
- ✔ No Stockouts
- ✔ On-Time Fulfillment
- ✔ Reduced Time to Market Product Cycles
- ✔ New Channels

Effectiveness

- ✔ Standardization
- ✔ Real-Time Inventory
- ✔ On-Time Order Fulfillment
- ✔ Real-Time Margin Markdowns
- ✔ Leveraging New Channels

Figure 12.2

Defining the fine balance of the successful e-business trading model.

in repeat end-user traffic. What this means for firms that have invested heavily in Internet site development is that, on average, for every 1 million site visits by customers, 40 percent of the customers will choose to go elsewhere, simply because of poor site performance. This is very costly, and oddly enough, it can be simply managed by the experienced designers of Internet sites and hosting technical infrastructures.

Another important reason for high degrees of Design Quality is that the user has now formed an impression of the company's brand, right or wrong—because of the site's performance. Although unexplained, it does happen. Customers who have bad experiences on an Internet site often leave these sites with a very negative image: This impression can have a rippling effect. If the Internet site is an exercise in futility, or if it wastes a customer's time, users will most certainly associate this with the particular brand; this holds true even in other, more traditional channels. This all relates to human factors and perhaps the notion of "first impressions."

To address some of these Design Quality problems, enterprises are rethinking their Internet site's goal (and initial design points) to analyze their usage failures. In some cases, the Internet sites were designed in pieces, with both old and new Internet designing tools. The customer experience in many cases was not even a factor for consideration.

The lack of clear design methods that leverage best practices of Internet site designs is an ongoing challenge. The extremely rapid rate of technology advances, plus new tooling and programming languages being introduced to the market, only complicates the challenge for the site designers. Continuous-learning is mandatory for the savvy Internet site designer.

Be it right or wrong, the mentality of "there are the rapid repair problems, where small and cosmetic changes can help alleviate some design flaws" is a constant. This attitude is sometimes apparent in a cyclical development approach.

SITE REDESIGN FOR DESIGN EXCELLENCE

If, indeed, some major redesign is required in the site, then this is what should occur— not a quick fix. The redesign effort may take more time now, but it may very well help minimize the costs of customer dissatisfaction because the site lacks ease-of-use functions, has poor overall performance or search capabilities, needs improvements, or is hard to interpret or understand.

The redesign team in this case sets out to fix poorly designed interfaces and other aspects based on unexpected end-usage patterns. The team usually consists of specialized network engineers, application architects, infrastructure architects, graphic designers, illustrators, and highly skilled programmers. This team applies fixes to improperly designed human factors and, following our current example, graphic or interface aspects that are errant. The specialized network engineers might evaluate the network infrastructure (routers, firewalls, traffic patterns, etc.), while the programming experts and application architects will repair or strengthen the site's architectural framework. If the site requires major repair due to a poor information architecture (while the content, transaction, and reliability areas are satisfactory) then major rework should be considered. Unfortunately, this rework approach might require a significant amount of time, as compared to the former redesign example. Either way, it may need to be accomplished.

Finally, there is the more traumatic redesign approach that basically involves tearing the site down and beginning again: Consider the initial site now a throw-away prototype. A learning example. This is necessary when the site has incomplete content, is not reliable, and lacks expected functionality or integrity. All of these problems could damage the brand image, if they are not handled in a proper and expedient manner.

It is unfortunate, but there will always be enterprises with sites in this state of disrepair. The rather drastic redesign step is taken only because the site design is ineffective and needs to be shut down and reconstructed. This requires major replanning and sometimes starting from the original concept or the brand objective. This next redesign might include designing prototypes during the early design phases that test usability functions. Be aware of being trapped into a nonscalable prototype design while entering the production phase: In other words, use caution in fielding prototypes into production environments. Measurements of *Design Quality* that validate the new design and ensure that the new component meets all the identified requirements and technical specification are key.

It should be abundantly clear by now that the focus must be on usability and the reengineering of business processes. *Usability* measurements are critical to the end users' experience, and all functions require testing and appropriate treatment. One very effective approach is to tie user experience metrics to the management compensation plan: Perhaps tie a measure of customer satisfaction and internal expectations to the management bonus plan. This can be achieved with metrics that yield quantifiable results of the customer's look-to-buy ratio: Thus, an interesting metric of innovation can be directly related to annual compensation. This approach attempts to provide incentives for IT managers to build e-commerce sites that have excellent *Design Quality* points and effective transaction system architectures. But, to be able to realize a design point inside of any design, the actual design itself must be specified in such a manner as to capture both positive and negative aspects of the design. This way one can monitor these design points into the future, while deciding exactly how to handle corrective measures.

In other words, Internet sites must be both effective and reliable. One example of a design guideline could be related to *performance*, and it could be stated as a Design Quality factor to be monitored. That would be to architect Internet sites that have multiple layers and pages, where each displays in 10 seconds or less at 28.8KB-per-second modem speeds (this is just an example). Complicate this by saying this is a global e-banking environment where global customer access must be maintained, 24 hours a day, 7 days a week. Transcontinental high availability can now be measured, once the design points have been specified.

An organized approach to tracking patterns of usage will help in the ongoing analysis of the site's effectiveness. The role of ongoing analysis is to insure that usability dovetails with anticipated e-business processes and long-term e-commerce strategies. Significant steps need to be taken to validate usage demands of the targeted vertical market segments, as well as any known customer dependencies and usage patterns within that vertical market.

Usability and customer hands-on simulation testing scenarios should be periodically conducted to ensure the best *Design Quality* practices remain focused at the site's objectives. Before going into a production state, the site should be tested with customer experience metrics (in a usability laboratory) that identify general performance characteristics of the site while being utilized by end users, both novice and expert. Once the site is in production, quarterly reviews should be executed to measure overall performance and to identify areas that may need attention.

On a regular basis, records should be kept of the traffic at all layers of the site, and temporal traffic trends at different telecommunication speeds should be tracked. In summary, it is clear that *usability* reigns in the design of an effective Internet e-commerce site. The bottom line in an e-commerce economy is this: The customer's experience relates to the usability of the Internet site. This remains the primary (and most strategic objective) of any Internet e-commerce site.

13
Utilizing the Internet to Extend Market Reach

....

Many business enterprises are challenged with new ways to extend their reach to new customers or end-user communities. Internet telecommunication portals, in part, play nicely into this requirement for end-user community extensions. Firms that manufacture products, for example, are paving the way to new customers, via sales strategies that utilize the Internet. To achieve this new reach, e-commerce applications and e-business technologies are emerging almost daily. These new instruments of e-commerce provide firms with the collaborative capabilities to reach across the value chain. And, yes, this will most likely require significant investments; however, the investments will potentially yield a very high return.

One area of Internet interest is new indirect channels to customers, via the Internet. Many enterprises that currently have fewer than 10 channel partners might plan to extend this number in their strategic horizon to as many as several hundred—all due to the Internet and its ubiquitous reach. They recognize that business-to-business e-commerce growth will be huge during the next five years; therefore, many companies may want to extend their reach as far as possible by linking with rather large numbers of channel partners. This is clearly seen as a primary tactical step of the business enterprise (that is, to include their resellers) in their e-commerce solution set.

BUSINESS PARTNERS LINKED VIA TECHNOLOGIES

One new e-commerce tool that these firms are planning to use is XML software to offset the CGI (common graphics interface) script language. XML stands for Extensible Markup Language; it is a subset of SGML that is easier to use and more flexible. XML is emerging as a (pseudo) standard in the industry for the development of proprietary rules, procedures, and systems—to link manufacturers and their channel partners. They are slowly beginning to bring their resellers on board, migrating them from CGI to XML solutions. There are concerns about getting XML to work with their legacy systems (for example, back-end order entry systems, accounts receivable systems, billing systems). Integration to back-end systems is always a major obstacle to overcome. In this context, resellers must often agree to share the order-entry information on their databases with the manufacturers. This enables the manufacturers to better understand what market upgrades are required to redirect to the reseller(s).

There is now, and always will be, general concern and fear over the inconsistency of data and security breaches: We should never lose sight of this concern. There are also concerns that resellers might expose customers to competitive products, sensitive information, or strategies of their services; even worse, they might unknowingly share customer data with competitors (contract information, for example). Enterprises planning to sell online need to form tightly coupled links with their own (preferred) indirect channels, with the expectation of huge growth in online indirect selling (see Figure 13.1). Companies need to consider linking to partners with distinct and separate technical standards and developing outstanding rules of doing business as partners.

Business-to-business commerce is expected to rocket to $1.3 trillion in 2003. This will cause every manufacturer to continually rethink exactly how they intend to fit into the ever-changing global e-commerce environment.

DISTRIBUTION CHANNELS LINKED VIA TECHNOLOGIES

Industries today manufacture and typically sell through several distribution channels to reach a large, diverse set of customer demands. One important question is how do premier businesses manage traditional channel partners, contrasted to how new channel partners are invited to alliances by other e-commerce solution approaches. How will these companies then manage direct customer visits to their enriched Internet sites and then electronically hand off to their channel partners critical order fulfillment and after sales customer support? How will these same companies face virtual intermediaries that provide product information not only to one manufacturer competing in a given industry, but perhaps to multiple competitors? This information might (unknowingly) include product strategies and key pricing information. How will these companies address the issues associated with customer relationship management, an area that the new virtual intermediaries consider an immediate threat?

Catalog maintenance and shared e-commerce transactions present other challenges. How will manufacturers deal with incompatible processes and technical nomenclatures? Part numbering schemes that have aggregated meanings, engineering changes to complicated manufacturing schemes, and (possibly) multiple pricing updates during the course of a normal business day or week are just some possible incompatibilities. These are all, in their own way, very difficult areas of focus across several areas of e-commerce.

Early Adopters Discuss Indirect Selling on the Net

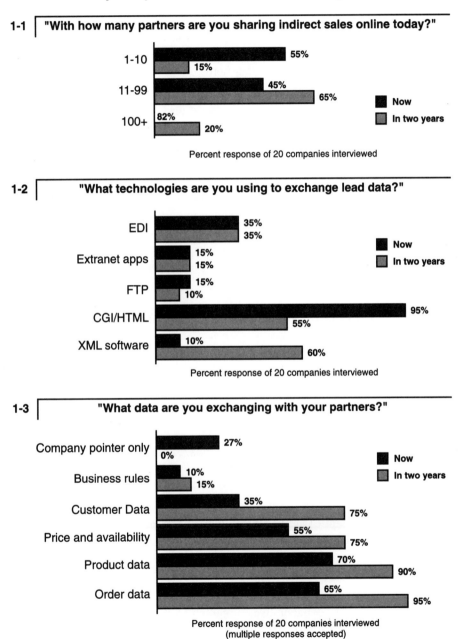

1-1 | "With how many partners are you sharing indirect sales online today?"

- 1-10: 55% (Now), 15% (In two years)
- 11-99: 45% (Now), 65% (In two years)
- 100+: 82% (Now), 20% (In two years)

Legend: Now, In two years

Percent response of 20 companies interviewed

1-2 | "What technologies are you using to exchange lead data?"

- EDI: 35% (Now), 35% (In two years)
- Extranet apps: 15% (Now), 15% (In two years)
- FTP: 15% (Now), 10% (In two years)
- CGI/HTML: 95% (Now), 55% (In two years)
- XML software: 10% (Now), 60% (In two years)

Legend: Now, In two years

Percent response of 20 companies interviewed

1-3 | "What data are you exchanging with your partners?"

- Company pointer only: 27% (Now), 0% (In two years)
- Business rules: 10% (Now), 15% (In two years)
- Customer Data: 35% (Now), 75% (In two years)
- Price and availability: 55% (Now), 75% (In two years)
- Product data: 70% (Now), 90% (In two years)
- Order data: 65% (Now), 95% (In two years)

Legend: Now, In two years

Percent response of 20 companies interviewed
(multiple responses accepted)

Source: Forrester Research, December 1998

Figure 13.1

Earlier adopters who relied upon selling over the Internet.

Some manufacturers have established an online presence with their customers, while at the same time maintaining tightly coupled channel relationships. They do this by linking interested customers that visit their sites to their resellers, via Internet site *hot links*. In this case the customer arrives at the new site and locates the product he or she wishes to order in the reseller's catalog. Sometimes, the customer might want to compare prices of other items.

The customers can now choose to order, or not to order, from this Internet site. Other manufacturers sometimes choose to host online product information, via their own catalogs, for resellers utilizing their sites; they thereby eliminate any need to send product information over the Internet. Other manufacturers send information via online shopping carts over the Internet to resellers to handle diverse types of customer fulfillment needs. In some cases manufacturers even carry information online about channel inventories.

Manufacturers experiencing online growth face some indirect challenges. As an example, there are issues related to performance and scalability. Formal relationships with the individual channel partners need to be carefully managed. These types of challenges will continue to accelerate as more and more new virtual partners are added to the supply chain and as the order of complexities continue to grow.

MAINTAIN UNIQUE RELATIONSHIPS

Each supply chain enterprise needs to maintain unique relationships with its trading partners. These unique relationships are sometimes based on legacy databases and complicated order-entry process rules. As a rule, these items seem to involve each of the trading partners. With high expectations of large online growth in the number of supply chain partnerships, complexities in the software and technical architectures to support these e-commerce linkages are increasing. Each enterprise within the supply chain will be compelled to deal with this issue in its own manner, ideally deploying solutions with a high-degree of Design Quality.

Producers in the supply chain appear to get adequate feedback, and on a fairly consistent basis. Feedback, while appearing to act as a benefit, can also result in a logistical nightmare for trading partners attempting to work together. Misuse of information and data exchanged between the companies can result in botched orders, lower customer satisfaction, and potential loss of customers.

Another significant challenge for members of the emerging virtual supply chain is the new collaborative computing environments that continue to emerge alomst daily. Trading partners will need to learn to work in a computerized, collaborative manner. All parties involved will be required to exchange information related to the dynamics of customer care and the sales of products or services. All parties involved must work together to accommodate customer preferences, products, service offerings, service requests, and other individual customer needs.

An analogy that can effectively describe a collaborative relationship is the requirements of track team members on a 400-meter relay team. It is critical for the runners to align themselves properly as one runner approaches the other to smoothly hand off the baton. Perfect execution in this case is a thing of beauty to watch. The same is true in supply chain business relationships that use e-commerce tools intended to provide collaborative trading environments. There is indeed a hand-off from one partner to the other. This hand-off also requires proper positioning and execution for the customer (see Figure 13.2). This is a balancing act that requires all trading partners to fully comprehend the strategic importance of combined business values, as well as the multitude of e-commerce technologies combined in the Internet site solution design.

Manufacturers must consider ways to execute smooth hand-offs to their trading partners. For example, virtual shopping baskets or carts should be electronically transferred to trading partners (in some form or another). The rules of engagement then become rather simplistic: perhaps involving only transfers of SKUs, quantities, or billing and payment information. This requires very little data management for both parties. Or does it? The actual processes involved in shipping can be handled via customized HTML links. What if the order has a split shipping requirement? Exactly how

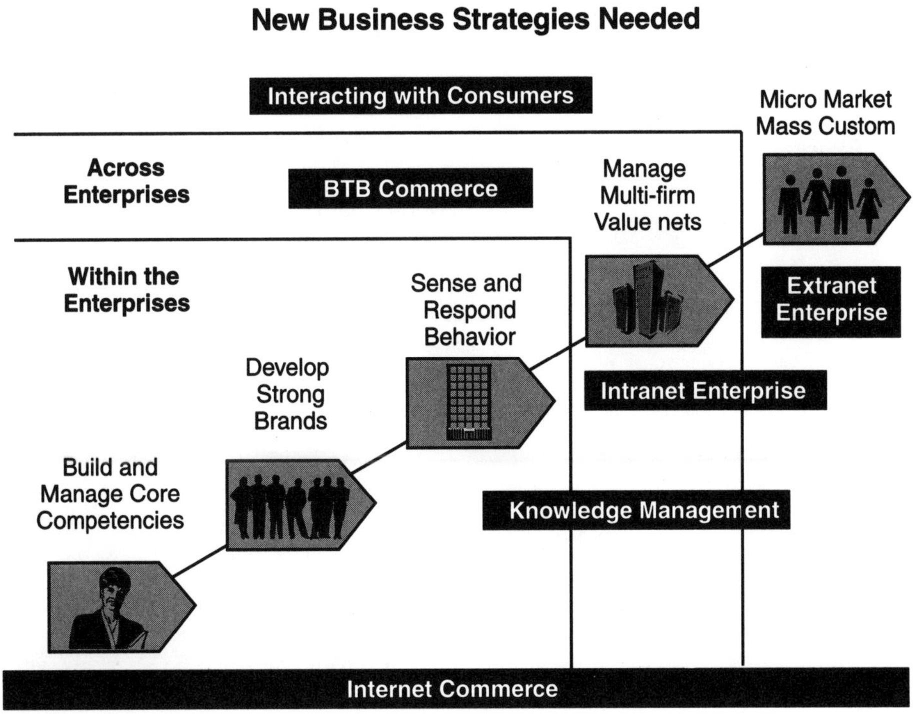

New Business Strategies Needed

Figure 13.2

It is important to rethink new business strategies.

does this get handled? For those solutions requiring more sophisticated moves from ERP-like systems, XML formats can be used. The entire point here is that e-commerce solutions demonstrating varying degrees of *Design Quality* can become complicated very quickly across several dimensions.

Alignment, smooth hand-offs to partners, and effective execution are essential to successful virtual channel relationships. In the case of indirect partnerships, business relationships need to be negotiated to include factors like order management, bill presentment and payment, and other key customer relationships. Next is the establishment of communities of interest. This means that trading partners in a virtual supply chain should be connected into each others' back-end systems, enabling the sharing of back-office data (see Figure 13.3). The potential capability for mining of customer data is another essential element requiring attention. New e-business tools provide valuable online customer profile information. In those cases where the manufacturer is not directly taking orders, it is still essential that the company has access to tremendous amounts of customer research data.

VIRTUAL BUSINESS COMMUNITIES

Virtual business communities in e-business relationships require online connections that enable the transfer of vital information in real-time including product or service

The E-business Value Chain

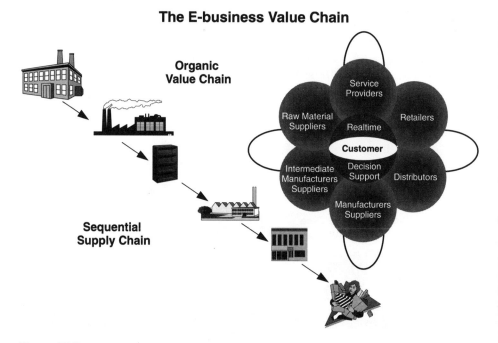

Figure 13.3

The e-business value chain is driven, in part, by knowledge of other enterprise values.

information, inventory data, end-user subscription information, and the status of customer orders, to name a few. This means that for all parties concerned, there must be a common customer-facing strategy that is a *single view* for the customer, yet is shared among multiple trading partners. This requires e-business and e-commerce technology synchronization across a set of complicated e-commerce environments. This is often achieved by sharing knowledge about the actions of customers, leveraging e-mail utilization patterns, buying patterns, and billing and payment requirements.

There is the global need to leverage message-based middleware to synchronize business processes throughout enterprise e-commerce boundaries. Because customers may be traversing sites, trading partners must have shared customer profile data, so that error tracking, for instance, can be achieved in real-time. It is equally important to standardize catalog capabilities, where utilized, as much as possible.

Product descriptions, pricing changes, imagery, currency differences, taxation, language barriers—all become factors in the equation. This equation is important to manufacturers and downstream trading partners that have had to deal with temporal aspects of refreshing catalog product information. To address this problem, e-commerce technologies like XML, for example, and Information & Content Exchange (ICE)—XML for the technology framework and ICE for content business guidelines—are favored. These e-commerce technology solutions (and others like Java and agent technologies) are available to all industries interested in e-commerce.

What types of costs are associated with the enablement of collaborative computing environments between trading partners? Some costs will be involved for manufacturers interested in providing smooth hand-offs to their trading partners. These costs could include provisions for shopping cart design metaphors, including HTML scripts and point-of-sale reporting capabilities. Costs are also associated with middleware applications and other e-commerce customization tools. There may be costs for external services to assist in engineering the networks and application designs, required for integrating enterprises in the supply chain. Finally, there are the system integration costs. Typically, software costs on average are 25 percent of the total cost for implementation of a virtual supply chain. The other 75 percent of costs include the cost of the skills required to do the seamless integration of e-commerce and other IT software into the newly aligned IT infrastructures. There are capital costs applied to the actual operations center required to support the e-commerce environment, even if outsourcing of infrastructure support services is the objective. Comparisons with ther typical e-commerce environments, their cost scenarios, their support scenarios, their lessons-learned will always help business leaders effectively plan for the associated costs related to enabling e-commerce environments.

What types of effects will the virtual supply chain communities have on channel partners? Figure 13.4 helps to shows these effects. It seems clear that in some cases the effect will be quite dramatic. The channel members, with robust and strong e-business/IT infrastructures (and staff resources), may have quite a competitive edge over those without the resources to support rapid movements away from the traditional models of supply

Importance of the Value Chain

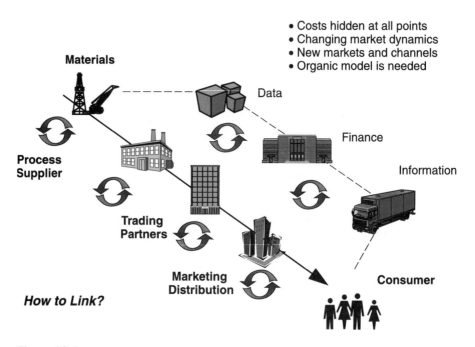

Figure 13.4

Dependence and cooperation must exist throughout the supply chain.

chains. This will cause channel partners to align themselves with the stronger players, leaving the weaker players to face reinvention as a viable e-commerce enterprise. Either they will have the skills and the investment dollars to compete, or they will not be able to afford the opportunity. Clusters of online communities will begin to form that will essentially lock out nonconforming players. Here is another paradigm shift.

Another intriguing phenomenon will occur with early global e-commerce engagements by setting (attempted) standards. Manufacturers in particular can take advantage of the "standards" of collaborative virtual communities being formed in any supply chain to enable them to gain valuable market intelligence information. Meanwhile, channel partners, like resellers, will strive to limit nonstandardized arrangements between trading partners and manufacturers, for converse reasons.

The formation of close-ended e-business alliances will therefore become popular for many global trading partners. The dynamics of these types of e-commerce environments will effectively launch new market spaces (like mobile Internet telephones) that were never previously imagined. For manufacturers that are significant players in e-commerce, significant competitive advantages will be presented. Some other examples of this trend may tend to lower inventory costs, as a result of leveraging supply chain partners carrying additions to their own inventories. This will be especially true in the distribution-oriented industries, for example, chip technologies. Another interesting paradigm shift might occur in the reliance on interenterprise e-commerce software, providing ubiquitous links between enterprises. This will mean that some systems will remain solid in back-end intranet usage, but the interenterprises will provide the supply chain direct channel links. The customer relationship models will tend to change as resellers begin to manage more of the customer relationships, including presale and after-sale support. Traditional customer care enterprises may have to reinvent themselves to be relevant constituents in the wide-range of e-commerce industry solutions.

We have discussed how enterprises will use e-commerce to extend their reach to new customers. New Internet portal sites will represent a tremendous window of opportunity for manufacturers and supply chain partners to extend their global customer reach. New technologies are being introduced at phenomenal rates to accommodate the growth of the emerging virtual supply chain communities of interest. These e-communities will leverage new e-commerce tools that will provide firms with innovative, collaborative computing capabilities across the value chain. And, yes, this will in turn require significant investments—but for those able to properly engage, it will be worth the investment.

14
E-business in Financial Industries

....

$\mathbf{T}$he growth of online revenues, for the insurance industry alone, is expected to be over $4 billion by 2003. There are, in fact, several outstanding predictions that traverse several of the financial industries. Although common consumer insurance sales (home, life, automobile insurance) will be significantly lower by utilizing e-commerce solutions (with some estimates as low as 2–3 percent) from that of previously implemented commerce solutions. The amount of sales resulting from the Internet operations will increase. This will likely grow three times as fast as more traditional methods of insuring individuals and property items. Attracting new customers and retaining older customers may be a challenge for insurers that decide not to leverage e-commerce applications to expand consumer reach and provide value-added services to new potential customers.

The insurance industry might generally be said to exercise more conservative approaches to the leveraging of technology for added business value. The insurance industry seems to be somewhat divided in its views about global e-commerce solutions. Business leaders in the insurance industry understand the implications of Internet e-commerce, as well as the dangers inherent in holding on to traditional approaches and old ways of thinking. Some of these business leaders assert that new metrics are emerging that will help them successfully manage their customer expectations. These new metrics include creative solutions in e-commerce that demonstrate a high degree of Design Quality.

E-COMMERCE AND INSURANCE COMPANIES

Consumers are clearly becoming more Internet and e-commerce savvy. It is therefore fair to view the savvy Internet user as an individual who recognizes tremendous value in access to important information. The savvy Internet end user understands exactly how to acquire vast amounts of information and how to transpose that information into knowledge. This, of course, helps any individual make the most intelligent buying decision possible. Consumers want convenience and control, which they generally can get by using the Internet. Recognizing this, some corporate executives and business leaders across industries are beginning to state that they, too, must adapt to the Internet—or face the possibility of becoming irrelevant and noncompetitive. This is yet another paradigm shift in industry.

Many critical e-commerce business solutions provide valuable portals for consumers to deal directly with insurers (and other financial industry enterprises) to gain more competitive prices for products or services. On the other side of the insurance industry equation, large numbers of carriers remain unconvinced of the enhanced business values associated with e-commerce solutions. Some research clearly illustrates the differing viewpoints held by insurance industry pundits. Some industry contenders may still believe that Internet e-commerce is a "passing trend." These believers might be wayward in their thought positions; therefore, from a business perspective, the consequences could be quite grave. Too little, too late may cause some to face the possibility of corporate disruption.

Although carriers have differing views of the business value of e-commerce and the Internet they are providing several forms of online services. One of these services involves allowing customers to review their own accounts or upgrade the services for their accounts online. Some insurers are beginning to strategically plan for e-commerce solutions that include the receipt of consumer applications and giving consumer online access to products and quotes. They also recognize the cost reduction potential related to e-commerce. In one example, reduced costs are realized by leveraging the Internet to link insurance agents and insurance brokers. There is a general feeling that providing consumers with e-commerce tools that enable access to a wide variety of insurance products may not result in wider consumer use. Other carriers feel differently and assert that the opposite is true— that more consumers will begin to find value in using online insurance-related services.

Insurers are certainly challenged with exactly how they can provide simplified ways for consumers to better comprehend their products, which sometimes can be very complex. Meanwhile, they remain concerned about corporate disruption for their agents, who have traditionally been the conduit to consumers. These agents can concisely and effectively explain the complexities of insurance products. Some feel that automating the "agent" process simply cannot be done. Many insurance products are just too complicated for the average and even above-average consumer to understand. Some also feel that selling insurance involves an emotional and human aspect that e-commerce technologies simply cannot project. Many insurers agree that channel partners will have to find ways to leverage e-commerce technologies and remain relevant. In conclusion, this is an interesting and somewhat unique paradigm.

To not only survive but excel, most carriers say that they now have to leverage e-commerce to gain competitive advantages through price points. Insurers are almost forced to provide value-added services, enhance their brands, and maintain high ratings. Failure is not an option, and survival of the fittest will be the rule for the day— even if survival means that these enterprises will evolve into offering products in specialized market segments or developing offerings with a variety of financial services.

E-COMMERCE, INSURANCE, AND BUSINESS CHANGE

Insurance carriers are very aware of the imminent changes on the horizon, and they understand that e-commerce will influence the way they deliver improved values to their customers. Basic services will be the first focus items that carriers will use to leverage e-commerce, with policy services being developed and offered over three to five years. Selling insurance online will not be easy, simply due to the complexity of the insurance offerings themselves.

The sale of insurance online will continue to grow, with some projections of more than $4 billion in revenues by 2003. The bulk of these dollars will be spent by young adults, those born in the early and mid 1980s. These people will use online insurance services on the Internet to obtain automobile insurance and other related services or offerings. Other types of insurance, like home owners and life, will lag due to their complexity. The degree of difficulty in presenting products to these customers online, without another human able to explain the details, is quite high.

Although consumers will leverage the Internet to search for insurance information, they will be more comfortable and therefore apt to purchase insurance policies offline with an agent or broker to help guide them through the products' complexities. Here we see a reversal of the benefits of utilizing the Internet to conduct e-commerce. The customer care offered by agents may prove a formidable challenge for any e-commerce insurance application to duplicate. Keep in mind that buying insurance is an emotional experience for most consumers.

Currently e-commerce applications lack very important customer value functionalities. For example, consumers find that while using these insurance e-commerce applications and shopping for information, a disconnect sometimes occurs as the leads are passed on to agents or brokers. Generally there is a time lapse before the consumer, who is ready to make a decision, is contacted. This clearly can result in loss of sales in a highly competitive environment.

Another challenge is that some online insurers do not provide full 24-hour services. Customers who visit their Internet sites have immediate questions, and there is right now a lack of call centers that are available 24 x 7 to provide the customer care functions. Most of these call centers operate Monday through Friday, from 9 A.M. to 5 P.M. EST.

CROSS-CHANNEL SELLING—ANOTHER SHIFT

Insurance enterprises face another challenge: to develop strategies that enable them to leverage selling insurance over multiple channels (see Figure 14.1). The customer becomes the ultimate arbiter who decides which channel to use. To achieve this, insurance enterprises need to implement several tactical objectives. One tactic is to reinvent

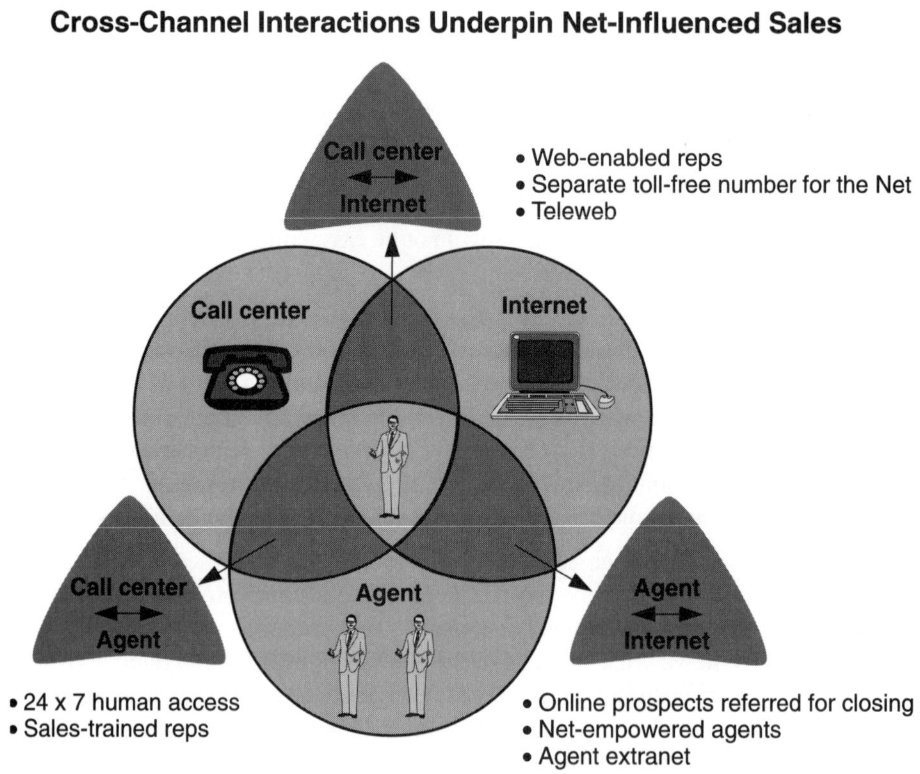

Cross-Channel Interactions Underpin Net-Influenced Sales

Call center
◄──►
Internet

- Web-enabled reps
- Separate toll-free number for the Net
- Teleweb

Call center

Internet

Call center
◄──►
Agent

Agent

Agent
◄──►
Internet

- 24 x 7 human access
- Sales-trained reps

- Online prospects referred for closing
- Net-empowered agents
- Agent extranet

Figure 14.1

The cross-channel interactions that will occur often in an e-business solution.

their agent services by accommodating a very informed consumer base with services like real-time claims status, extension of the enterprise (via extranets), and provision of leads to agents so that they can effectively close business with customers.

Another challenge to the insurance enterprises involves immediate availability of customer data. This is critical for the success of cross-channel selling. Middleware can be leveraged to maintain online databases that provide customer information. This type of business intelligence is critical for several reasons. It gives insights about the buying behaviors of customers, what types of information about insurance they were searching for, whether they are already customers, and how often they visited the site. This information is invaluable to the agents who receive the leads electronically. Customer care processes and e-commerce telephonic-Internet solutions are another important tactic because they allow customers to talk via the telephone to insurance-savvy representatives, who can provide guidance to the customers and who are trained to close business over the phone. Finally, there are dynamic online insurance e-commerce applications that empower consumers to identify their insurance requirements and suggest the best coverage, enabling them to buy without human intervention.

Early e-commerce contenders will gain strategic competitive advantage, as well as market share, as carriers develop new channel strategies that leverage e-commerce. Direct writers are most likely to go after this market space first. However, some larger carriers with established brand and marketing savvy will also get in the early mix and establish significant presence on the Internet. How these players move to establish their position will be fascinating to observe.

SUBSIDIARIES VERSUS AGENT SELLING

One approach that some insurance enterprises will leverage is to use direct subsidiaries instead of traditional agents. This approach clearly will be a significant change to the current channel models. Another, even more powerful e-commerce approach is to make the use of the Internet a branding experience for both new customers and established customers. This will mean that customers will view the Internet as simply another channel for doing business with their insurance carriers. A word of caution is in order, though: Carriers need to ensure that the customer experience with the brand is relevant and meaningful; otherwise, customers will click their way elsewhere to competitive sites they find more interesting, user friendly, relevant to their needs, and simpler to use.

Other significant strategies will include tactics that leverage new Internet-based distribution models. It is important for these enterprises to consider that most consumers do not surf the Internet seeking insurance company Internet sites, at least not yet, even though a growing portion of consumers do choose to visit insurance carrier sites.

One tactic that appears quite promising is to plant points of sale at every place where consumers may make insurance-related buying decisions. For example, consumers will visit relevant sites when they are expecting a new baby, purchasing a new home, or buying an automobile. Carriers can partner with these sites and include relevant insurance information (essentially their brands), specifically tailored to the potential needs of these consumers. Another tactic could be to establish points of sale on corporate intranet sites, where employees obtain information about their benefits.

Carriers can leverage important intermediaries that are already established players (for example, InsWeb) in the insurance industry. This will provide carriers with significant economies of scale and efficiencies, as they work on a referral fee-based model, instead of the commission models offered by many online agencies. Finally, carriers need to continue to explore partnerships with key financial services communities, including securities firms, banks, and brokerage houses. A great deal of research has been completed in this area and supports the fact that the financial community is, and will continue to be, a significant conduit for online distribution of insurance. Some research firms report that by 2002, there is a potential for 90 percent of the large online banking communities to sell insurance over the Internet. Insurance carriers need to move quickly here if they expect to be relevant enterprises in the future.

The real question is this: What role will insurance carriers play in the strategic horizon? A number of research reports indicate (from a consumer perspective) that there are two new e-commerce portals for consumers that will provide access to a new financial services models: financial providers and financial specialists. Because consumers visit Internet banks and Internet brokerage sites daily we can observe the role of the financial providers; insurance carriers will aggressively move to become financial specialists. The financial providers will be in a position to provide their customers and potential new customers with product offerings from many enterprises, being able to consolidate account data and offer sound financial guidance. The financial specialist, on the other hand, will concentrate on the development and distribution of its products. The carriers that compete in this space will have to be more innovative, provide superlative customer support services, and leverage distribution portals via their finance providers and others who maintain specialized Internet sites.

OPEN-FINANCE SPECIALISTS

Financial providers and financial specialists will introduce new products that provide added values to consumers. One example of this will be insurance policies that are based on real-time value to customers. These dynamic insurance offerings will provide adjustable policies based on consumer requirements, on a real-time basis. The financial providers will have the advantage of comprehending their client's complete financial situation. In those cases where carriers have partnerships with the providers, there will be the advantages of adjusting life policies, for example, in a real-time manner, utilizing the Internet e-commerce site.

Insurance carriers will strive to differentiate themselves by the value-added services they will offer customers, thereby avoiding the problems associated with pricing competition. One example of this would be automated e-commerce tools that will be used for underwriting and claims processing, in real-time, that guarantees immediate processing and payments.

The lower costs that insurance carriers will establish with the Internet as a major distribution channel will empower them to offer more creative forms of insurance. This will also help insurance enterprises have a greater customer reach and provide protection for niche markets risks (for instance, insurance for snow skis, expensive mountain bikes, roller blades, jet skis, and boats). One last area that will afford carriers potential revenue boosts will be the offering of low-end insurance, especially in the middle-class consumer segments.

In contrast, there are no better examples of exactly how an industry will be challenged to adapt to e-commerce than the insurance industry. This industry, as with other industries, will realize tremendous benefits through effective utilization of e-business utilities—embellished in creative e-commerce Internet solutions.

15
E-commerce Crossing Several Dimensions

....

The term "e-commerce" implies several methods of conducting electronic business through various transaction mediums. This refers most notably to those business practices conducted through methods of Internet telecommunication practices. E-commerce is accepted on a global scale, in the sense that its services are found around the world, connecting business partners and consumers electronically through use of many complicated Internet subnetworks.

The term *content-hosting* refers to the method in which any party is able to board and operate its e-commerce business applications, while storing them for managed operations in an ISP, or Internet Service Provider. The notion of an ISP is that any electronic business, or e-business, can be hosted for many individuals and/or companies to access the intended service that the e-business is designed to provide. For instance, many e-business services focus on buying and selling. This is quickly becoming a preferred method of conducting e-commerce, on a global scale.

Many systematic design concepts cross several dimensions, and they represent options that one has to consider when deciding on design concepts for creating an e-commerce, or e-business, application. For example, security is of prime importance. It is also very important to understand exactly how a company wishes to maintain its specific e-business content information. If, for instance, a company is providing a buying and selling e-business (sometimes referred to as e-procurement forms of e-business applications), then areas of interest rely primarily on the catalogs being hosted on the Internet and the methods of payment to be provided to the end user.

Staying with this e-commerce example of buying and selling, the most common aspects of electronic catalogs, which continually present themselves as difficult challenges, are product information, product pricing, and the continual need to update this information. Then, of course, if you are catering to a global community, both language and global trade/taxation laws become challenging issues to resolve. These are only a couple of examples where e-commerce developers, on a global scale, continually strive to design the most efficient methods in e-commerce applications.

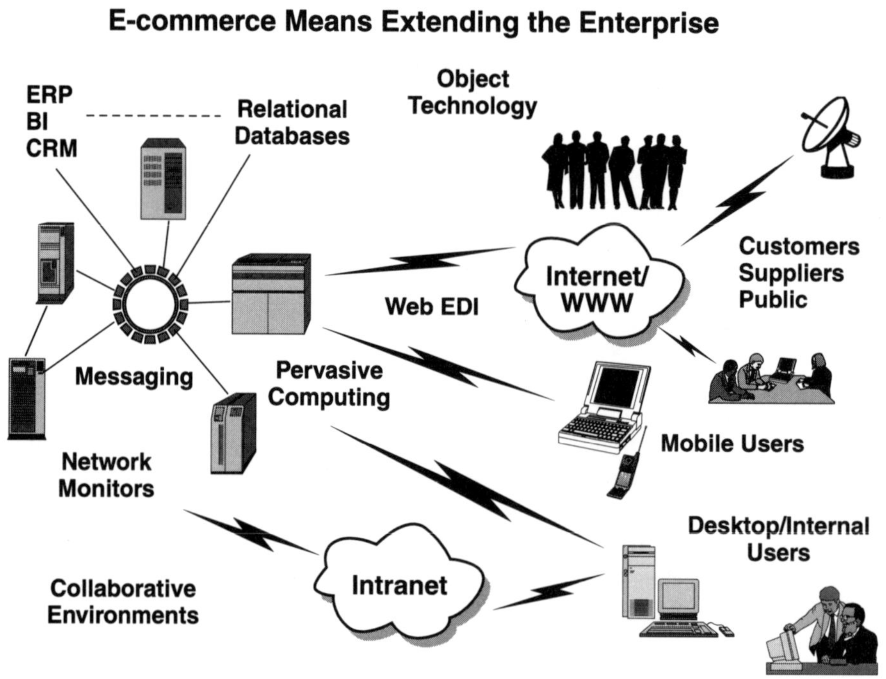

E-commerce Means Extending the Enterprise

Figure 15.1

Successful e-business solutions require expansive collaboration.

Many factors contribute to the ability of e-commerce technologies to reach out across several dimensions. Figure 15.1 illustrates the many e-commerce providers and their product lines that "reach out" to many sectors of the e-commerce end-user communities.

INTERNET SERVICE PROVIDERS

Internet Service Providers (ISPs) are rapidly becoming very lucrative businesses. ISPs are the commercial organizations that provide Internet service access; most often an ISP also provides content-hosting for those applications that are Web-based.

Designing and creating ISPs around the world involve many complex implementations of technology. These include various networking and telecommunication protocols, security schemes, billing and payment approaches, and content-hosting of server-dependent Internet applications. An ISP will typically charge per endpoint or per end user. There are also ISPs that charge flat rates based on usage.

The telecommunication companies, which are commercial-grade telecommunications carriers, find the business of ISPs quite natural. These corporations are the key element to any ISP, mainly because all of the endpoint usage traffic is transmitted through the global telecommunications infrastructure.

The typical technology components of any ISP include networking routers, which are complex, automated switching units that route end-user traffic from one geographical region into another. These routers also appropriately channel end users to other subnetworks within the ISP (that is, servers).

In conjunction with routers, technologies that exploit security (or filtering) measures are found. These devices are commonly referred to as "firewalls," and they enable end-user security. Firewall devices authenticate specific end users to access specific subnetworking areas of the Internet. In order to provide hosting capabilities for any end users that require secure environments, many complicated designs need to be considered carefully when filtering needs are required.

The enablement process of any e-business environment depends on an ISP. ISPs store the application services that represent the e-business itself, and then they route end users into (and out of) the e-business environment. The growth projections for business-to-business e-commerce are breathtaking. Within the next five years Internet commerce transactions are estimated to be equal to or well over $300 billion worldwide (see Figure 15.2).

1997	2002	2008
$8 billion worth of business was transacted on the Internet	$333 billion worth of business will be transacted on the Internet	
80 million users of the Web around the globe	329 million Internet users expected, some 80 million will be based in Europe. (*InfoWorld*, May 11, 1998)	One billion users of the Web around the globe

Figure 15.2

The global business consumption suggests very aggressive growth patterns for e-commerce solutions.

Global business consumption represents over 40 percent of the global economy and will reach over $13 trillion by 2001 (see Figure 15.3). This business-to-business consumption growth is what will drive the e-commerce transaction traffic to well over $300 billion. With estimates of well over 1 billion consumers worldwide using the Internet by 2002, the 38 percent projected global consumer consumption will sky-rocket e-commerce in the business-to-consumer market space to spectacular levels; it may even reach hundreds of billions of dollars.

THE GLOBAL E-COMMERCE THEATER

The growing global business-to-business opportunity among first-tier countries is projected to be almost 60 percent (see Figure 15.4). Enterprises investing in retrofitting their Information Technology global infrastructures to enable e-commerce will be significant in first-tier countries as their corporate missions will drive them to take advantage of the shift from manual trading models to electronic trading models. Although the growth rate in second- and third-tier countries will not be as great as in the first-tier countries, they may very quickly succeed in the global market space by leapfrogging to electronic trading models, driving e-commerce growth to even higher levels around the world.

The evolving new electronic trading model of Internet commerce is supported by exciting and innovative technologies (see Figure 15.5). This will enable pervasive computing. The e-commerce evolution is progressive, and as businesses begin to adopt these technologies they will advance. Their clear goal is to advance from establishing a presence for their brand to a becoming content model and ultimately an integrated e-commerce model.

The Internet has proved beneficial as a common practice for businesses to start with Internet sites that may have *buy-buttons* and *offline transaction* capabilities. Typically, there is no link to their legacy systems and virtually no customization. The next step usually taken is to create dynamic cataloging capabilities

1996		2001	
$11 Trillion		$13 Trillion	
Business-to-Business	42%	Business-to-Business	42%
Business-to-Consumer	38%	Business-to-Consumer	38%
Business/Consumer-to Government	20%	Business/Consumer-to Government	20%

Figure 15.3

The global theater of e-commerce is tremendously large and growing in volumes each day.

Segmentation	% BTB Market	Opportunity Assessment
First-tier countries	59%	High
Second-tier countries	19%	Medium-Low
Third-tier countries	8%	Low
Rest of the world	14%	Very Low

Figure 15.4

Business-to-business opportunities on a global level.

with shopping carts; users can use search engines to navigate throughout the catalog, loading their shopping carts with those items that they want to purchase. Next they begin to customize their sites with a view to the enablement of end-to-end e-commerce (see Figure 15.6). More advanced buying and shopping models are developed, leading to more advanced merchandising techniques with personalized services and some back-end integration. The next steps lead to a complete integration into a fully customized and advanced catalog and merchandising model (see Figure 15.7).

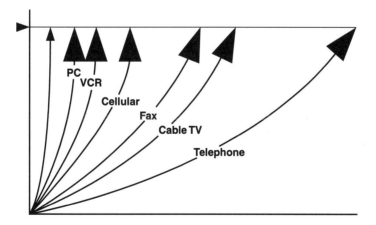

Figure 15.5

The electronic trading model and popular instruments utilized in some e-business solutions.

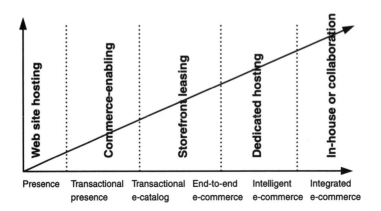

Figure 15.6

Information technology is racing to embrace the diverse needs of the Internet commerce end users.

The Historic Growth of E-business

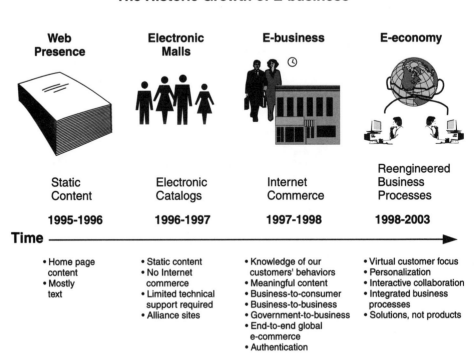

Figure 15.7

The historic growth patterns of e-businesses—almost a business transformation of a sort.

GLOBAL E-BUSINESS SERVICES ADD VALUE

The e-commerce progression provides a value-add proposition. This value-add proposition takes the form of an e-commerce *Value-Added Service Model* with four stages of progressive growth, from a commerce-enabled Internet presence to a fully integrated global enterprise site (see Figure 15.8).

The global Information Technology industry will experience a major metamorphosis during the next few years. Innovative platforms and new technologies will transcend the limits of traditional information technology, leaving the IT industry pundits to answer the key question of greatest importance: How will these changes affect the bottom line?

Some researchers in this area predict that the Internet will represent 10 percent of information technology revenues by 2001.

E-commerce Value-Added Service Models

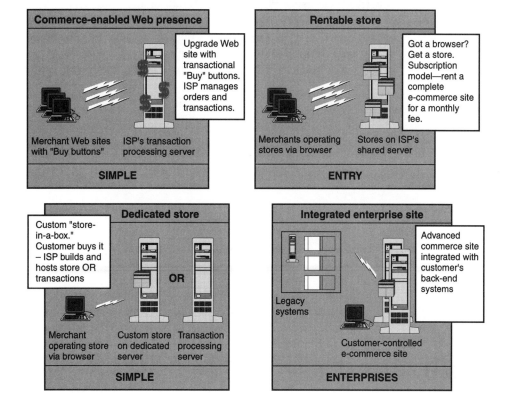

Figure 15.8

Examples of e-commerce value-added service models.

During 1996, the Internet market totaled $19 billion, or 26 percent of the information technology market's growth; it is currently experiencing a 50 percent annual growth rate, making the Internet market the leading area of new growth in the IT market. In 2000 the Internet market space will amount to $92 billion in revenue and will supplant the PC as the engine of growth in the industry. The Internet's impact on business will be profound. It will have significant effect on the information technology industry.

There are a number of reasons why global businesses and consumers are using the Internet for business. One-third (33 percent) of the consumer market with online access stated that they bought products using the Internet, and two-thirds (66 percent) reported they use the Internet to research products online before purchasing them through traditional channels (Ernst & Young/*American Banker*, 2/24/98). Online e-commerce transactions are projected to reach 1 million in 1998 (*Financial Times*, 2/1/98) with more than 70,000 merchants accepting online payments (*Financial Times*, 2/1/98). A key reason for this is the cost of bank transactions. For example, it is currently estimated that the cost of one bank transaction over the Internet is $.13 versus using PC software at $.26 or the telephone at $.54. This same type of bank transaction at a bank branch office would cost $1.08 (Booz-Allen & Hamilton). Consider the cost of purchasing an airline ticket online at $1.00 versus $8.00 through traditional channels (Booz-Allen & Hamilton). Other examples would include the North American automobile industry, which reportedly has the potential of saving approximately $1 billion a year, or roughly $71 per car, using e-commerce technologies (Automotive Industry Action Group/Forrester Research/Bloomberg, 1998).

Several business and technology research groups have provided a variety of forecasts about the growth of buying and selling goods and services over the Internet. Consider the following reports:

- Approximately 10 percent of global companies utilize the Internet to conduct sales transactions.
- Approximately 44 percent of global companies will begin to utilize the Internet over the next two years (Zona Research).

According to forecasts from Piper Jaffrey Investments, $228 billion in goods and services will be acquired and paid for over the Internet by 2001.

SPEED IS A BARRIER

The Massachusetts Institute of Technology (MIT) Media Laboratory predicts even faster and more incredible growth rates involving e-commerce—$1 trillion generated annually through e-commerce activities by 2000, with 70 percent in the business-to-business market (Nicholas Negroponte, director, at the Seybold/Wired Internet Publisher Conference, March 1998, New York). Therefore, the market for e-commerce will grow (at least) 100 percent between now and 2011 (Datamonitor/Financial Times, 1/27/98). Online music sales are expected to reach $1.7 billion by 2001, from $71 million during the past year (International Herald Tribune, 1/26/98).

These reports clearly support the projected phenomenal growth rates anticipated as a result of the e-commerce evolution; e-commerce is also being realized (financially) in all of the global stock exchange markets. This raises several questions regarding the growth in various industry segments: Who are the key players in the e-commerce evolution and what are they doing? What types of new e-commerce technologies are emerging? How are businesses using them to earn a profit?

The e-commerce phenomena is also viewed in other interesting, yet somewhat puzzling ways. For instance, in the United States there is an automobile bumper-sticker that simply says, "Internet for President." Now there is an interesting thought.

INTERNET ELECTRONIC BILL PRESENTMENT AND PAYMENT

The following information describes in some detail various efforts to establish Internet bill presentment and payment solutions. These are nontrivial concerns when we consider the technologies and the liabilities involved in delivering integral environments such as this. These are just a few of the innovative corporate partnerships that have recently been announced, involved in bill presentment and payment.

Banc One

Banc One Corp. plans to roll out an online program that will allow its customers to view and to pay bills completely—electronically. A bank representative made the announcement at the Online Banking Association's Electronic Bill Presentment and Payment Conference in San Francisco in 1999. If Banc One remains on schedule, it will be one of the first institutions to offer its customers fully electronic, Internet-based bill presentment and payment services. But it will not be alone for long, as at least half a dozen other institutions are currently involved in pilot programs.

Several banks now allow customers to pay bills over the Internet. As of yet, though, no banks are able to offer customers a service that presents the actual bills on the screen; no one can combine bills from different sources, like utility companies, telephone companies, and online grocery companies.

Banc One will launch the service along with Philadelphia-based Integrion Financial Network and Columbus, Ohio-based CheckFree Corp. CheckFree is currently working on individual pilot programs with Wells Fargo, KeyBank, Norwest, and Mellon. At least one electronic banking source agreed that Banc One is likely to complete its product first.

The new integrated services will enable Banc One customers to receive, view, and scrutinize a wide range of bills electronically. Customers can pay these bills through their computer, transferring funds from their bank accounts to pay any biller that presents an online bill through CheckFree. The system will connect Integrion's Interactive Financial Services (IFS) platform, CheckFree's Bill Presentment and Remittance system, and Banc One's internal bill payment technology.

"Banc One's launch of the Integrion/CheckFree solution clearly marks a new era of sophisticated online financial services being offered to consumers through the industry's trusted agent—their bank," said Peter Knight, chairman of CheckFree. "Institutions like Banc One—which offer consumers all critical financial transactions in a seamless Internet environment and provide an important distribution channel for billers—are clearly the driving force behind the rapid expansion of online financial management."

A spokesperson for Wells Fargo, which started a six-month pilot program in July 1999, said the testing phase has "been very successful" so far. In 1995, Wells Fargo became the first bank to offer customers banking over the Internet.

Electronic bill payment promises to reduce paper and transaction costs for banks while expanding the services a bank can offer its customers. "Receiving bills online instead of waiting for snail mail to arrive is the ultimate in convenience," said Dudley Nigg, executive vice president of Online Financial Services at Wells.

Although Citibank has yet to set a completion date for its bill presentment technology, it recently announced a pilot program with Redmond, Washington-based TransPoint that aims to couple several advanced features already in use by the two companies.

As part of the agreement, TransPoint, which was originally launched by Microsoft and First Data Corp., will take advantage of the bank's "pay anyone" technology. This enables consumers to pay any bill or make any payment regardless of whether the participating biller delivers the bill electronically.

First Union and TransPoint Announce Internet-Based Bill Delivery and Payment

First Union Corp. and TransPoint announced that, together, First Union will pilot the TransPoint Internet bill delivery and payment (IBDP) system, enabling First Union home-banking customers to receive and pay bills over the Internet quickly and easily.

TransPoint, formerly MSFDC, is the joint venture of Microsoft Corp. and First Data Corp., with Citibank as a minority equity investor.

"Internet bill delivery and payment adds tremendous value to First Union's service offerings, and TransPoint is one of the strategic companies we plan to work with in this arena," said Edgar Brown, senior vice president of First Union. "TransPoint has demonstrated its commitment to enhancing financial institutions' customer relationships, and its business model provides significant opportunities for us to better serve our customers."

First Union Corp., based in Charlotte, North Carolina, is the nation's sixth largest bank holding company. It serves more than 16 million retail and commercial customers and constitutes the nation's third largest branch network on the East Coast.

"The addition of First Union allows consumers throughout the Eastern seaboard to pay Internet e-bills through one of the largest banks in the country and enhances TransPoint's strong regional and national presence," said Lewis Levin, vice president of desktop finance at Microsoft. "We look forward to working with First Union and enabling the company to offer TransPoint E-Bills to its customers."

With the TransPoint pilot service, First Union customers will benefit from an efficient, easy-to-use bill management system that collects bills from participating billers and displays them at the First Union bill presentation Internet site.

TransPoint has announced pilots with several financial institutions, including Banc One, KeyBank, Norwest, Merrill Lynch, Wells Fargo Bank, Citibank, and Mellon Bank. More than 24 billers are also included in the pilot, including PECO Energy Company, J.C. Penney, Mobil, and Xerox.

First Union

First Union Corp. is a leading provider of financial services to more than 16 million retail and corporate customers throughout the East Coast and the nation. First Union is the nation's sixth largest bank holding company, based on assets of $234.6 billion as of September 30, 1998, and ranks among the top 15 financial services companies in the world, based on market capitalization. The company operates full-service banking offices in 12 states and Washington, D.C. For more information, visit http://www.firstunion.com/.

TransPoint

Formerly MSFDC, TransPoint is a joint venture of Microsoft and First Data Corp., formed in June 1997. Citibank is a minority equity investor in TransPoint. In 1999, the company introduced the nation's first end-to-end system for Internet bill delivery and payment. TransPoint's service, uses existing payment systems, and allows consumers to access and pay their bills through the branded home banking services of participating financial institutions. TransPoint is based in Englewood, Colorado. For more information, visit http://www.transpoint.com/.

(Note: Microsoft is either a registered trademark or trademark of Microsoft Corp. in the United States and/or other countries. TransPoint is a trademark of MSFDC. Other product and company names herein may be trademarks of their respective owners.)

If you are interested in viewing additional information on Microsoft, check out the Microsoft Internet page at http://www.microsoft.com/presspass/ on Microsoft's corporate information pages.

Mellon Bank

The Financial Services Technology Consortium (FSTC) announced that another Bank Internet Payment System (BIPS) working prototype has been implemented. Participants are Mellon Bank, PP&L, Inc., and NCR.

In the prototype, customers of PP&L, Inc., a Mellon corporate customer, were able to pay their PP&L utility bills over the Internet, even though the customers did not have an account with Mellon Bank.

The Mellon Bank demonstration builds on a previous BIPS prototype by Illinois-based Glenview State Bank in which Glenview received payment instructions from a corporate customer over the Internet. The Mellon prototype expanded on the Glenview prototype to demonstrate how payment instructions can be initiated by parties whose banks are not BIPS-enabled, using digitally signed automated clearing house (ACH) debit authorizations and certificates to ensure the initiator's identity. The Mellon prototype is a first step toward enabling secure, spontaneous transactions over the Internet between parties unknown to each other.

In the Mellon prototype, customers of PP&L view their PP&L invoice on an Internet site. When a customer decides to pay his invoice, he accesses the BIPS interface and fills in the data necessary to instruct Mellon Bank to debit his account at his bank and to credit PP&L's account at Mellon Bank. The customer then digitally signs the ACH debit authorization message, and the message is encrypted, certified, and transmitted to Mellon Bank over the Internet with BIPS technology.

Using equipment supplied by NCR, Mellon Bank receives the customer's instruction to pay the invoice, authenticates the customer using the customer's digital signature and certificate, and translates the instruction into an Automated Clearing House (ACH) debit origination transaction, using the existing ACH clearing and settlement system for transmission via the ACH Network.

Normally, this type of transaction would have consisted of the receipt of a paper bill and payment via either check or a preauthorized debit. While the preauthorized debit improves on the speed of check payment, it forces the payer to relinquish control over the dollar amount debited (it will be whatever is billed) and the date of the debit.

The BIPS method allows PP&L's customers to retain control of the payment process; they specify the dollar amount of the payment and the date that the debit to their account will take place. PP&L receives the payment quickly, and PP&L's accounts receivable system is electronically updated to more quickly reflect the payment from the customer. In addition, use of the ACH network is generally less expensive for both the payer and the payee than is the issuance of paper check payments and the clearance, settlement, and posting of those payments to the payee's accounts receivable system.

According to Nancy Atkinson, Vice President, Mellon Global Cash Management, "Mellon Bank can see the tremendous potential of using the Internet as an efficient and low-cost medium for transmitting payment instructions. BIPS does not require a large investment in equipment or development time and leverages our existing ACH system. Most importantly, it provides flexible new payment initiation options for our corporate clients to offer to their customers."

The integrity of the relationship between PP&L and its customers is maintained throughout the process. Mellon Bank acts on behalf of its customer, PP&L, and with its authorization to do so. The PP&L customer's digital signature and certificate provides the security mechanism to authenticate the originator of the instruction and the integrity and nonrepudiation of the instruction.

Customers participating in the Mellon Bank prototype required only Internet access, an Internet browser, a digital certificate, and an account at a domestic bank. PP&L required only an account at Mellon (a BIPS-enabled bank) to receive the payment. The prototype program with Mellon Bank is a further extension of PP&L, Inc.'s commitment to providing high-quality service to its customers at low prices. The Allentown, Pennsylvania-based company consistently earns customer satisfaction ratings that are among the highest in its industry. One of the ways PP&L, Inc. earns those ratings is by anticipating—and responding to—the needs of customers.

Treasury Services, PP&L, Inc. indicates that "using BIPS offers a new, convenient method for our customers to pay their power bills. The ability to control the exact time and amount of payment from the convenience of their computers is something many of our customers desire. We are excited to be part of this groundbreaking prototype."

PP&L, Inc. is pleased with the results of this prototype and plans to pursue an Internet-based payment option for its customers. PP&L, Inc. indicated that Mellon Bank was an excellent partner in the effort.

Mellon Bank's BIPS prototype system is supplied by NCR, using its High Availability Internet server and custom software to receive BIPS-formatted payment instructions. The NCR system enables acknowledgment that the instruction has been received, performs reason checks, and creates audit trails to track the progress of the payment instruction. The BIPS project developed an open specification for a secure server and a network payment protocol that can be used to provide payment transactions via the Internet to banks. BIPS allows payers and payees to agree on payment terms and mechanisms, be able to access multiple bank payments systems, and enable customers and banks to choose the most cost-effective way to make a payment. In addition, BIPS may provide the intelligence to select the appropriate payment mechanism for the payer based on the payer's requirements for cost and speed of settlement, and it provides online authentication of payers and payees and authorization for the transaction.

The BIPS prototype projects are designed to demonstrate its interoperability, test the feasibility of the BIPS method, and identify any payment system risks and operational issues. These prototypes validate the specification in multiple scenarios and focus on reducing risks to the systems and participants and identifying and resolving organizational issues.

Organizations participating in the BIPS project, which is an effort of the FSTC, include Citibank, Compaq-Tandem Division, Glenview State Bank, Mellon Bank, Fujitsu Research Institute, GlobeSet Inc., and NCR. Project advisors include @Work Technologies, CommerceNet, The Federal Reserve Bank, The National Automated Clearing House Association (NACHA) Internet Council, The Open Group, and SWIFT.

The Financial Services Technology Consortium is a not-for-profit research and development organization composed of banks, industry partners, financial service providers, technology companies, academic institutions, and government agencies. Founded in September 1993, the FSTC fosters the development of technology-based solutions to meet the financial services industry needs and opportunities. FSTC sponsors project-oriented research and proof-of-concept activities on interbank issues, with a focus on interoperability requirements and standards. In addition, particular emphasis is placed on payment systems, electronic commerce, and information delivery. Current FSTC programs include Bank Internet Payment System (BIPS), Electronic Check, Risk Management, and Paperless Automated Check Exchange and Settlement (PACES).

Mellon Bank

A broad-based financial services company with a bank at its core, Mellon Bank Corp. ranks among the nation's largest bank holding companies in market capitalization.

With approximately $350 billion of assets under management and approximately $1.8 trillion of assets under administration, Mellon provides a full range of banking, investment, and trust products and services to individuals and small, mid-sized, and large businesses and institutions. Its mutual fund companies, The Dreyfus Corp. and Founders Asset Management, place Mellon as the leading bank manager of mutual funds. Headquartered in Pittsburgh, Mellon's principal subsidiary is Mellon Bank, N.A.

NCR Corp.

NCR supplies banks and other financial institutions with banking solutions in the age of the consumer—solutions that are tailored to the NCR customer's individual needs, so that it can offer the best services to its consumers. These solutions cover the areas of self-service, payment, channel delivery, and customer management.

Customers in more than 130 countries around the world use NCR's computer systems, store automation, banking systems, consulting and support services, and consumables. NCR is located on the World Wide Web at http://www.ncr.com/. The Financial Solutions Group pressroom is at http://www3.ncr.com/product/financial/press/.

PP&L, Inc.

PP&L, Inc., a subsidiary of PP&L Resources, Inc., provides electricity delivery service to 1.2 million customers in eastern and central Pennsylvania, sells retail electricity throughout the state of Pennsylvania, and markets wholesale electricity in 22 states and Canada. Other PP&L Resources subsidiaries include PP&L Global, Inc., an international independent power company; PP&L Spectrum, Inc., which markets energy-related services and products; and H.T. Lyons, Inc., an energy management and heating, ventilating, and air-conditioning firm.

CheckFree to Provide Processing for EDS' Electronic Bill Paying Service

CheckFree and EDS announced in the first half of the year a six-year agreement in which EDS will use CheckFree's remittance processing services for the electronic bill paying service that EDS provides to financial institutions.

CheckFree is the leading provider of bill presentment and payment processing for financial institutions, processing more than 10 million electronic bill payment transactions per month. EDS, a global information technology services company, has more than 5,000 financial institution clients in 32 countries.

"Consumers increasingly are using electronic delivery channels to bring speed and convenience to such tasks as paying bills, and financial institutions are responding by offering Web- and telephone-based electronic bill payment services," said John A. Meyer, president of EDS' Diversified Financial Services business unit. "Teaming with CheckFree, the industry leader in remittance back-office processing, is enabling us to provide more efficient bill payment services to our financial institution clients."

"With its large customer base, EDS is one of the major players in the financial transactions market, and we're very pleased to work with them and provide an even greater level of service to their client base," said Sean Feeney, executive vice president, Electronic Commerce Sales at CheckFree. "Behind the scenes, CheckFree will provide EDS' clients a highly cost-effective option to process and deliver bill payments. This agreement expands our third-party relationships and continues EDS' strong support services for financial institutions."

EDS

EDS, the official information technology services provider for World Cup 1998, is a leader in the global information services industry. The company's more than 110,000 employees specialize in applying a range of ideas and technologies to help business and government clients improve their economics, products, services, and relationships. EDS, which serves clients in 45 countries, reported revenues of $15.2 billion in 1997. The company's stock is traded on the New York Stock Exchange and the London Stock Exchange. Visit EDS via the Internet at http://www.eds.com.

CheckFree

Founded in 1981, CheckFree (http://www.checkfree.com), the operating subsidiary of CheckFree Holdings Corp., is the leading provider of financial electronic commerce services, software, and related products for more than 2.5 million consumers, 1,000 businesses, and 850 financial institutions. CheckFree designs, develops, and markets services that enable its customers to make electronic payments and collections, automate paper-based recurring financial transactions, and conduct secure transactions on the Internet.

In summary, this long list of electronic commerce corporations have demonstrated what they all perceive to be very healthy relationships, forming with each other to compliment their own best interests. The synergy between these type of corporate entities will not cease, instead continue to grow in immense and perhaps never considered ways—simply by virtue of combining e-commerce tools, practices, and business transformation efforts.

Part 4
Global Segmentation

$\mathbf{T}$his part of the book explores customer relationships involved in e-commerce engagements. Financial services involved in the process of conducting e-commerce will also be explored. The value chain, the supply chain, and many other forms of ongoing relationships will be discussed. Customer relationships in a global segmentation are varied, and many of the solutions in e-business discussed in this part of the book cover aspects of establishing valued customer relationships.

This part of the book will explore many facets of e-business that incorporate concepts of e-commerce, such as the aerospace industry and the innovative approaches in e-business demonstrated in a spare parts business. The automobile industry also has demonstrated leadership, shown in some excellent e-business examples. The value chain management process and aspects of e-procurement will be explored in this part of the book. And finally, the supply-chain will be discussed.

16

Customer Relationships: E-contracts, E-bills, E-payments, E-care, E-trust

....

Business leaders responsible for developing and implementing e-commerce applications need to explore several areas of e-commerce service delivery and service support. These organizational functions must provide business value while demonstrating corporate strategies and key business objectives. The first area is in payments. Bill payment is enhanced by bill presentment applications. As enterprises bill their customers based on invoice data, transactions (when executed) are automatically applied to customer accounts, and electronic feeds are then made to the electronic accounts receivable ledger systems. From a consumer perspective, bill payments must integrate seamlessly into demand deposit accounts and update their account balances in real-time. Another important area is the scheduling of payments. Financial enterprises require that bill payments be integrated into the baseline electronic funds transfer systems to avoid the costs of adding still another payment operation.

E-BILL PRESENTMENT

Another area that requires examination is the actual management of customer relationships as they apply to billing and payments. This requires that an end-to-end framework for the processing of transactions be in place, ensuring that the transaction(s) can be audited for all parties concerned or by those with the rights and need to know. Specifically, this means an audit capability must be in place that tracks electronic bill presentment, electronic payments, and account adjustments and that updates the account ledger. This audit capability is provided to customers with all vital statistics and information relative to their accounts. These business functions must provide an accurate depiction of accounts and payment status. For all parties concerned, bill presentment must be integrated into the already established baseline processes.

Other key areas of importance to all parties involved in the billing process include the retention of billing data, ownership of the data, efficiencies, and profitability.

ONLINE CONTRACTING: E-CONTRACTS

Perhaps one of the more interesting areas to explore in e-commerce is online contracting, or e-contracts. The recognition of legal documents electronically is important in e-commerce. In the United States alone, numerous legislative actions are designed to put some *controls* on the electronic contracting process. For many global enterprises, there remain a great deal of debate and many unanswered questions surrounding the topics of governance and controls.

Many firms are moving ahead in the use of online e-contracts. They are driven by the opportunities and cost savings realized by doing business online. This means that these organizations are willing to bear the responsibility and accountability that goes along with managing e-contracts over the Internet. This is despite the fact that the Uniform Commercial Code (UCC), which has been adopted throughout the United States by many states, has the proviso that contracts require a handwritten signature for goods worth more than $500. Verified and validated electronic signatures remain at the center of the debate.

The hyper-growth and obvious importance of Internet e-commerce have been compelling factors for many states to draft new legislation that allows online contracts. Standards for online contracts are just beginning to be developed, although none currently has been widely embraced.

The current state of affairs relative to online e-contracting is in some turmoil with pervasive inconsistency in addressing different laws drafted by each state or, even more complicated, by different the global regions. The stakes are very high for enterprises that are entering into e-commerce because consideration of electronic contractual agreements is of utmost importance. Industry is about to discover solutions for both the public and private sectors. How will the laws in this area develop and get enforced? Will they be consistent? Will they be uniform? Most important of all, will the laws be acceptable to customers? Here lies several yet unresolved subject areas. To date, regulation of international Internet operations is virtually unchallenged although regulatory controls seem to be a natural next step. International independence makes this notion difficult, if not impossible, to resolve.

Part of the problem dealing with laws and integrity has been that in the United States, independent states have typically provided contracts and laws that apply in the case of online contracts for their specific state. Considering global issues in this area, the problem becomes more fractal. There are several consumer-related concerns that governments have to consider for their own public sectors, not others. For example, the government is interested in protecting its citizens, who may unwittingly enter into electronic contracts without properly understanding potentially adverse or unknown consequences. Consumers need to be properly protected when they are involved in authentication of contractual agreements online. Regulatory laws need to be passed (and are) that allow for electronic signatures to replace handwritten signatures. There are several viewpoints on how to resolve the complexities of e-commerce, specifically e-contracts that are written and "legally" signed online. The key motivation for many different industries remains with the government's legislators and other officials. That is, exactly how do we protect consumers?

An important question that governments are addressing is whether legislation should be technology-oriented. Some issues surround the term *lecturing signature,* which is a generic term that applies to authentication and accountability. The electronic signature can be a simple electronic mark (of some sort) or the capture electronically of an actual handwritten signature. A variety of encryption methods are also being introduced to resolve this difficult problem. Today, biometrics and other advanced signature identification methods can be used to verify handwritten electronic signatures. Most states have passed some form of electronic signature legislation. Many of these laws differ; it seems that very few, if any, of these laws are identical.

For the most part, much of the U.S. state legislation applies to government or healthcare proceedings. The issues surrounding the legal implications of electronic signatures remain pervasive in every country. There has been a reduction of global efforts to develop legislation that focuses on digital signatures and public key infrastructures; however, the U.S. government is trying to reduce restrictions on complicated encryption schemes, allowing portions of this problem to be resolved.

This market space is still nascent; therefore, it will take time before laws are developed that address the issues involving electronic authentication, consumer acceptance, unfair liability, cross-state utilization, and transcontinental authentication problems. The costs and complexities related to building infrastructure capable of supporting electronic authentication are causing many global governments to pause and consider alternative ways to approach the problem. Meanwhile, the U.S. government continues to challenge the ability of introducing regulatory legislation to regulate online contracts. The banking and financial services industry has introduced regulatory initiatives that permit the use of electronic authentication.

Enterprises engaged in business-to-business e-commerce will depend on mutually agreed-on ethical rules of governance to oversee their e-commerce deals. They can (if they find it necessary) refer to other examples from model contracts developed by other enterprises (for example, UNICITRAL and the ICC).

It is important to consider that any enterprise that requires online e-contracting capabilities to conduct normal business sometimes will need to determine who their potential contract parties are—for example, world government(s), other national or international businesses, or consumers. This allows the enterprise to investigate all legislation relevant to the contracted parties. These enterprises should be especially careful in the business-to-consumer scenario. The reason for this is that very little legislation covers consumers and online electronic agreements. This type of consumer legislation will probably be unlikely for quite sometime, due to territorial politics and the sensitivities of legislators involved in protecting the citizens they represent.

A company's legal team, IS teams, and unit managers should all participate in risk-assessment studies for each potential customer group, thereby developing sound policies and safeguards (or guidelines) for the governance of both the business-to-business and business-to-consumer markets.

FINANCIAL SERVICES—TRUSTED AUTHENTICATION

In 1998, a consortium of eight global banks including ABN AMRO, Bank of America, Bankers Trust, Barclays Bank, Chase Manhattan, Citibank, Deutsche Bank, and HypoVereinsbank made an innovative e-commerce announcement. They introduced a *for-profit* company, as a consortium, that offers certificate authority (CA) services. This newly formed company will utilize the public key infrastructure (PKI) technology. This global consortium will provide the capability (or role) of a "global trust enterprise," and it will offer services in several major e-commerce areas.

First, this trusted enterprise will offer authenticated security solutions that guarantee a trading partner's identity between enterprises; that is, partners that are engaging in e-business trading through the utilization of e-commerce technology solutions. This will mean that firms using e-commerce can engage in business-to-business e-commerce (on an international basis, if desired) with PKI guaranteed authentication. Second will be the actual establishment of internationally recognized CAs that are concentrated in business-to-business electronic e-commerce. This trusted enterprise will then enable interoperable trusted applications, by virtue of the PKI technology, and across several heterogeneous systems (utilized by the various enterprises) engaging in business-to-business e-commerce trading. Third, this trusted enterprise will leverage the aforementioned services to better position banks (obviously, as trusted intermediaries) in the e-commerce world.

As e-commerce thrives in the forthcoming decade, the CA market space will grow significantly. The role of CAs will gradually grow in both the business-to-business and the business-to-consumer e-commerce areas. An excellent example of a commercial CA e-commerce provider is a company known as Verisign, found at: http//www.verisign.com/.

To achieve this kind of trusted enterprise success, the enabling PKI technologies will have to be simple to establish and transparent to customers. The CA must be a simple programmatic item to manage security authentication, and it must also be held in complete security and safety by the owner. Over the last couple of years, CAs have been well established as a trusted method for doing business on the Internet: Therefore, the CA seems to be a dependable transaction medium. Obviously, financial institutions are well positioned to establish this trusted CA approach. Therefore, banking alliances are a good starting point; the success of CA acceptance may very well be based on specific industry best practices—which implies reengineering business practices in those areas that require trusted forms of e-commerce enablement (for example, CAs).

The banking and financial services industry is undergoing a global metamorphosis of a sort. This industry seems to be moving from a slower, non-Internet-based world (in terms of consumer-related services) to a virtual online agent with a plethora of new services including investments, account management, credit services, and brokerage services. Many of these Internet-based services use PKI technologies to satisfy complicated security and encryption requirements. Many banks that cannot keep up with the rapid pace of Internet-based e-commerce technology adoptions simply may not be able to afford the required investments; in some cases, they are being acquired by other more aggressive banks.

The banking industry continues to consider innovative ways to redefine its core businesses, its industry relevance, and its business values. For example, deregulation has led to intense competition from nonbanks (investment companies, insurance companies, and software companies, for example). There seems to be a great deal of pressure resulting from Internet commerce, a seemingly continuous state of banking mergers, and corporate consolidations. This is a phenomenon that is forcing banks to seek new revenue channels.

A key area of interest in the banking industry has been triggered by evolving corporate supply chains and the innovation of e-commerce initiatives that introduce causal effects on their own business. Consequently, many banks have reengineered their core business systems (and customer care interaction processes) to the point of almost eliminating the need for human intervention. This seems to be the current direction in both retail and commercial banking markets. The danger for banks is the emerging role of increased transaction efficiencies and commodity executions. This new business model, as innovative as it may seem for the banking industry, has pundits concerned about banks' exposure to considerable competitive risks.

One way that banks are outflanking this "competitive risk" issue is by attempting to reposition themselves as value-added services providers, by creating services that help companies validate the identity of partners, suppliers, and customers. Thereby, they are confidently able now to engage in e-commerce as trading partners. One example of the global trust enterprise is the concept of the consortium of global banks. Their strategies are to establish a global financial network that will act as a single (trusted) focal point for use by financial institutions, other participating corporate trading partners, and general consumers. Some examples are Internet-based business-to-business banking applications for processing letters of credit, electronic funds transferal, wire transactions, check authorization services, international trade, corporate purchasing, securities purchase and exchange, commercial real estate, government services, and a tremendous amount of other content-based delivery items.

The banking industry today is in an excellent position to enable this type of global trusted infrastructure. It is unclear, however, exactly how this global banking industry will be regulated, and what governance will be imposed on banks as service providers. It is clear that the banking industry has the necessary resources and experience in risk management, and it has enough technical expertise to support CAs. For the global trusted enterprise to be a reality, it will require near-term support from other global financial institutions; security companies will also be required to participate. Then, the participating banks will have to cooperate in issuing CAs to prospective corporations (and their employees) based on a standard set of system rules, contracts, guidelines, and business practices.

The banking industry will not be the only form of institutions that will compete in this space. Other corporate entities will include business enterprises, such as IBM, Equifax, WorldCom, EDS, Verisign, and Entrust. It is most likely that these enterprises have established their own PKI technologies to enable them to process CAs. Furthermore, the competition will be fierce as different competing entities maneuver for position and seek to gain significant shares of the CA market space.

To successfully compete in this arena, the global trusted enterprise (formed by the global banking community) will have to differentiate itself from its competitors. One set of functions that the global trusted enterprise currently has appears to be significant. This function is differentiated from traditional security methods, as it involves the enablement of a multistep signing capability that divides the (electronic) private key in pieces and then stores these pieces in distinctive hardware signing devices. Multistep signing techniques enable an enterprise to assign select groups of the "key" pieces (that are stored to be used by approval officers) to accept certificates and certificate revocation lists from other points. By designating multiple approvers, a single point of failure is virtually eradicated, resulting in a realizable reduction of fraud and private key compromises. This approach is complex across several dimensions, yet it seems to be quite effective.

Another unique function that serves to differentiate the global trusted enterprise from more traditional banking enterprises is a function that integrates technology, law, risk management, and business conduct guidelines. In order to establish a relevant position in the business-to-business e-commerce market space, this type of function is a requirement. This also means that the banks that have developed (and support) the global trusted enterprise are extremely well versed in industry-specific supply chains, e-commerce business processes, ethical practices, and technical architectures. Although their reach is extensive, it is not clear that the banks that support the global trusted enterprise have expertise in important market segments (for example, retail and manufacturing). To be successful in this space, banks will have to earn recognition as key trusted e-commerce intermediaries.

17

Examples of E-business Solutions

ming more and more vital in many industries as e-commerce
to deliver value-added services via the Internet. One way that
this is to leverage e-business to enhance the customer expe-
mple of this is the Boeing Company's work in e-commerce.
of Boeing established an Internet site that enabled its cus-
needed spare parts. The advantages of this site were much
t cycles, a greater reach to more customers (including non-
r customer ordering costs.

y is one of the global giants in the aerospace industry. It is a
of commercial jetliners and military aircraft. The Boeing
on was designed to provide more comprehensive information
o allow these customers to quickly process online orders for
formed e-business enterprise had some core business issues to
ded to explore (and then implement) new ways to augment slow-
ties in its core businesses. Consequently, Boeing had to create other
usiness value to its enterprise and subsequently its stakeholders.

demanding customers and Boeing's self-imposed requirement to
doing business, and thereby improving its competitive position in
t, were two driving factors. The need to increase revenues and prof-
cantly improve customer satisfaction by providing real-time access to
extranet, indeed presented an admirable challenge (for any enterprise).
With   access to its corporate networks, Boeing customers would soon have
an online "portal" to Boeing's parts information and order status systems. To achieve
this, Boeing's answer was an e-business solution called PART (Part Analysis and
Requirements Tracking). This Internet e-business site has been very successful and
has helped Boeing to process 13 percent of its total orders after the solution was in
production for a year. This has significantly reduced costs because it is replacing more
expensive methods of processing orders. In fact, the company has eliminated 25 percent of its order-processing costs.

The creation of new e-business solutions has helped Boeing to level out the number of people in the spare parts data entry group even as the order volume has increased by approximately 30 percent. This has demonstrated a cost avoidance of 10 percent in additional resources.

Boeing is also enjoying a windfall of savings on the paper, printing, and labor costs previously required to produce weekly order status reports. This is all a direct result of customers being enabled to access Boeing's online order status information. The potential in annual savings is estimated at over $300,000. Also of interest are the intangible results that do not have the normal metrics. This includes the outreach for new customers (that is, other companies' maintenance and engineering departments).

BACKGROUND ON BOEING'S SPARE PARTS E-BUSINESS

The Boeing Company, like many other companies in the age of information and e-commerce, is going through a metamorphosis. It is transforming at least one of its key enterprise businesses into an e-business. This change will permanently alter the way its customers, trading partners, employees, and business analysts view it as a global enterprise—a transformation that is very good for any business.

The design points for its aircraft have matured to the extent that passengers can now fly halfway around the world, on any one of the equipment categories of Boeing's fleet of aircraft products. There are no current plans to extend that range; therefore, improvements to the company's current aircraft designs are expected to be incremental rather than major breakthroughs. The new challenge for Boeing executives is to generate more revenue streams from other sources.

One area that represented a significant opportunity for Boeing was the aircraft spare parts business. More specifically, four areas in the spare parts space were identified: aircraft maintenance, supply chain improvements, reductions in workflow time, and lowering of overall costs. In total, this area would mean substantial additional revenues for the company. Boeing chose an e-business solution to enable its new spare parts venture. A key reason for doing this was the significant improvements that the e-business solution offered to the front-end of Boeing's spare parts supply chain. This is one of the first major business processes changed by Boeing's adoption of e-business technologies.

A number of applications (on a corporate level) make use of e-business technologies and solutions. Technologies like e-mail, knowledge networks, and the migration of paper documents from print to the Internet all contribute to any company's innovative ways of transforming their business to an e-business.

Boeing executives felt the value to its e-business solutions would enable reductions in required lead times, in addition to reducing errors and adding real-time order status information capabilities. The aircraft spare parts business manages *time* as one of its major strategic control points. The bottom line is to significantly reduce the time it takes to order and receive an aircraft part. This means that e-business solutions that offer real-time query capabilities were, and remain, a critical success factor in this part of Boeing's business. In this business (to which Boeing is a supplier), time is everything. The objective is to reduce the time it takes to get a part to an aircraft that needs it. The real-time status information must include answers to the following questions:

- When, and by what route, will each part be shipped?
- Which carriers have the part(s)?
- In what phase of the shipping process is the part?

The spare parts business is based on both planned acquisitions and unplanned acquisitions. It is the unplanned part of the business that the e-business solutions really address. The spare parts industry maintains delivery schedules that require responses in terms of hours and minutes, not days. Boeing's focus in providing this e-business solution was to enhance the customer experience in processing and fulfilling unplanned orders of spare parts.

These types of unscheduled customer requirements mandate fulfillment in hours. It is extremely important to deliver order status information to customers, online and in real-time. This solution turned out to be significantly superior to the traditional ways in which spare parts requirements were met.

A FEW OF THE E-BUSINESS CHALLENGES

To understand the magnitude of the business problem that it needed to tackle in the aircraft spare parts business, Boeing first examined who were its customers and how the company traditionally processed the customer orders for spare parts. The most significant customers were the large airline carriers and aircraft maintenance companies. This segment is the largest revenue producer in spare parts for Boeing, and it accounted for approximately 60 percent of Boeing's orders for spare parts. These customers generally operated in EDI environments with batch, or non-real-time, EDI capabilities. This worked fine for normally scheduled orders but proved insufficient for "Aircraft On the Ground (AOG)" emergency replacement part scenarios. AOG orders were given the highest priority because an airplane could not be back in service without the part replacement. Typically, these orders were made by telephone, telexes, or faxes. The customer would place a confirmation order on the EDI system and send it to Boeing at night.

On the other hand, about 20 percent of the spare parts sales come from smaller customers. These customers are typically airlines or repair companies in Europe, the Middle East, Latin America, and small companies in the United States. These companies tend to use outdated (that is, telex-based) EDI transactions that are entered manually. The error rates are high—in many cases over 30 percent. There were several reasons for the errors including language barriers and the lack of standard message formats utilized around the world. Because these orders were entered manually this process was labor-intensive. Finally, some customers sent in their orders via fax machines. This group of customers accounted for another 20 percent of the spare parts revenues. Typically they were distributors that provide special services for certain airlines that find it difficult to deal directly with U.S.-based distributors, some because of language barriers and some because of political problems.

About one-half of the company's spare parts business is considered high priority. This situation generally occurs as a result discovering a missing part during normal and routine maintenance checks. This is different from the AOG scenario when the plane is scheduled for flight. This situation can be classified as AOG, though, if the plane requires an additional part other than the scheduled part replacement.

Boeing's policy for high-priority parts is to ship AOG orders on the same day, ready to ship in four hours (the internal target is reported to be two hours). Normal scheduled maintenance parts orders are typically shipped the day after the order is received, with delivery occurring during the early morning.

Interestingly, the two groups of smaller customers required more of Boeing services than the larger airlines, although they generated smaller revenues. They tended to be much more labor-intensive, more demanding, and often required more hand-holding than the larger customers. Therefore, these customers were much more expensive to service than the larger airlines. The reasons for this were their reliance on more labor-intensive means of communicating with Boeing, such as the phone, faxes, and telexes rather than EDI (generally, EDI was too expensive for these smaller customers).

Boeing's services organization was set up to accommodate the three groups of customers described in the following ways. Boeing organized several teams to work with their customers. One group typically addresses the technical issues and problems. Another group addresses the more trivial customer queries and provides data entry services. One team consisted of 13 people who managed a couple of thousand non-EDI orders daily. This team's activities were generally data entry of new orders, correcting errors, and doing other clerical tasks. This team was very labor-intensive and represented a cost-challenge for Boeing from an organizational viewpoint.

Another important team (about 17 members) is Spares Information Services (SIS) that operates on three shifts providing general nontechnical customer information (including part numbers), pricing, availability, and order status. The SIS team usually handles several hundred calls per day, in addition to some fax and telex inquiries. The team members use a company database to research answers to customer queries. Many of these queries are answered on the same first call, while others are answered via fax. Still another Boeing team (about 15 members) addresses approximately 900 customer queries daily for high-priority AOG orders. The Spares Technical Information team is the final team that Boeing established. This team is responsible for inquiries that are more technical in nature (for example, interchangeability of parts or engineering changes). Because of the technical nature of this type of query, as well as the complexity of the customer call, it is an unlikely candidate for automation. Online access in real-time to engineering drawings, illustrating the latest engineering changes, will be a productivity enhancement in this process.

Boeing has automated many of its internal processes and had been using EDI for years; however, its e-commerce customer links were now the challenge. Too much time was being spent (three to four minutes) handling trivial customer queries. Its data entry capabilities were inefficient and not adding a realizable business value, at least not at the levels it was accustomed to achieving. Many customer calls were not being handled as efficiently as Boeing wanted, and therefore customer satisfaction ratings were not as high as previously hoped. Clearly, Boeing was a prime candidate for a comprehensive e-business solution strategy.

BOEING'S E-BUSINESS SOLUTION

The PART system was designed by Boeing e-business technologists to improve the company's spare parts processes. PART provides an Internet-based front-end link to process customer orders and resolve status inquiries. Boeing developed an e-commerce application based on code originally written more than two decades prior to PART's development. By doing this, Boeing created significant business values through incremental business realized from a faster and more efficient ordering capability. This e-business solution provides an Internet-based front-end that allows customer access to Boeing legacy system information and spare parts databases. This has proven to be extremely valuable to Boeing's customers for several reasons:

1. It eliminates costly labor-intensive data entry resulting from faxed and paper orders.
2. It reduces the errors that can result from transcribing orders, which could mean shipping errors and the lengthening of time to service and maintain planes.
3. The customer status queries are now easily handled in real-time.
4. It provides customers with real-time status updates that track shipments right to delivery.
5. It reduces significantly the wayward shipment of incorrect spare parts.

One of the key hurdles for Boeing in implementing this parts e-business solution was gaining the buy-in of other internal business units. This initiative represented the first time the company had given its customers information access to its back-end systems. In other words, Boeing had created an extranet for its customers to use. This meant that the IT organization had to get involved to provide a secure IT infrastructure that would prevent customers from gaining access to areas in Boeing's intranet that they were not entitled to access. Boeing went to great lengths to ensure that all of its business units' fears were placated by clearly demonstrating the business value of the e-business solution to the company as a whole. The architecture for this solution environment includes an application server that transparently links clients, via a fire-wall filtering design, from the Internet to Boeing's back-end systems. Client queries and orders are passed to and from the mainframe database via middleware that is loaded on a different server.

The PART system is currently being used by 50 percent of Boeing customers on a regular basis. These include both EDI and non-EDI customers, and they are driving usage rates to as high as several thousand accesses per day. Although much of the use has been from U.S.-based customers, more and more online usage comes from the other global geographies as they, too, adopt e-commerce solutions.

In summary, the business value for Boeing has been a reduction of its SG&A through elimination of labor-intensive data entry costs, a reduction in the use of older telex-based EDI technology (that was sometimes error prone), and a significant drop in the number of orders made by phone, which created heavy data entry workloads.

Although the metrics cited are impressive, the impact of this e-business solution to the bottom line is difficult to quantify, due to the overall increase in revenues resulting from aircraft production demands. Considering this, and adding to this the increase in airline travel business, which has generated significant business in spare parts replacements, the best Boeing could do is to estimate cost avoidance metrics.

In this case, savings resulted from not increasing personnel (about 10 percent more staff) that would normally have been required before the implementation of the e-business solution. Boeing estimated that it was able to eliminate over 25 percent of its order processing costs. Another very important metric that Boeing has benefitted from is the improvement in customer satisfaction, resulting from online order status updates and significant reduction in errors and shipping problems.

The e-business approach for Boeing has also meant that customer access to information is a best-practices solution. Boeing enjoys significant leadership in providing innovative e-business solutions, and it has also gained substantial brand recognition for being a leader in using e-business solutions to reinvent itself. As a direct result of this exercise in reinvention, Boeing discovered new ways to provide business value for its shareholders. The company also gained recognition from its peers (other airline manufacturers) as a global leader in providing customers with faster service and service that is virtually error-free. Equally important is that Boeing has been able to significantly add to the bottom line by reducing its costs of doing business. Boeing has enhanced its after-market support services business, and consequently it has also influenced the way customers and channel partners do business with it.

Boeing is clearly a leader in adoption of e-business technologies that provide business values to all of its shareholders, and enhanced value-added services to its customers and the entire aerospace industry.

18
Automotive Industry E-business Solutions

....

Automobile manufacturers are currently in the process of exploring new and innovative ways to add business values to their enterprises by implementing Internet e-business solutions. During the second quarter of 1998, a U.S.-based automobile parts manufacturer was able to develop, build, and implement an e-business solution that focused on its dealer and distribution networks. Strategically speaking, this manufacturing enterprise wanted to provide better information access and online transaction processing capabilities to its channel partners. Like many other auto manufacturing companies, this firm leveraged EDI as the primary link to its channel partners.

The problem was that most of its dealer networks were not EDI networks. The dealers generally lacked adequate IT infrastructure to accommodate an EDI capability, or the costs to install EDI processing systems was considered to be too expensive. By linking its channel partners, this auto manufacturer could provide real-time inventory status, supply delivery updates, and process claim submissions and product orders.

The dealers (for the most part) are pleased with the system, which is essentially an extranet solution. They are now reporting significant improvements in the quality of their service to customers and a much more collaborative working environment for dealer employees. The number of channel partners using the extranet solution has grown rapidly and substantially. In fact, orders over the extranet are not far off from the number of orders processed via EDI. The reduced transaction costs versus the EDI transactions costs has resulted in a significant cost avoidance for the dealers and distributors that use the extranet.

BACKGROUND ON THE MANUFACTURER'S PROBLEM

This automotive manufacturer decided that its channel-based extranet solution would provide added business values by giving better service to its customers, dealers, and distributor networks. It was correct in this supposition.

The high costs of implementing EDI, as well as the lack of IT infrastructure, prevented its customers from access to timely information about inventory and triggered long lead times for processing claims and product orders. This meant that its customers and channel partners had to rely heavily on manual, labor-intensive processes for product order information.

Another major problem for its customers was the lack of timely information regarding inventory status. This resulted in consumer dissatisfaction with dealers and distributors who were not able to provide an accurate updated status about orders and product availability. Therefore, the business value proposition was clearly linked to the customer, and ultimately to consumer satisfaction improvements.

The overall solution for this automobile manufacturer was based on its strategy to extend its enterprise by designing and building an extranet that could be used by its customers. A brilliant strategy. It was the company's belief that this solution, which had as its focus improving supply chain efficiency and improving business processes, would provide significant business value. The company was correct.

The more traditional dealer and distributor relationship management process starts with way the manufacturer communicated with their dealers and distributors. This was mainly by telephone, fax machines, and normal postal mail. Complicating the situation, there were hundreds of field representatives and more than 80 telecommunication call center representatives who handled a large portion of the communications between the dealers, distributors, and the automotive manufacturer. About 30,000 monthly calls (approximately half of the total of 60,000 monthly calls) were order-related calls. The next highest volume of calls came from the dealers or distributors inquiring about inventory items. Other lower-volume calls were related to product information, queries about marketing programs, special incentives, financing, account information, order status, and other consumer-related situations.

This enterprise used the following metrics table (see Table 18.1) for customer satisfaction surveys (that is, for its dealers and distributors) to quantify the effectiveness of its communications.

Table 18.1   Customer Satisfaction Metrics from 1995 Survey

Customer Satisfaction Dimension	Rating
Overall service quality	
Customer service effectiveness	
Timely order delivery	
Accurate billing and delivery	
Willingness to work together	
Simplified billing	
Respect for customer	
Local market assistance	
Back order fulfillment	
Training	

These survey metrics measured the company's performance on a competitive scale of 0.00 to 1.50, with a score of 1.00 being equal to competitors' performance. A score of 0.90 would indicate performance 10 percent lower than that of competitors, while a score of 1.10 would indicate performance 10 percent higher than that of competitors.

THE AUTOMOTIVE BUSINESS PROBLEM

In 1995, the company received the ratings shown in Table 18.2 from its dealers.

Table 18.2   Customer Satisfaction Metrics from 1995 Survey

Customer Satisfaction Dimension	1995 Rating
Overall service quality	0.82
Customer service effectiveness	1.04
Timely order delivery	0.86
Accurate billing and delivery	1.00
Willingness to work together	0.78

It was quite clear to the executives running this enterprise that their firm ranked lower than their competitors in providing service in some very critical categories, such as "Timely order delivery," and the firm was only average in other critical categories, like "Accurate billing and delivery." After doing some strategic analysis of the problem, a solution was proposed and accepted that involved e-business technologies and the Internet.

THE AUTOMOTIVE E-BUSINESS SOLUTION

Improving customer satisfaction ratings would, in turn, provide added business values to this firm. To achieve this improvement, an e-commerce extranet solution was chosen as the e-business solution. The solution was intended to provide improvements in information access and to better support the network of dealers and distributors.

This turned out to be quite an innovative and attractive solution for several reasons:

1. The solution reduced dealer access costs.
2. The solution was simple to use.
3. The solution was interoperable across a variety of computing platforms.

The dealers immediately benefitted because they were already electronically linked to the company, enabling them to be somewhat self-sufficient and to service their own requirements on a 24 x 7 basis. This would encourage more pervasive use than the EDI system the company had previously used for a number of years. This e-business solution provides not only 24 x 7 access but real-time access to information via almost any Internet browser.

This commonly available Internet browser approach enabled a solution with much greater flexibility for their dealers and distributors, and at a much lower cost. A number of transaction capabilities were enabled as a direct result of this e-business solution, including the following:

- Simple methods for improved visibility into product inventories
- Highly improved claims submission processing
- Improved time-related factors throughout the ordering processes
- Advanced shipping notifications
- Online product information and technical specifications
- Online marketing and sales promotion information
- Enhanced communications and collaboration via e-mail

A very key element in this e-business solution is the support of the line organizations, especially support to the sales units. The executive responsible for sales decided to improve the satisfaction of the company's dealers, and this executive wanted to significantly improve communications with the dealers. Various line organizations participated in the overall development of this e-business solution. When the new system was designed, it went through an initial proof-of-concept and a testing phase with a select number of dealers. The tests were very successful, and subsequently the e-business solution was hardened for production and immediately rolled out for use by all the dealers. Very important in the success of this e-business solution was the involvement of the dealers in providing valuable input to the solutions. These steps are commonly referred to as the "human factors" evaluation stage of a design analysis: This stage is critical to any new Internet e-business environment.

Although extremely successful, the implementation of the solution was not necessarily simple—in fact, it was just the opposite. An important part of this e-business solution was the link to back-end systems (parts, ordering, inventory, etc.), which was complex. The system development team was required to outsource this part of the solution because they did not have the expertise required for this difficult integration step. This particular step in any e-business development stage is always difficult to achieve, primarily because these back-end systems are typically older technologies, and skills for managing the low-level programming are often difficult to acquire. The development team worked very closely with a vendor who had significant expertise in integrating legacy systems to Internet-based applications; as a direct result, they gained critical skills that then transferred into their team.

Another complexity that needed some attention was the variety of platforms used by each of the vendors; in some cases, the vendors actually had no systems at all. Incompatibility among dealer platforms was a major issue that required an immediate resolution. In addition to providing installation support of the new platforms that were standard (and tied into the corporate Intranet) training was provided to the dealers and distributors.

This e-business system included a tutorial application that guided users in its use. It also provided a fool-proof Internet browser (if required) so that dealers would not have any problems linking to the company through the Internet. All these efforts greatly improved the dealers' e-commerce adoption rate. The dealers have been very pleased with the new system(s), and they now view leveraging of Internet e-commerce environments as an extremely efficient and cost-effective means to improve their own internal business processes.

E-BUSINESS SOLUTION RESULTS

Approximately 250 dealers are now using the e-business system. About 50 dealers use this solution regularly. The number of orders through the extranet is growing daily. This is important because the the orders submitted over the extranet were much larger: The company experieneced almost a compounding effect. The costs of using the extranet e-business solution for processing orders is 10 percent of the costs of processing orders using the previous, more traditional EDI approach. That is an incredible savings, not to mention a welcomed business process improvement.

As more dealers and distributors begin to adapt to this e-business environment, this manufacturer expects significant reductions in the cost of processing orders. Even more important to the enterprise's executives is the improvement in overall customer satisfaction, customer service effectiveness, timely order fulfillment, improved accuracy in billing, and significant improvements in teamwork. A key strategic benefit is the building of greater dealer loyalty and trust—a benefit that any company would applaud.

Future enhancements to this e-business system include automated payments, even greater access to inventory levels, improved accounting information, and improved feedback capabilities. The improvements offered by this e-business solution will have significant effects and added business values, as the company extends its reach as a global contender. This is an excellent example of a paradigm shift, by virtue of the Internet and an innovative e-business strategy. Indeed, a job well done.

19

Internet E-business Value Chain Management

....

$\mathbf{T}$he subject of corporate value chain management extends across several dimensions. In this chapter, we will explore one of the early e-commerce solution areas being recognized by many global companies. This area is procurement. The following pages will explore exactly what about the corporate value chain lends itself so well to considering the "procurement" business function as a likely candidate for crafting e-business solutions. The procurement business function, in both corporate and government settings, has grown over the years to be a costly activity. It often involves slow manual business procedures, and even slower systematic processes for handling procurement transactions.

During the early 1990s, many of the larger global corporations recognized that they needed to aggressively pursue this area of procurement and, at the same time, that they also needed to understand exactly how the Internet would play a role over the next decade. Today, almost every company Fortune 500 company has its own Internet e-business site for selling to consumers and internal sites designed for managing corporate procurement activities (usually intranets). Some industries have accelerated more quickly than others in this area. Oddly enough, it appears that many governments are also acting quickly to lower operational costs; this is one area that has been looked at intensely around the world.

PROCUREMENT E-BUSINESS SOLUTIONS

Many enterprises in the manufacturing industry are beginning to integrate e-business technologies to reduce costs while remaining profitable and competitive. For many of these firms, a significant area is extending their reach to their customers and suppliers—in faster and more efficient ways. For example, one consumer electronics and semiconductor manufacturer has developed an e-business solution that significantly enhances its procurement function. In this case, the e-business function(s) focused on procuring nonproduction materials and services.

To reduce procurement costs, executives and business leaders need to consider exactly how to leverage combinations of e-business technologies. The e-procurement solution space is (in part) intended to provide an enterprise with an improved negotiating position with its suppliers. This means that the company will realize (as just one example) a stronger volume discount on billions of dollars in annual nonproduction procurement. This could lead to significant savings (perhaps millions of dollars annually). In general, the costs of processing procurement transactions may drop significantly, let's say, from a range of $100–$250 per transaction to approximately $20–$25 per transaction.

Let's focus on a large computer manufacturer and global services corporation. This Fortune 100 company developed a new e-procurement e-business solution that simplified the overall process and provided many improved efficiencies in its procurement process. The e-procurement solution reduced the time required to research suppliers, simply because it identifies only preapproved suppliers. Another important benefit was that procurement personnel were redeployed into other, more business-critical areas of the enterprise, which in turn brought more business value to the enterprise. These areas included using redeployed resources to help identify cost-savings opportunities and the renegotiation of prices with suppliers. These newly redeployed skills provided tremendous enhanced values to the business, compared to the previous tasks involving manual tracking of purchase orders and resolution of payment issues.

To successfully implement an e-business solution, most firms will almost always want to reengineer some of their core business processes. This theme continues throughout this book, only because of its importance. In the procurement areas of any business, there are traditionally labor-intensive activities that translate into higher dollars than desired. The virtues that e-business solutions bring to any business enterprise (especially involving procurement) are improved productivity and enhanced revenue streams. Most enterprises depend heavily on more traditional channels to reach their supply chain partners. This includes paper requisitions, regular postal mail, telephone, fax, and e-mail.

The new e-procurement solution now provides employees and business partners with online access to the enterprise procurement information. This extranet type of solution provides a much lower-cost practice for communicating with the suppliers and, likewise, for the suppliers to access information that they seek on the company's legacy systems. This, too, is often critical to improved efficiencies in any business. Using Internet EDI capabilities, when one is bound to using EDI, presents a much less expensive mechanism for information exchange than the more traditional (dedicated-line) EDI practices.

This firm, like many other firms implementing e-business solutions, is typical of a high-growth company that strategically wants to move along the e-business continuum, passing through the security chasms, and then moving toward other adoptions of e-commerce. This type of e-commerce growth can lead to new business units being formed from loosely coupled enterprise entities. There is often no centralized process for managing procurement for nonproduction materials and services (like office supplies and office equipment). Therefore, needless to say, this area of procurement is ready for automation that uses creative e-business solutions.

Senior executives recognize the business problem that comes from the lack of a standard process for managing procurement, especially of nonproduction materials. Recognizing that they might be losing the opportunity to leverage millions of dollars of purchasing power when dealing with their contracted suppliers, they set forth to deploy more strategic solutions. Without standards, the enterprise has no way of tracking procurement transactions, identifying parallel transactions, and controlling rogue purchasing patterns. Furthermore, without standard supplier channel partnerships, assessing many areas on a consistent and regular basis was difficult. Another challenge for many firms (including this firm) is the understanding that comes with being a global enterprise, especially in areas of standard practices and procedures of Internet e-commerce. This is not a trivial or straightforward challenge to overcome. A major business priority for any firm is to realize its vision of an integrated supply chain framework (global if necessary), for both production and nonproduction procurement practices.

Visionary business leaders recognize that effective strategic supply chain partnerships are critical to any manufacturing strategy. It is still true that most manufacturers use traditional EDI formats for production procurement; few such procurement systems exist for the procurement of nonproduction materials. What is required is an e-business solution that promises to make the integrated supply chain vision a reality while supporting changes to the reengineered business processes.

An e-commerce solution often provides greater access to suppliers and extends the company's reach to smaller yet key suppliers. This improves information flow, which in turn allows the enterprise to negotiate more profitable deals, while providing a baseline for consolidating purchasing strength with its suppliers.

E-PROCUREMENT BUSINESS PROBLEMS

There are corporate examples where an enterprise might have more than 30,000 nonproduction suppliers. These companies utilize traditional means of communicating with their suppliers (for example, phone, fax, postal mail). A variety of products and services were purchased from these suppliers, including items like office equipment, office supplies, office furniture, and outsourced labor contracts.

As many as several hundred employees might be responsible for managing the traditional nonproduction procurement process. For the most part, the procurement processes for nonproduction products is disparate and not standardized. This accounts for significant time being lost as employees negotiate, validate catalog content, update pricing, and communicate new pricing to retailers; without a centralized approach, they lacked significant leverage to get better deals.

It quickly became clear to the business enterprise that the traditional ways of processing nonproduction procurement goods were not very efficient: The complexities encountered to audit a series of transactions could sometimes be far more time-consuming than necessary. Yet the process of audit is an absolute must. This often prohibits companies from completing a meaningful analysis of trends in the procurement industry, which causes them to rapidly fall behind the curve in earnings. As with any other form of initial change, it is difficult to define areas of opportunity. Any improvement introduced by e-commerce solutions in nonproduction procurement (an area that involves billions of dollars, millions of transactions, and hundreds to thousands of people) would bring significant business values and dramatic increases in profitability to the enterprise.

E-PROCUREMENT BUSINESS SOLUTIONS

A nonproduction e-procurement system is often a first key design objective. An Internet site, with a simple Internet browser that enables company employees to procure preapproved products and services, alone will begin to leverage the company's buying power with its suppliers. This system can be (and most often is) an extranet solution, allowing suppliers (using their Internet browsers) to access, on demand, critical information on a real-time basis. This eliminates traditional, more manual processes, and it significantly improves the speed of processing transactions.

Another value proposition is simple; that is, online order processing capabilities. The company will then, of course, have to offer electronic delivery of orders (sometimes even split-order deliveries), enabling suppliers to reduce manual transactions. As simple as this may seem, the process can become very complex.

Online e-billing and e-payment solutions will provide incentives to suppliers to use the e-procurement applications. These types of solutions are integrated into back-end systems for completion of the end-to-end processing required to complete the transaction. The enterprise has therefore provided business value to its trading partners, as well as its corporate shareholders. The value e-business solutions bring to the business is that they are always available to preferred suppliers, thereby gaining more business for the enterprise. The nonproduction e-procurement solution needs to be designed for simplicity and ease of use, while requiring very little training (close to none at all) for suppliers to effectively interact with it.

The launch of these types of e-procurement solutions needs to be carefully controlled, while slowly bringing more suppliers into the system. This allows for any discrepancies in the system to be immediately corrected, with the least impact to the business. This approach also acts as an effective instrument for acquiring usage information related to improved human factors. The business value of this type of e-business solution is transferred to the suppliers, who now can deploy their employees on tasks that provide more value to their own businesses: another nongoal benefit.

These types of solutions almost always lead to other areas of the enterprise, seeking e-commerce initiatives that will further drive added business values. For example, across an enterprise there may be an interest in trying to leverage e-commerce solutions to improve the supply chain processes. This achievement can be accomplished by utilizing both internal and external resources. The initial investments in development costs for these types of e-business implementations often show a significant return on investment.

E-BUSINESS SOLUTION RESULTS

This type of e-procurement e-business solution renders significant business values to any enterprise by greatly improving the system used to procure nonproduction products. The reduction of costs resulting from this type of solution can be enormous. Internet-based e-procurement solutions can eliminate the problem of employees ordering from nonapproved sources. These solutions can improve price change practices, and they can be open for business 24 hours a day, 7 days a week.

Many e-procurement solutions enable an enterprise to leverage billions of dollars worth of buying power, and, in turn, they offer better pricing through larger volume discounts. The use of e-procurement solutions also provides a data repository of information that tracks all aspects of every transaction, and this information is available for audits of any specific transactions. This gives the company's business analysts the ability to evaluate suppliers through historical data; often inspections can be performed at random. Furthermore, this historical data then can be leveraged to help identify methods to improve their future supplier relationships in areas like faster delivery times, lower prices, and better payment terms.

Another important result is the huge amount of time savings related to vendor searches. Instead of hundreds of employees engaging in extensive research on vendors and suppliers, these searches are controlled by the preselected vendor lists from which they may choose to order. This greatly reduces labor-intensive search time. Even more significant is that the former, less-productive time of employees is now spent on activities that have increased business values to the business enterprise.

Shipping and delivery errors can be significantly reduced with e-procurement solutions. Moving from a manual paper process to an automated procurement process means fewer errors in the order fulfillment process. In addition, there is cost avoidance in that employee time to resolve order errors is greatly reduced (for example, correcting problems such as order quantities, special shipping instructions, errant delivery locations, billing information, tardy deliveries, misspellings, and products ordered by mistake).

Another direct benefit of the e-procurement solution is that it renders enormous reductions in transaction costs. The executives for many enterprises already utilizing e-procurement will agree that during the next couple of years, over 90 percent of nonproduction procurement will be handled via the Internet. They also project that the average costs for processing an order will be reduced from $100–$250 for manual procurement, to $20–$25 for e-business procurement. In some cases this reduction will be even greater.

Another area of business value will be related to the reduction in the size of an order, as employees gain better visibility to existing stock levels. Some additional benefits of the e-procurement solution include audit trails of orders in real-time, visibility to individual department purchases, liabilities issues, consolidated buying for nonnegotiated items, and decreased out-of-stock situations.

The enterprise that aggressively pursues launching these types of e-procurement solutions (and other e-business initiatives) will demonstrate leadership within its industry. These companies are most likely planning to integrate e-commerce applications to replace their legacy systems (for example, e-billing and e-payment solutions). These e-business solutions will be delivered to marketing areas (supporting the field), service delivery disciplines, field engineering experts, many consumer-related areas, and almost any area capable of being managed through Internet-based practices. These leadership companies might also want to consider integrating an existing production schedule-sharing system with their e-business platform(s), providing more suppliers with enhanced access to critical information (for example, an extranet solution).

The leaders in this area consider developing e-business solutions so that their suppliers will strive to work more closely with them, simply because, by virtue of their accepting the new e-business approach to performing business, they find that their own internal business practices are substantially improved. This can often be seen in technical infrastructure areas, in that these complicated environments might be offset by (let's say) an inventory system, now accessible through Internet-based methods. This yields a much simpler and more cost-effective solution for both parties.

20

E-business Enhances the Supply Chain

....

$\mathbf{A}$ very large home products manufacturer that earned revenues last year of approximately $10 billion chose an e-business solution to provide real-time access to its trading partner networks. Approximately 10,000 trading partners are involved in this e-business solution. The e-business solution is designed to enable these partners to access product information, specifications, and availability—on a real-time basis (see Figure 20.1). Each of these trading partners has links to the enterprise's inventory management system, where the trading partner can execute orders, change orders, and check the order backlog.

One key business value in this collaborative e-business solution is the reduction of staff required to maintain trading partner support cost centers. This will result in a staff cost savings of millions of dollars per year. The ultimate goal in this solution is to Internet-enable the entire supply chain, including suppliers, vendors, trading partners, and consumers—to have simple access to required information through Internet browsers. The company executives believe this solution significantly improves customer relations and helps to solidify consumer loyalty to their brand. All of these initiatives will result in improving the enterprise's competitive posture.

SUPPLY CHAIN E-BUSINESS CHALLENGE

The senior leadership team feels very strongly that an important factor in the firm's competitive positioning rests on its core business competencies. Three corporate competencies have been identified:

1. A strong relationship with its channel partners, that is, its trade, procurement, and manufacturing partners
2. The ability to demonstrate manufacturing excellence, that is, providing superior quality at the lowest manufacturing cost, and with the fewest incidents of service requirements
3. Customer knowledge

191

Supply Chain management includes 7 macro business processes, all supported by *transaction and planning* systems.

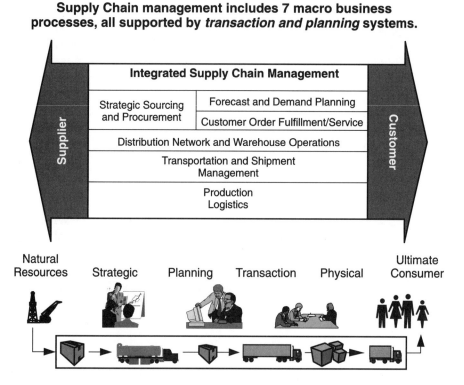

Figure 20.1

Some of the macro-businesses related to the supply chain.

Competitive threats are looming as a result of a new virtual economic climate that fosters new business models. This climate is creating new requirements from customers and, conversely, new competition. The enterprise is concerned about the risks involved in not moving into an e-business competitive posture. Many questions are being asked, as with any company considering the same types of initiatives. Will the company become noncompetitive and irrelevant in the new virtual economic climate? Will the company ultimately face some form of corporate disruption? What future corporate opportunities will not be realized if the company does not enter into Internet commerce? These are all very good questions to consider when developing a transformation plan that utilizes the Internet and e-commerce.

The threats seemingly appear from all sides, as nontraditional trading partners become virtual competitors, and from other corporate enterprises that influence customer purchasing decisions. The virtual competitive climate includes third-party competitors who are not directly in the same business, but who can influence customer buying behaviors. These new intermediaries provide value-added services to customers by providing assistance through cost and product comparisons. What makes this very dangerous is that these third parties may have no brand loyalties, yet they are focused on helping guide customer buying behaviors. They represent a nongoal benefit to the consumer.

This enterprise established two parallel e-business initiatives that would bring added business value to its shareholders, its customers, and its trading partners. The initial strategy was to service its consumer base by linking consumers directly to its trading partner Internet site(s). These sites provide product, services, and promotional information. The objective here is to provide better and faster services to consumers, which, according to their profile of customer buying behaviors, would lead more consumers to engage in similar trades.

Another key initiative that this enterprise sponsored was the forming of an e-business strategy team to identify ways that the company could more efficiently and cost-effectively manage its intranet, extranet, and Internet sites. Equally important was this team's responsibility to introduce e-business strategies that improved services for its customers and trading partners.

The strategy team conducted a cross-industry and competitor analysis, simply to determine what other enterprises were doing that was either effective or ineffective. This team identified a number of important e-business initiatives, one of which includes adding more functions for customers and trading partners. Some of these improved functions were in the following areas: product choices, outlet choices, order handling, presales and postsales support, and literature on demand. Two significant results of this solution were enhanced functionality and improved communication with the thousands of trading partners with whom the enterprise executes transactions.

SUPPLY CHAIN E-BUSINESS PROBLEM

This enterprise segmented its trading partners into three categories: national retailers, retail trading partners, and contract trading partners. The national retailers provide the channel coverage for the large volume accounts: There were (at the time) approximately 10 of these very large accounts. These trading partners represent almost 66 percent of the sales and volume. The retail trading partners account for approximately 25 percent of the sales and volume. The contract trading partners represent the rest of the sales and volume (only about 9 percent).

The national retail accounts were processed mainly via EDI (approximately 80 percent), and the rest of the orders were processed by telephone. The large-volume orders are generally represented by low numbers of SKU assortments, shipped from the enterprise's manufacturing warehouses.

Any manual orders are typically emergency orders, and they are somewhat atypical; therefore, they require special attention outside the norm for EDI processing. On the other hand, the retail trading partners represent medium-sized orders with a wide range of SKUs, often requiring split deliveries to more than a single regional warehouse. Very few (if any) of these trading partners use EDI. Finally, the contract trading partners require more customized orders and tend to be smaller with a wide range of SKUs. The bulk of these orders are manual. The larger trading partners in this group fulfill orders through the regional warehouses, whereas the smaller trading partners fulfill orders through local warehouses. The customized orders require a great deal of attention and are typically more complex. Additional factors in this area include these: the management of smaller packages, the variety of product sizes, different shipping requirements, custom deliveries that may include installation, and damaged goods processing.

The mechanics for supporting each of these trading partners is rather different and requires separate call center support. Each of the three channels has its own dedicated call center support, which is divided between major products and accessories. Generally the call centers provide presales support, order processing, order status, customer sales support, and marketing support. A separate call center is responsible for telesales in the retail channel, and still another call center for channels outside of the United States. There is also a customer support center that deals strictly with credit, claims, and other financial support services.

The bulk of the orders from all three channels are funneled mainly through a company 800 phone number (sometimes more than one 800 number). There are also some fax order-handling capabilities. The call centers are generally staffed 12 hours per day, Monday through Friday. These types of operations typically require approximately 175 people, handling an estimated 4 million contacts, most of which are manual queries. On average, about 250,000 orders are processed out of the 4 million calls. The vast majority of the queries are for product pricing, order status, product availability, or customer assistance. The personnel in the call centers typically handle the requests by researching the query. This might require the call center staff to call the trading partners back with the information they seek: This is not the normal process, but it is done for more complicated support issues. The company provides product-based workshops, product literature, and pricing information so that, for the most part, the trading partners know their order requirements.

Here is how the order process was traditionally handled: A trading partner calls the 800 number, where a call center support team member answers the partner's questions. The order is keyed into the enterprise back-end system and then confirmed. The large account trading partners, large retailer trading partners, and the contract trading partners use EDI for order placement. More than 66 percent of the orders are from trading partners, with much smaller and more frequently placed orders to maximize inventory turns. The majority of the calls handled by the call centers come from these trading partners. What this means is that the bulk of the company's resources are being used to handle the thousands of trading partners that account for only 10 percent of overall sales revenues.

Furthermore, there are a number of problems with this traditional process. For example, there is often no single point of contact for the trading partners. Each call is most often handled by a different person. Key service functions are in different reporting areas. The data repository is not centralized, and it may not be standardized, thereby complicating some research practices. Key data transfers are slow and inefficient. This really complicates matters for trading partners who may have more than one problem or issue and may have to place several separate calls to get each issue resolved. This also means that the call center representative has to requalify the trading partner on each separate call. Added to this is the amount of effort required to reenter data.

Pervasive throughout the supply chain are manual, slow, and inefficient processes for ordering, claims, fulfillment tracking, service calls, providing customers with instructions, and fulfilling customer requests for product information in the form of literature. These are for the most part paper- and telephone-intensive processes, which sometimes require a great deal of human interaction. Generally speaking, the error rates were very high. Then the company realized that its systems were poorly integrated. This had adverse effects on production and procurement processes. This also resulted in high inventory levels because the enterprise lacked a better way to track customer order requirements.

SUPPLY CHAIN E-BUSINESS SOLUTION

The enterprise has launched several e-business initiatives including an e-commerce ordering application. This enables electronic ordering capabilities for its customers over the Internet e-business service environment. It provides one-stop shopping capabilities, as well as a self-service environment that pushes significant amounts of information to its channel partners. This application will ultimately act as a front-end to an enterprise resource planning (ERP) implementation. The ERP implementation complements the e-commerce order interface application and will enable the legacy system to be totally integrated. This will result in significantly improved accuracy, through more consistent data made available to trading partners, real-time and pervasive, throughout the supply chain.

The benefits to the supply chain trading partners will be significant. For example, channel partners will be in a position to manage orders better and to have real-time access to the enterprise inventory management systems. Another key initiative is literature on demand for channel partners. That is, if a customer requests a single brochure or hundreds of pieces of literature, the enterprise could fulfill this request within hours or minutes, as opposed to days. These e-business solutions will also help to improve the company's annual catalog processing costs, which runs in the millions of dollars.

Many enterprises view an electronic solution as crucial to their business for several reasons. First, an electronic e-business solution brings forth the strength of personal contact and channel expertise to support the channel partners. This is viewed as a competitive imperative. While implementing the e-business initiatives, the enterprise call centers were being transformed into total service centers. The personal customer touch is still viewed as mission critical and is therefore tightly coupled with e-business solutions. One major factor resulting from this e-business transformation will be that Internet-based orders will cost approximately 10 to 25 percent of the traditional order's cost. This savings represents a significant improvement, which can then be passed on to the customer.

SUPPLY CHAIN E-BUSINESS SOLUTION RESULTS

The implementation of this particular e-business solution is anticipated to deliver quantifiable metrics that will help to evaluate and better shape this particular e-business endeavor. One key expectation is that trading partners depend less on the call centers. The specific goal is to dramatically reduce call volumes and dependence on the call center. This means significant labor savings, resulting in savings of millions of dollars. Another key factor is the creation of added business value in the form of loyalty and allegiance among the trading partners. The trading partners will appreciate the removal of non-value-added work, and they will most definitely welcome the improvement of order and shipment accuracy.

Another key goal of this e-business solution is for the enterprise to improve profitability in all of its channels. The challenge with this e-business solution is to manage delivery costs, which vary by channel. The data captured from the execution of this e-business solution will provide the necessary information to help the enterprise determine the independent channel delivery costs. This will, in turn, help the enterprise make choices that are more profitable.

Another key goal is to focus on the consumer. The consumer market represents a great opportunity for the enterprise to leverage its strength in manufacturing, managing inventories, and mass-merchandising of products to consumers. This is accomplished with interactive product information and interactive transaction capabilities, by virtue of the e-business solutions. Their approach is go directly to consumers to enhance loyalty and convert shoppers to buyers. The enterprise also wants to use e-business solutions to promote products to consumers, especially those products that are more profitable to the enterprise. Another important cost reduction resulting from this e-business solution is the literature-on-demand capability. This solution enables consumers to download and print product brochures on demand, thereby reducing the company's printing and handling costs.

As consumers visit any Internet site, the hosting enterprise can capture important consumer data. This is often accomplished programmatically (that is, by using cookies) and can be transparent to the end-user. This data can be varied in form, but it usually includes preferences and buying patterns. Other e-business initiatives include inventory management, reduction of stock-outs, and significantly improved supplier relations. This enterprise believes that its entire supply chain will be enhanced as a result of this solution. This is a welcome paradigm shift in the methods that supply chains use to perform day-to-day business transactions.

Part 5
Unique Management and Organizational Challenges

This is the final part of the book. The term "exploration" is an appropriate term, when one considers the various aspects involved in an excellent e-commerce or e-business solution. In this part, we will explore a couple of other areas where e-commerce has served a major role in "change." We will explore how by virtue of implementing e-commerce and e-business solutions, an enterprise is able to reduce costs and increase revenues.

Many of the issues surrounding security extend beyond the scope of this particular book; however, there are some key concepts that apply directly to the content of this book. Some we have already explored, such as trusted authorities and other information privacy issues. We will explore digital signatures and extending the business enterprise in this part of the book. We will explore an excellent example of a travel industry e-business enterprise, and finally we will conclude with our thoughts and observation encountered while researching and writing this book.

We hope that you have found this book to be both interesting and informative about the many facets of e-commerce. It is truly an "exploration" when one attempts to describe an area such as e-commerce. We would like to respectfully offer our thanks for your interest in this book, and we also encourage any comments or requests readers might have regarding this material.

21
E-insurance: Reduces Costs and Increases Revenue

....

The global networked e-business economy is beginning to change traditional businesses. For example, in the insurance industry, consumers are starting to migrate toward investments in stocks and bonds, versus whole-life and term insurance. There are some good economic reasons for this growing trend. Leveraging the stock market is a viable practice to plan for retirement, as opposed to the use of insurance policies. This is largely due to the low returns on the insurance policies as investment instruments. This has led some insurers to develop strategies to reinvent themselves. One way to approach this reinvention is to develop and execute a few strategic e-business solutions.

An industry example of reinvention is demonstrated by some specific strategic actions of one insurance company that also serves as an annuity provider. This firm took strategic actions to lower its costs of doing business by the design and implementation of an online *agent* information system.

E-BUSINESS CHALLENGE OVERVIEW

This new e-business solution would have to provide an automated solution (a virtual world of a sort) for the company's key administrative activities. These activities include the submission and processing of new insurance applications, where policy administration and access to forms is accomplished electronically. Although this e-business solution was implemented just recently, at least 10 percent of this enterprise's agents are currently using the system; there still needs to be greater involvement, though. The company's overall business volume has increased five times in a very short period of time.

This insurance carrier expects that in just two years, at least 50 percent of its new business opportunities will result from e-commerce on the Internet. This will occur by virtue of the creative e-business solutions being deployed. It is also expected to attract at least twice as many new independent brokers during the next three to five years.

199

Background on the E-business Problem

Insurance companies face a difficult challenge: new investment options being offered to their traditional customers. Investors have had opportunities to experience real-time access to investment data, through electronic securities Internet trading sites.

The flexibility of these creative Internet securities trading front-end applications has enabled e-investment enterprises to push timely and significant Internet-hosted products (for example, stocks, bonds, mutual funds, initial public offerings) to their customers, thus enabling them to make better-informed trading decisions. By pushing Internet-hosted investment-related content to many customers, they hope to leverage a growing trend of lack of interest among consumers in purchasing traditional insurance product offerings.

This company relied heavily on the more traditional means to support its approximately 3000 agents. It used a call center to handle the bulk of the incoming inquiries. Customer service representatives handled approximately 2500 calls per week from the agents. Representatives used personal computers on their desktops to access an online system and retrieve the information required by the agents in the field. Most of these personal computers had an Internet browser-based interface. For routine queries such as account balance and status information, this enterprise implemented an automated voice response system.

The E-insurance E-business Problem

Consumers are becoming more and more inclined to invest in the stock market as a viable retirement investment rather than traditional insurance. They generally are better educated and much more informed than previous generations. For example, consumers are beginning to recognize that traditional insurance offers lower returns than the stock market. As a result, there is a shift away from buying traditional insurance policies such as whole and universal life.

The time has ended for insurers who have relied on insurance agents alone to maintain tight customer relationships and to retain their clients. The younger, better educated, and sometimes better informed customer now wants to manage his or her financial resources for greater returns and ultimately greater wealth. Consumers can do this quite simply by taking advantage of many Internet financial portfolio management systems. To remain relevant in the e-commerce environment, the insurance enterprise decided that to survive it must seek new channels to retain and reach out to its customers. It also felt that it was imperative that it create innovative products to attract 21st century customers.

This particular insurance company decided to develop strategies for the use of e-business technology to establish new channels to reach and retain its customers. A key tactic was to use market-based mutual funds to attract customers to buy insurance in the form of tax-deferred variable annuities. Several e-business technologies were also viewed as a cost-effective way for the company to more efficiently execute its own internal business processes.

During the mid 1990s, this enterprise transformed its legacy computing environment from a mainframe to a client/server model. This was a radical change that included implementing new financial, workflow, and imaging systems. The next step was the integration of Internet-based front-ends that were linked to the legacy systems in the new computing environment. Once the company executives recognized the value of using e-business technology as their primary interface to their systems, a new corporate vision emerged.

The new corporate vision included the newly formed intranet, an extranet for business partners, and the Internet for attracting new agents—the best of three worlds. The intent was to simplify systems for the company's many customers, making it easier for them to conduct business and process transactions. This would also attract new agents who are interested in insurance firms that have Internet-enabled e-business methods.

The added business values that this enterprise desired were threefold:

1. The insurer wanted a way to keep independent agents satisfied while making it easier for these agents to do business with the company. This was of great importance to the insurer because a key criteria in independent agents' choosing to sell one company's services over another was an easy and reliable interface for the agents to use. Furthermore, providing access to internal information systems for the agents meant a higher level of support than they got from other providers. This was seen as a clear, sustainable, and substantial competitive advantage.

2. The insurer knew that linking its agents to an Internet-enabled system would have the most direct bottom-line impact in two ways. One, it would reduce its costs by leveraging e-business technologies in a distributed computing environment; two, it would attract new agents and therefore new customers with its easy-to-use Internet-enabled front-end interface.

3. The insurer felt that many insurance products are very complex and therefore customers would still rely on agents to help them make informed decisions. Although customers may shop around, it was felt that ultimately they still required the expertise of an expert agent to best explain the choices. (This is a notion that may never be automated.)

The E-business Solution

The e-business solution project was motivated by executive leaders from both the business lines (the customer services team) and the IT organizations within the business. A nongoal benefit was that the e-business solution was to be fully integrated with the company's existing systems and processes.

This project had the support of the company's CEO, who fully understood the potential of Internet-enabled e-commerce applications. The CEO also pushed for the company to have a strong Internet presence. This executive commitment minimized any political issues that were seen as impediments to the progress of the e-business solution.

The application was developed after several months and was then tested. It went into production following the test period. It was developed using primarily in-house staff. The company contracted the development of the actual e-business Internet site. It also worked with a vendor that provided security consulting services, to ensure that the site was secure.

The e-business solution included the following functions for field agents:

- New customer submissions
- New business status (access to images)
- Current policy value updates
- Online transaction history log
- Policy queries and reporting
- Historical investment performance online reports
- Online company forms
- Download capabilities for proposal writing and other sales tools
- Online access for calculations and other planning tools
- Online catalogs
- Company updates and news

These functions represented about one-fifth of the transactions that a field agent typically would do with the *call center*. The company's goal is to gradually extend the Internet-enabled functions to one-half of the agent's interactions with the company. The overall costs to develop the linkages of the Internet site to back-end systems, the e-business applications, and the security controls were approximately $800,000. This total includes internal and external sourcing requirements, hardware, and software product costs.

CRITICAL ISSUES IN THE E-BUSINESS PATH

This enterprise faced some critical issues that other firms may also face as they create Internet sites that link to their back-end legacy systems. Keep in mind the rapid growth and change associated with e-business technologies and software products: This is a constant challenge for any company to comprehend.

This company also found that the bulk of existing Internet development tools were still in the early stages of development, and some of them were not very reliable. A big challenge for the chosen development tool was to interface with the company's data warehouse; the warehouse databases are optimized (normalized) for decision support, not general data access.

There were staffing issues especially related to acquiring critical skills and experience for Web/database integration, combined with insurance industry knowledge and agent experience. A significant advantage, however, for this firm is its ability to support a large end-user base. The enterprise had a strategy in place to support all standard Internet browsers, which most of their customers already maintained on their computing units. This was an enabler.

The Internet site for this enterprise is heavily promoted to its customers and potential new customers. A significant campaign was launched to educate the agents about the functionality of the company's new e-business solution. The company's technical services group delivers education and presentations to regional groups of agents. They have also launched mass-mailing campaigns to their agents, announcing the site, the features it offers, and the advantages end users realize while using the new e-business site. Promotions were used to offer incentives to agents who registered for a user ID and then used the e-business site. As a result of this excitement, this insurance enterprise has been recognized as a leader in the insurance industry.

The E-business Solution Results

The application has been online for quite some time now, and the growth of new users has been consistent and rapid. The current plan is to have over two-thirds (66 percent) of the agents online and using the new solution on a regular basis within two years. Three important areas that provide added-business values to the enterprise are these:

1. The ability to serve new channels
2. The ability to maintain stronger channel relationships
3. Added traffic volumes of end users now able to register for their own user ID and then use the site and its e-business functionalities

The company indicates that the abilities to serve new channels and maintain stronger channel relationships are the most important benefits realized from the site. By providing an easy-to-use system, with a standard client interface, and simple ways for accessing complex networks of data, it now becomes easy for anyone to conduct business with the company.

Perhaps the most measurable aspect of this solution that truly demonstrates real added-business value is the *cost of processing* transactions. The company basically performs 200 to 300 transactions per week using the new business site. Current industry estimates are that traditional costs of processing transactions are $8–$10 per call versus negligible processing transactions via the Internet. This has resulted in savings on the order of $10,000 each month. This has been achieved (remarkably) with only 10 percent participation in the use of the new e-business sites. As more users adopt the new system, the cost reductions will grow, reaching as much as $1 million within two years.

Another area where the company expects added-business values resulting from this e-business solution is the area of *application processing*. Last year alone, this firm expected to achieve the goal of 10 percent of its new policies being handled over the Internet, with expectations that in two years it would achieve an increase of 50 percent.

Online processing of new business offers improved efficiencies, time savings, and cost reductions over the traditional processes. The company estimates that it will reduce the cost of processing a new application by 75 percent with its e-business solutions. To achieve further cost savings, the company has an established objective to print three-fourths of its new policies directly from the new Internet site (eliminating handling, mailing, printing, and additional paper costs).

Other benefits are expected as a result of this solution. One key area is the growth of the number of agents. This is projected to be quite significant due to the attraction of an Internet-based agent support system. The firm's executives believe that this e-business environment will help to foster new business relationships and build constructive partnerships with other organizations that may not be able to afford to invest in this type of Internet-based system of their own that lack the skills and technologies to create their own Internet-based agent support system.

The senior managers of this insurance enterprise feel strongly that the site provides them with tremendous leverage as they seek to build and reinforce their business partnerships. For example, they experienced some difficulty distributing through banks. They can now leverage their system to attract banks that might want to offer financial services.

The firm's executives have concluded that banks will find the system advantageous for several important reasons. As an example, it is easy to implement and use while requiring very little administration. The company could also use the system as a source of outsourcing for other insurers, banks, or financial services organization—for example, private labeling where an extension of its site looks like part of another insurer's or bank's online presence. This approach could lead to business-to-business seamless integration. This would be especially attractive to smaller companies that don't have the resources to invest in building an e-business solution that provides full online transaction capabilities. For this company, the Internet site is a market maker, enabling it to access new markets while expanding opportunities in those markets it currently supports.

22
Security and Privacy

....

$\mathbf{T}$he topic of security is a very complicated field to describe as it relates to e-business operations. This is due simply to the need for computing complexities in many of the security implementations on the Internet. Information privacy has always been one of the drawbacks to users of Internet e-commerce services, that is, in the form of trust in any transaction. Security and information privacy are being implemented more and more, in almost every e-commerce transaction.

Several topics are involved in giving Internet end users the level of comfort they need to complete their e-commerce transactions. For example, digital signatures has long been a topic that both e-commerce suppliers and legal counselors have been pursuing for years. There will always be sites that can be trusted and end users who can be trusted. There will also be those sites that cannot be trusted and those end users who cannot be trusted.

DIGITAL SIGNATURES

The digital signature mechanism provides legal proof of authenticity, satisfying the need for an electronic form of a handwritten signature. These nonrepudiation services are implemented by digital signature mechanisms (for the most part), such as the RSA public key encryption algorithm. This helps to ensure integrity measures related to the security while operating on the Internet and in other various forms of e-commerce.

A straightforward explanation of the concept utilized by the Rivest Shamir Adleman (RSA) public key security algorithm is based on the difficulty of the mathematical factorization problem. Specifically, the *factorization problem* is to find all prime factors of a given number n. The factorization problem is believed by mathematicians to be very difficult to resolve when n is sufficiently large (for RSA, n is typically 512 bits or more), and when n is the product of a few larger prime numbers (for RSA, n is the product of two large prime numbers).

This technique of digital signatures can therefore be used to implement the non-repudiation services required to secure Internet e-commerce transactions. In the case of Internet e-business solutions, the digital signature has been challenged as a replacement for the handwritten signature, as a legal proof of authenticity. This form of digital authenticity is becoming trusted worldwide at a rapid rate.

The digital signature can be used to provide proof of origin, proof of delivery, proof of submission, and proof of electronic transport. A digital signature directly provides valid proof of the identity of the data sender (or end user). A digital signature is used to sign an acknowledgment "receipt" for the latter three proofs.

What all of this really says is that cryptographic methods are employed in using the RSA digital signature mechanism in global e-commerce. Specific products that use RSA encryption and global services that use RSA encryption are commonly found in a global e-business theater.

ESTABLISHING SECURITY POLICIES

Establishing security policies involves a set of decisions that determine the enterprise's position toward security. A policy, in this case, establishes the limits of what is to be considered acceptable behavior, from one networked environment to another.

Firewalls are computer devices designed to act as filters, allowing and disallowing traffic within a network to gain rights of passage via certain routes. These filters determine (packet by packet) which way to direct the network traffic request. Therefore, by defining what is considered to be "acceptable" behavior, it becomes fairly straightforward to understand what rules need to be implemented in the firewall architecture. Firewalls are then able to better ensure *information privacy*, according to the rules in which they have been programmed.

One of the early steps is to determine what is not permitted. For some reason, that comes more naturally than determining what is permitted. For example, some companies that deal with very sensitive information may want to consider restricting network traffic outside of their own infrastructure, to best protect aspects of sensitive data integrity measures.

The best measures of *Design Quality* related to firewall designs attempt to provide all firewall designs with fail-safe design points, and in many cases with routing redundancies for enhanced network high-availability routings. This might even allow for advanced forms of security software related to "intrusion detection." In many e-business sites today, various forms of intrusion detection software are used that may be operational on a 24-hour basis. This software detects environmental abnormalities, records the event, and initiates communications to the individuals responsible for information protection. Policies related to exactly *how* intrusion detection will be managed, from a business viewpoint, need to be established.

23

The Extended E-business Enterprise

....

There have been many business enterprise advances in the various disciplines of e-commerce. The enterprises that have advanced their businesses through the e-commerce and e-business continuums, to a large degree, have reinvented their businesses. Generally speaking, this implies extending their enterprise by linking their customers, supply chain partners, and consumers to their back-end systems. Internet commerce requires that companies can link their IT infrastructure through the firewalls to enable their customers and trading partners to get to the appropriate data. An excellent example of this is in the travel industry; it is known to many to as the Travelocity Internet site.

Travelocity is one of the largest Internet sites to date. Travelocity is a business unit within American Airlines Reservation's (AMR) SABRE Group. The Travelocity site is tied to AMR's back-end systems that are required to support the enormous airline reservation system. This site requires 24 x 7 availability and very rapid response times. Loss of transactions means loss of revenues to the travel industry; therefore, it is critical that Travelocity be available at all times. This e-commerce application is an early pioneer of Internet commerce.

Our discussion of Travelocity will provide an example of a framework for an e-commerce strategy that includes the ability to link Internet commerce transactions to the IT infrastructure in the enterprise's back-end systems. It will therefore illustrate the basic IT considerations required for Internet-enabled e-commerce in an extended enterprise.

TRAVELOCITY'S E-COMMERCE DESIGN OVERVIEW

Travelocity is the first full-service online travel system that also provides real-time information to consumers who need to make travel arrangements. The service provided by this e-commerce application was put in place for approximately 1 million business and leisure travelers throughout the world. It has reportedly booked as much $100 million of travel business each year since its inception in 1999 all via the Internet. It is purported to be able to process 50 million viewing pages each month, servicing over 3 million registered end users.

To design this e-commerce environment, the development team had demonstrated significant technical skills in Internet design methods, computing resources, infrastructure architectures, and multitier transaction processing environments. The entire AMR enterprise-wide staff also needed to embrace the importance of the Travelocity Internet site. The rationale for this would be that during the early stages of the deployment, there would be very little return on investment (ROI). In general, a common vision had to be conveyed throughout the enterprise because all the staff needed to support the new e-business portal site as a new e-business channel. This was very important because immediate payoffs were not going to be readily apparent. Also very important was that the new site needed to perform fast and efficiently. The new Internet site also had to be scalable, highly secured, and capable of 24 x 7 availability. The speed and rapid response required by Internet commerce sites mandated costly hardware computing resources. In essence, Travelocity represented another channel for distribution and the Internet extension of the SABRE reservation system. The support for the Travelocity e-business solution was there from the very beginning, with the SABRE corporate parent supporting its launch and rapid growth. This support turned out to be instrumental in the success of the Travelocity e-business solution; SABRE is the reservation systems for many global/domestic airlines, and thousands of travel agents around the world use it on a minute-by-minute basis.

An important factor that needs to be understood is that the SABRE system is really an extremely complicated legacy system with which Travelocity had be integrated to succeed. This meant that from the very beginning the SABRE design/support team was involved in the Travelocity project. This provided a solid channel of communication between the two teams and spawned a great deal of synergy. It also meant that the SABRE team staff members had to understand how changes in the legacy systems would affect the Travelocity e-commerce environment and, conversely, how changes to the Travelocity e-commerce environment could affect operations in the SABRE system environment. This enabled the two teams to anticipate and address problems earlier and to avoid unexpected problems in the Travelocity Internet commerce site.

THE TRAVELOCITY LOGICAL ARCHITECTURE

The Travelocity technical architecture can be best understood by an examination of both the physical and logical views of the environment.

Visitors enter the Travelocity Internet site by simply using their computer desktop's Internet browser (almost any browser capable of security encryption keys can be utilized). They begin their interaction on the Travelocity home page, the main page for the site. They are then able to browse the home page, viewing content from the primary servers. They gain further access to other areas in the site through hot-links and dynamically viewed Internet pages—all based on the level of security they have been granted within the site. At this level, the end user can also view content from the proprietary transaction server(s). Visitors are given access to this part of the site based on their agreement to be a guest (that is, on a limited basis) or their registration as a member.

The servers we have discussed to this point are linked directly into the SABRE legacy systems. These servers send the end-user request to the SABRE system, requesting arrival/departure information and other reservation-related information. Visitors access (or are unable to access) this information by virtue of the firewall computing security devices. This secured access procedure is transparent to the end user if the end-user authentication is confirmed. If it is not, a rejection notice is sent to the end user, due to the system's inability to authenticate the end user. This rejection could occur for several reasons: forgetting the password, discrepancies in the registered end-user information, or sometimes even network routings.

In order to explore this e-commerce environment further, let's say (for example) a customer who is a registered Travelocity member wants to make an airline reservation. The process begins with the customer signing into the system with a user ID and a password. This initially validates and verifies (or authenticates) that the customer's identity in the Travelocity end-user profile is correct.

Once the customer's identity has been authenticated, the customer's flight request (perhaps based on personal criteria stored in an online form) is transferred through the firewall to the transaction server(s), where it is then processed and converted from an Internet-based HTTP (secured) request to a SABRE system database request.

The request now moves through a second firewall and further into the SABRE legacy system. At this point, the customer's request has completely transitioned from the Internet into the SABRE legacy system. The end-user client device is now awaiting a response from the SABRE environment. The SABRE system processes the customer's request and sends the response back to the transaction server, which translates the information back into an Internet-based format (for instance, HTML) and passes it to an Internet server. At this point, the end user is able to view a dynamic Internet page containing the requested information. At the same time, the transaction server notes that the request has been completed. This process continues until the customer completes his or her transactions or exits the Travelocity Internet site.

LEGACY AND INTERNET ENGINES ARE COMPLEMENTARY

The Travelocity e-business system and the SABRE system complement each other. The SABRE travel reservation system maintains one of the world's largest private networks. The SABRE system has an enormous database that is built on a very secure legacy infrastructure. It is too costly and impractical to build a data repository and legacy environment for Travelocity and to dispose of the database currently in use. Therefore, this e-business solution was designed to tightly couple with the already mature and well-established SABRE system database. In essence, Travelocity provides a new market to which the SABRE Group can extend its reservation services, all by virtue of the Internet.

Currently the vast majority of the world's largest enterprises run on legacy systems that also include some type of distributed computing systems. The growing use of the Internet for e-commerce will not force these enterprises to change their legacy engines into Internet engines. Instead, organizations are connecting their Internet-enabled systems to their mature back-end systems where their data resides. The typical mainframe (or minicomputer-based) legacy systems are designed to provide comprehensive solutions for public- and private-sector enterprises. They are often considered to be very costly, and they may have rather high maintenance costs. There is another problem in that the older legacy environments sometimes require skills that are somewhat obsolete in the workplace, making maintenance and support even more costly. It has also been demonstrated that older technologies often take significant time to design, build, and operate. Over the years, as many legacy systems mature, they are often enhanced, changed, redesigned, and reengineered: This too becomes quite costly. These legacy systems typically included complex business logic (sometimes undocumented), and they are almost always used by large end-user populations.

The Internet offers a way to extend the reach of legacy system user organizations into the world of e-commerce. Travelocity is proof in that it is a system that links with the SABRE legacy system and then uses this environment as its large-scale repository of data and business logic rules.

The benefits realized in the Travelocity project were accelerated due to the universal use of the SABRE system throughout the travel and transportation industries. A key issue that needs to be addressed is this: Because many legacy systems (like SABRE) are not designed to be quickly converted to Internet e-commerce systems (like Travelocity), they are sometimes subject to unexpected usage spikes (and at warp speeds) depending on how the two systems are integrated. The Travelocity system is designed for Internet-based dynamic e-business change requirements: Each week the site changes. On the other hand, the SABRE legacy system exists in a very stable, secure, and mature IT environment. The legacy environment changes with a much slower and deliberate pace. Travelocity was built (as are others) with the ability to respond to requests for changes rapidly. It is complementary to the SABRE system, as it almost extends its life and allows for changes to occur around SABRE without directly causing changes to occur within SABRE.

Travelocity was designed with isolated Internet-specific processes (and data) outside of the legacy system. Travelocity processes consist of Internet transaction-processing capabilities and Internet-centric data. This data generally includes customer profiles and commonly accessed reference tables. The advantage of essentially integrating these two systems is that the Travelocity system is enabled to make changes to data schema, business rules, and content on the fly, whenever and wherever required. The introduction of Travelocity (utilizing SABREs complementary, almost "parent-like" system) is of enormous business value. The Internet-based commerce applications provide speed, ease of use, and global public access; the legacy environment provides integrity, stability, and reliability. Essentially, the Travelocity system draws on the strength of the SABRE system and leverages the speed and global reach of the Internet. This hybrid system-like combination is becoming a standard practice in distributed computing environments (like client/server), where the objective is to move the data and business logic as close to the enterprise-wide end users (and general public) as possible.

TRANSACTIONS: THE INTERNET TO LEGACY SYSTEMS

Enterprise executives and business leaders realize the importance of data and commands being converted, as this information moves between Internet and legacy systems environments.

The conversion and mapping of data elements are first processes that must be planned and completed as any company moves from a legacy IT model to a legacy IT/Internet environment. This all begins where a plain and simple text-based terminal is typically used for processing transactions electronically, utilizing more traditional automated machine-to-machine communications. Automated e-business tools are then used to invoke a series of events, starting with screen scrapes (parsing data directly from screen views), moving to generic data streams of more structured data. Next, this structured data travels through application programming interfaces (APIs) to the legacy system. Travelocity's design concept is based on the use of generic data streams and screen scrapes. This requires that the linkages between the Internet commerce site and the back-end systems have to enable efficient data and command conversion processes. Ideally, this is a tight coupling of information.

When airline reservation transaction traffic moves from the Internet to the legacy systems, the data must be converted from an Internet-based format to a legacy-standard format. Concurrently, the commands must be converted from Internet formats into legacy and database queries.

Generally speaking, legacy systems maintain designs for manual data entry and batch data entry, using terminals that are directly linked to the legacy environment. This means that many legacy system interpretations of direct system commands cannot be applied: They do not have designed into them the abilities for Internet format translations. What this implies is that the Internet-connected portions of the Travelocity system must convert its commands into SABRE queries, which can then be automatically executed by the back-end systems. In turn, the legacy systems generate a response that is either converted to a data stream or is screen-scraped and transmitted back to the Internet system (where the "scrape" actually reads and maps characters from a specific location on a terminal screen into new data fields and then transfers the data to the Internet environment).

Although the data acquisition methods we have discussed in this area have several (perhaps more innovative) solutions that can be applied, the systematic procedure of screen scraping seems to be a generally accepted method for data gathering across many global industries. The process of mapping data from one format to another can be extremely difficult, and the advanced technologist might want to encourage more innovative methods to perform data acquisition. Screen scraping is (let's say) a natural way to acquire data from legacy environments. There are indeed other utilities that enable this process of data acquisition to occur, through more programmatic methods.

PERFORMANCE AND SPEED

As the Travelocity e-commerce site has evolved, the company has carefully monitored end-user demands, adding new features and content as required. However, Travelocity found that these strong features and broad content capabilities were but one of several drivers of Internet site activity and revenues. In fact, Travelocity has also found that the Internet site's success (as measured in revenues derived from reservation bookings) is directly related to speed and site performance. Thus, speed is always a key consideration in software development and system design.

The Travelocity system comprises many UNIX servers, Netscape Internet servers, and proprietary high-speed transaction processing servers. These servers provide the services for dynamic content to be served (in most cases). This enables Travelocity to deliver highly customized data and allows one to make changes on dynamically served data, thus easily accommodating custom entry points. The Travelocity system designers have found that the transaction systems that drive Internet commerce produce an even greater strain on resources. In summary, Travelocity employs more powerful servers for dynamic content and transaction processing capabilities.

To achieve optimal performance, the Travelocity Internet commerce site has combined applications and content in a server machine. This enables quick access from and to the legacy SABRE system for the Internet commerce site. For the purposes of speed, the Travelocity system has transferred dynamic content into the server's RAM (random access memory) as opposed to a hard drive (a physical disk in the server). This is achieved via an API and provides the fastest access to information. Equally important are the speed, reliability, and lower cost of RAM, as opposed to the hard-drive approach.

The Travelocity system consists of two types of servers: home page servers and transaction servers. Each server is designed to accommodate either secure or nonsecure Internet traffic. The nonsecure traffic includes home pages, various forms of catalog content, and travel information pages; the secure server traffic includes purchase transactions for tickets and other types of personal information being passed back and forth between servers. The higher-volume traffic is run on high-end transaction e-commerce servers, and the lower-volume transaction traffic runs on smaller e-commerce servers. The management of both types of traffic is directed by an *enterprise server*, which basically oversees the traffic between all servers throughout the enterprise. Enterprise servers are generally high-end, high-performance computing machines that logically sit at the apex of the entire e-commerce environment.

The majority of the data is located on the legacy SABRE system. Legacy systems like the SABRE system operate at varying capacities. The Travelocity e-commerce site has built automated response systems that make adjustments to slower responses from the legacy systems, preventing system bottlenecks. This helps keeps the traffic flow consistent. Speed varies on the legacy system because it provides services for internal users running many different applications, usually on an enterprise-wide intranet.

The Travelocity system automatically regulates its traffic flow to the legacy system, thus ensuring that bottlenecks and slower response times do not occur. Automatic switching can occur, transferring traffic loads to other servers, to enable this enhanced response time. On the other hand, if the Travelocity system is running slow the legacy system also has built-in automated capabilities to regulate traffic flow to and from the e-commerce site. This ensures consistent user response time in processing the many transaction requests.

TESTING

Another key service that provides excellent results is the stress-testing tools that emulate network traffic. Excellent tools are available to do this. The key is to stress-test the e-commerce environment before the system is put in production, as well as on an ongoing basis. It is especially important to test under heavy loads. Load testing is quite valuable for the anticipation of scalability problems. This entire topic of "load balancing" involves complex theories in architecture, which (for the purposes of this book) guarantee the end user adequate response times.

Adequate hardware scaling of the Travelocity system was required to handle unpredictable high-bandwidth requirements. When this occurs, points of failure have to be quickly identified to allow support organizations to scale additional machines into the environment. Peak loads (or spikes) that occur without warning are handled via system-performance and capacity-planning instrumentation. New servers are generally on hand based on predictable growth and high peak-traffic volume patterns. The system is designed to accommodate new servers with very little downtime, and without reconfiguring the entire system (or upgrading existing servers). One important element in capacity planning is the correct understanding of the nature of the content. Transaction traffic based on business processes is much slower than Internet traffic, which changes at more frequent intervals and faster rates.

The Travelocity e-commerce solution has matured, and it has added several new capabilities. Some of the features have enhanced the uses of the legacy system data and also support new e-commerce applications that do not require legacy system support. In addition to basic services like flight, hotel, and rental car schedules and reservations, it now has been enhanced to include equipment descriptions and seat maps.

FIREWALL SYSTEMS

Travelocity has firewalls placed between the clients and the Internet servers. Its other firewall is located between the Internet system and the SABRE system.

The firewall systems provide access security to help prevent intrusions by hackers and unauthorized access into the corporate intranet and legacy system. Basically, a firewall has two sides for hauling network traffic: an open-side and a secured side. End-user authentication (or lack thereof) determines which side the end user will be allowed to access.

The SABRE system's complex business rules, corporate databases, and legacy applications are safe and secure. This is important because the SABRE system is widely used by the public, businesses, and governments for travel transportation needs.

SYSTEM RELIABILITY AND AVAILABILITY

The Travelocity system uses load-balancing tools and techniques to ensure the reliability and performance of its Internet servers. There are early warning tools that measure unusual trends in user traffic. Tools that dynamically monitor Internet pages are desired because they ensure that content has been delivered and that the content is accurate. These types of dynamic tools (and methods) are required to monitor online processes and the frequency of error page occurrences. Furthermore, they provide dynamic monitoring of round-trip time for requests to the legacy system and identify problems that might occur in the database environment(s).

24
Conclusion

....

$\mathbf{T}$he exploration of e-commerce is vast. The topics that enable the various forms of e-commerce to occur are present in both horizontal and vertical segments of global industry. Social structures are affected in sometimes very dramatic ways. One thing is for sure, this change will not stop: It is the evolution of socio-economic structures. Many businesses, electronically enabled through forms of e-commerce technologies, will find new segments to operate. These companies will be referred to as "e-businesses." The small to medium-sized business segments may realize the most fluid levels of change as they adopt to their new market segments.

As a society, we as people expect change. In fact, change is the catalyst that makes a society strong. Many obvious changes have occurred in societies as a direct result of the Internet and e-commerce solutions. WebMD, Dr.Koop.com, Stamp.com—many enterprises are forming to address public needs for coping in this ever-changing state

The only concept that will remain unchanged is "change itself." Virtually anything a human can do that does not require tasting, touching, or smelling can be performed by some form of automation. The question is this: Is automation the right way to solve a particular issue, and if so, is the Internet, and e-commerce, the preferred way to perform the automation? The global infrastructure exists to automate tasks worldwide: It is the Internet and all of its subnetworks. Does this imply that the next step of Internet/2 will bring even more capabilities for change to occur in industrial and public sectors? What is next?

As explorers and practitioners in the field of the Internet e-commerce and e-business, we (the authors) submit that innovation, and the ability to manage this innovation, will continue to be the driving force in global e-commerce. E-commerce is a challenge for us all to face. We would like to encourage the many global participants in the field of e-commerce to continue to work together for the good of the cause. The possibilities are virtually endless—to bring forth the best-of-breed in both technologies and global practices of e-commerce. We are amid a vast change in both industry and the social structures surrounding our daily lives. Endure the change. Invite the challenge. And finally, partner with other global team members, to develop what is best for the e-commerce challenge at hand. Once a business is on the Internet, it is global. Let us continue to think in global terms, and ultimately we will improve many lives around the world—through simple, tenacious management of innovation.

Appendix A
Further Reading

....

This is an extended list of additional reading materials, which the reader may find helpful. The works listed here are directly, or in some cases, indirectly, related to fields of e-commerce.

Bolthouse, D. 1996. *Exploring IBM Client/Server Computing*. Florida: Maximum Press.

Burros, D. 1993. *Technotrends: How To Use Technology To Go Beyond Your Competition*. New York: Harper Books.

Champy, J. 1995. *Reengineering Management*. New York: HarperCollins Books.

Chickering, A.W. 1993. *Education and Identity*. 2nd ed. San Francisco: Jossey-Bass.

Goleman, D. 1995. *Emotional Intelligence*. New York: Bantam Books.

Hammer, M., J. Champy. 1993. *Reengineering the Corporation*. New York: HarperCollins Books.

Hammer, M. & S. A. Stanton. 1995. *The Reengineering Revolution*. New York: HarperCollins Books.

Kegan, R. 1994. *In Over Our Heads: The Mental Demands of Modern Life*. Cambridge, MA: Harvard University Press.

Laszlo, E. 1996. *The Systems View of the World*. New Jersey: Hampton Press, Inc.

Lucas, Henry C. 1996. *The T-Form Organization: Using Technology to Go Beyond Your Competition*. San Franscisco: Jossey-Bass.

Miles, M. and A. Huberman. 1994. *Qualitative data analysis: a sourcebook of new methods*. 2nd ed. Beverly Hills, CA: Sage Publications.

Orfali, R., D. Harkey, J. Edwards. 1996. *The Essential Client/Server Survival Guide*. New York: John Wiley & Sons, Inc.

Scott, R. W. 1992. *Organizations—Rational, Natural, and Open Systems*. New Jersey: Prentice Hall.

Senge, P. M. 1992. *The Fifth Discipline: The Art and Practice of the Learning Organization*. New York: Doubleday.

Tapscott, D. and A. Caston. 1993. *Paradigm Shift*. New York: McGraw-Hill, Inc.

Tapscott, D. 1996. *The Digital Economy*. New York: McGraw-Hill.

The Learning Organization. (1996). The Economist Intelligence Unit, IBM.

Global Insurance to the Twenty-first Century. 1996. The Economist Intelligence Unit, IBM.

Vaskevitch, D. 1995. *Client/Server Strategies*. Foster City, CA: IDG Books.

Yin, R. K. 1994. *Case study research: design and methods*. 2nd ed. Thousand Oaks, CA: Sage Publications.

Appendix B
Exploring E-business Industry Events

....

This is an extended list of miscellaneous industry events, which one may choose to research for details regarding specific events related to e-business. This list is also directly, or in some cases, indirectly related to fields of e-commerce. (Information source: CNNfn Internet Site):

http://search.cnnfn.com/query.html?col=cnnfn&qt=e-business&qc=cnnfn&qm=1&st=61&nh=10&lk=1&rf=1

INDUSTRY EVENTS

Many of the industries around the world are progressing each day toward their strategies for managing e-commerce and e-business. What follows is just a few of the events that are being traced related to accomplishments in the field.

IBM Surges on Positive Growth Outlook—
May 17, 1999

PALO ALTO, Calif. (Reuters)—IBM plans to announce on Monday a new version of its database software which it claims makes it easier and faster for customers to develop electronic business applications. International Business Machines Corp. said the latest version will . . .

IBM Stock Surges On Net News—

May 14, 1999

USA TODAY (NB)—By Sara Nathan, USA TODAY. IBM shares soared nearly 9% Thursday, propelling the market to record levels, after CEO Louis Gerstner said Big Blue makes more money from the Internet than the top 25 Internet companies combined. The computer giant gets $20 billion, or 25% of . . .

Philippine Firms Explore E-Commerce,

Compaq Leads—May 13, 1999

MAKATI CITY, PHILIPPINES (NB)—By Jennifer B. Malapitan, Metropolitan Computer Times. Compaq Computer [NYSE:CPQ] is staying focused on what it wants to do after the integration drill with Digital and Tandem—satisfy customers by providing them the best "solutions" . . .

QWest Leads New E-Commerce Alliance

with SAP, HP—May 11, 1999

LONDON (CNNfn)—Qwest Communications, Hewlett-Packard and Germany's SAP signed a strategic alliance Tuesday designed to boost their share of the booming market in Internet-based business software. The rapid spread of computer-based management systems known as . . .

C&W Announces New IDC Offer—

May 11, 1999

LAS VEGAS (Reuters)—Britain's Cable & Wireless Plc said it plans to unveil on Tuesday a new e-business service for U.S. small and medium-size businesses using equipment supplied by International Business Machines Corp. Cable & Wireless's WebReady system provides U.S. . . .

Sage Shares Rocket on IBM Deal—

May 11, 1999

LONDON (Reuters)—Shares of British software services company Sage Group jumped nearly 10 percent Tuesday as the company outlined plans to expand its Internet activities in partnership with computer giant IBM. Sage, which has made a number of medium-sized acquisitions in . . .

Intel Creates $250M Internet Venture

Fund—May 10, 1999

SANTA CLARA, Calif. (Reuters)—Computer chip giant Intel Corp. Monday confirmed it is forming a $250 million fund to invest in technology companies. Compaq Computer Corp. (CPQ), Dell Computer Corp. (DELL) and Hewlett-Packard Co. (HWP) are among the . . .

Intel Execs Outline 'e-business' Strategy—

April 22, 1999

NEW YORK (CNNfn)—Intel Corp. executives outlined a strategy Thursday to be a leader in Internet commerce and said the chip giant will derive 90 percent of its revenue from electronic commerce by 2002. "Our goal is to be the building-block supplier to the Internet . . ."

Extranet: The Next Internet?—April 6, 1999

CHICAGO (internetTelephony)—First up was the Internet. Next came private business Intranets hooking up company employees, local and remote, for the exchange of corporate information and intelligence of all sorts. Now, according to many industry readers, enterprise Extranets are . . .

3Com Corp. Eyes $100 Million Savings—
March 17, 1999

NEW YORK (CNNfn)—Computer networking company 3Com Corp. said Wednesday it expects to save about $100 million in calendar 1999 because of streamlining from doing more business electronically. The Santa Clara, Calif.-based company projected that so-called "e-business" . . .

Attachmate Partners with ASL in Hong
Kong and China—March 16, 1999

HONG KONG, CHINA (NB)—By Staff, IT Daily. Attachmate has partnered with systems integrator Automated Systems to offer host access management "solutions" in Hong Kong and China. Under the partnership, ASL will integrate Attachmate's Unix and OpenVMS-based host . . .

Developer Pow-Wow Highlights Intel's
Pentium III—February 23, 1999

SAN JOSE, Calif. (NB)—By Prudencia R Orani, Metropolitan Computer Times. Intel's [NASDAQ:INTC] Developer Forum, called "Designing Connected Computers," runs today through February 25 at the Palm Springs Convention Center. More information about this . . .

Internet World: E-Commerce Challenges
Canadian Businesses - February 4, 1999

TORONTO, ONTARIO, CANADA (NB)—By Grant Buckler, Newsbytes. Pop quiz: What is the difference between electronic commerce and electronic business? A lot of business people are having trouble answering that question, according to Gary Simkin . . .

CEOs See E-Commerce as Major Source of Revenues—Survey—January 29, 1999

DAVOS, SWITZERLAND (NB)—By Adam Creed, Newsbytes. Company chief executive officers (CEOs) are optimistic about the growth of their business, even those from Asian companies, and chief executives are especially bullish on the potential of electronic . . .

CEOs See Online Threat—January 28, 1999

DAVOS, Switzerland (CNNfn)—Forget all the hype about the dreaded Y2K bug, today's business leaders say the biggest threat could be from non-traditional competitors using the Internet to hawk their wares. In the latest survey of 800 global bosses, released Thursday at the World Economic Forum . . .

Correction—IBM and Hong Kong's ABC Offer E-Business Tools—January 28, 1999

HONG KONG, CHINA (NB)—By Staff, IT Daily. (Note—this corrects a version of this report dated January 26. The URL in the earlier version was wrong—this version corrects it.) IBM [NYSE:IBM] and ABC Interactive, the interactive auditing unit of the . . .

HP to Market German E-Services Platform—January 26, 1999

FRANKFURT, GERMANY (NB)—By Staff, CHIP Online and Newsbytes. The U.S. subsidiary of a German electronic commerce software company has announced a joint marketing agreement with Hewlett-Packard [NYSE:HWP]. German Brokat Infosystems AG said Hewlett-Packard will sell Brokat's . . .

The Pitfalls of E-Commerce—

January 21, 1999

NEW YORK (CNNfn)—As a six-month veteran of online retailing, Toys R Us thought it was prepared for anything. The purveyor of children's playthings entered the e-commerce scene last summer with relative ease, patting itself on the back for its innovation and efficiency in filling Web site . . .

IBM Beats Street by Pennies—

January 21, 1999

ARMONK, New York (NB)—By Craig Menefee, Newsbytes. IBM [NYSE:IBM] on Thursday announced record fourth-quarter 1998 diluted earnings per common share of $2.47, beating the consensus First Call estimate of $2.45 by two cents but falling well within the estimated range of $2.39 . . .

Internet Tools Inc. Bought by Axent—

January 20, 1999

ROCKVILLE, Maryland (NB)—By Newsbytes Staff, Networking Roundup. Information security company Axent Technologies Inc. [NASDAQ:AXNT] has acquired Fremont, Calif.-based Internet Tools Inc. Under the terms of the merger deal, Internet Tools' stockholders and option . . .

"PC as King" Era Over—IBM Researcher—

January 20, 1999

NEW YORK (NB)—By Matt Hines, Newsbytes. As part of a series of speeches focusing on the next century, IBM Corp.'s [NYSE:IBM] top researcher, Dr. Paul M. Horn, said an emerging breed of hand-held and embedded devices will revolutionize the ways computers . . .

Intel Outlines PC Roadmap for E-business—

January 4, 1999

MAKATI CITY, PHILIPPINES (NB)—By Joel D. Pinaroc, Metropolitan Computer Times. Intel's [NASDAQ:INTC] roadmap, specifically for its microprocessor product line, is well-suited to accommodate emerging and more complicated electronic business (e-business) applications that . . .

Internet IPOs Likely to Stay Hot in 1999—

December 21, 1998

NEW YORK (CNNfn)—The last year of the 20th century will be the year of the rabbit, the year global economic growth is expected to slow to a crawl, the year set to begin under a cloud of political paralysis—but what will 1999 usher in for IPOs? If past is prologue, then one . . .

Zergo Snaps Up Baltimore Technologies in

$55 Million Deal—December 18, 1998

BASINGSTOKE, BERKSHIRE, ENGLAND (NB)—By Steve Gold, Newsbytes. In an interesting development for the IT (information technology) security marketplace, Zergo Holdings has announced plans to merge with Baltimore Technologies, the Irish headquartered . . .

Attachmate Forms Asian E-Business

Consulting Group—December 15, 1998

HONG KONG, CHINA (NB)—By Staff, IT Daily. Host access management solutions provider, Attachmate has announced its formation of a regional consulting solutions team for organizations that are moving their business to the Internet. Managed from the company's . . .

Intel Raises E-Commerce Bid—

December 14, 1998

MANILA, PHILIPPINES (NB)—By Prudencia R Orani, Metropolitan Computer Times. Expecting to earn by year-end $2.5 billion from intel.com geared for electronic commerce (e-commerce) only five months ago, Intel Corporation [NASDAQ:INTC] announced plans to further fine-tune its . . .

Internet Commerce Facts and Figures—

December 10, 1998

NEW YORK (CNNfn)—Online retailers are rejoicing. The figures look good. Experts expect online sales to triple this year to roughly $3.5 billion, and it's only getting better. The total value of goods and services traded by American companies over the Internet will reach . . .

AT&T Buys IBM Unit—December 8, 1998

NEW YORK (CNNfn)—AT&T Corp.'s desire to jumpstart its global networking plans, and IBM Corp.'s wish to focus more on e-business applications, combined to create Tuesday's series of transactions that include the $5 billion sale of IBM's global network to AT&T, the companies said. As part of . . .

Global IT Majors Team Up to Supply

Equipment to Indian ISPs—

December 6, 1998

CALCUTTA, INDIA (NB)—By C.T. Mahabharat, Newsbytes. If the new Indian Internet policy is spurring prospective ISPs, technology providers are getting ready the feed the enthusiasm. Information majors like Microsoft, Compaq, Intel, Cisco and Loral Orion . . .

Comdex India/IT World 98 Opens—

December 4, 1998

NEW DELHI, INDIA (NB)—By C.T. Mahabharat, Newsbytes. The much awaited IT World '98 Comdex India, billed as the largest infotech show in the subcontinent, finally got rolling in the capital's Pragati Maidan on December 2. With the country poised for the Internet boom, it does not . . .

IBM Mounts Aggressive Philippines

Campaign for Business—November 26, 1998

MAKATI CITY, PHILIPPINES (NB)—By Joel D. Pinaroc, Metropolitan Computer Times. Leading IT vendor IBM Corp., through its local subsidiary, reported recently that it will mount an aggressive campaign for its software and Internet businesses in the . . .

IBM Adds to E-Business and Privacy

Services—November 20, 1998

SAN JOSE, Calif. (NB)—By Newsbytes Staff, Networking Roundup. IBM [NYSE:IBM] says it has expanded its electronic business services and added a new privacy consulting service to help companies utilize the Internet. IBM adds that the new services also . . ..

Java-Based Enterprise Resource Planning

Software Debuts— November 17, 1998

STOCKHOLM, SWEDEN (NB)—By Sylvia Dennis, Newsbytes. Intentia has taken the wraps off, what the company claims is, the first enterprise resource planning (ERP) package developed in Java. The software is actually a complete write-thru of the firm's Movex . . .

IBM/Lotus/Xerox Simplify Electronic Paper Mgt—November 2, 1998

HONG KONG, CHINA (NB)—By Staff, IT Daily. IBM [NYSE:IBM] and Xerox [NYSE:XRX] have announced an initiative to deliver a new "solution" to help customers easily manage paper and electronic documents across the enterprise. This knowledge-sharing "solution" will ...

IBM and CompUSA Target SOHO Market— November 2, 1998

NEW YORK(NB)—By Craig Menefee, Newsbytes. IBM [NYSE:IBM] and CompUSA [NYSE:CPU] are rolling out a "comprehensive computing solutions" joint initiative for small businesses and small office/home office (SOHO) operations that want to turn their businesses into . . .

Poor Info Mgt Threatens Growth of E-Business—Report—November 2, 1998

BRACKNELL, BERKSHIRE, ENGLAND (NB)—By Sylvia Dennis, Newsbytes. According to a report just published by Novell [NASDAQ:NOVL], organizations which recognize that information is their chief asset and manage and protect it properly, will be the future winners . . .

IBM Consolidating Net Ad Business— October 26, 1998

ARMONK, New York (NB)—By Bob Woods, Newsbytes. IBM Corp. [NYSE:IBM] said it is consolidating its interactive media buying, design and Web strategy efforts by trimming its agency list from 60 such shops to six: True North Communications Inc.'s [NYSE:TNO] Modem . . .

IBM Opens Disk Drive Manufacturing Plant in Ireland—October 23, 1998

DUBLIN, IRELAND (NB)—By Newsbytes Staff, Networking Roundup. IBM [NYSE:IBM] has opened a new hard disk platters manufacturing plant in Dublin, Ireland. The company says it made an initial investment of $250 million in the plant, which will lead to over 700 . . .

Internet Services to Soar, But Not Profits—October 15, 1998

LONDON (CNNfn)—Internet service providers in Europe are facing a massive surge in demand, but recent research suggests that doesn't mean they are going to make much money. Telephone call charges are set to drop over the edge of a cliff, . . .

Internet Services Will Soar, But Profits Won't—October 15, 1998

LONDON (CNNfn)—Demand for Internet services in Europe is set to surge massively, but recent research says that doesn't mean there are profits to be made. Telephone call charges are set to drop over the edge of a cliff, according to U.K. telecoms . . .

Merrill Offers Free Research In Internet Trial—October 15, 1998

LONDON (CNNfn)—Merrill Lynch will offer its stock research free over the Internet during a four-month trial period. Merrill, the largest U.S. brokerage firm, is a long standing critic of online trading. It denies the move marks a softening of its . . .

Asian CEOs Upbeat on E-Business, Says PWC—October 13, 1998

SINGAPORE (NB)—By Adam Creed, Newsbytes. Asia's chief executive officers (CEOs) see electronic business (e-business) as revolutionizing the way they will interact in the future with customers, suppliers and employees, according to a PricewaterhouseCoopers survey . . .

IBM Signs Encryption License Deal with Hi/fn—October 12, 1998

LOS GATOS, Calif. (NB)—By Sylvia Dennis, Newsbytes. IBM [NYSE:IBM] has signed a licensing agreement for Hi/fn's IPsecure, a suite of portable source code toolkits that are used for Internet security (IPsec) protocols. The move is an interesting one for . . .

E-Business Set to Rocket in the Next Five Years—October 12, 1998

LONDON (CNNfn)—Senior executives across the globe believe that e-mail, Web sites and Intranets will transform the way they do business in the next five years, with the number of online transactions soaring, according to two new surveys of corporate attitudes to . . .

France Telecom, IBM Offer Low-Cost Internet Access—October 6, 1998

PARIS, FRANCE (NB)—By Steve Gold, Newsbytes. In a move that could have a profound effect on the way in which the general public accesses the Internet, France Telecom has linked with IBM [NYSE:IBM] to develop a low-cost superphone that can access the Internet. . . .

Equant Forms Lotus and IBM Network

Integration Practice—October 6, 1998

HONG KONG, CHINA (NB)—By IT Daily. Equant has announced the creation of a worldwide Lotus and IBM [NYSE:IBM] Network Integration Practice to deliver Lotus Notes and Domino-based communications and collaborative "solutions" with related services for . . .

IBM's HotMedia, For Audio/Video Without

Plug-Ins—October 1, 1998

SOMERS, New York (NB)—By Jacqueline Emigh, Newsbytes. By the end of this year, IBM [NYSE:IBM] plans to add video Java applets to HotMedia, a new World Wide Web content creation tool now being piloted by sites ranging from PGA Interactive to The Jim . . .

CashWare Turns to Entegrity for Secure

Cash Flow—September 28, 1998

OREM, Utah (NB)—By Newsbytes Staff, Networking Roundup. Public key cryptography security company Entegrity Solutions says it is providing the security for CashWare's new extranet-based, e-business cash management system. The company also says it is . . .

Responsiveness Follows Year 2000—

Report—September 17, 1998

PALO ALTO, Calif. (NB)—By Craig Menefee, Newsbytes. The Year 2000 or so-called Millennium Bug is taking the headlines now but what happens after the bug has struck? A new Killen & Assoc. study says the Next Big Thing for information technology (IT) . . ..

Attachmate and IBM Propose Open Web to Host Standard—August 26, 1998

BELLEVUE, Wash. (NB)—By Steve Gold, Newsbytes. Attachmate and IBM [NYSE:IBM] have taken the wraps off a proposed new standard for universally compatible Web-to-host access. Known as OHIO, short for Open Host Interface Objects, the proposed standard . . .

IBM Launches Software Company— August 11, 1998

WHITE PLAINS, New York (NB)—By Jacqueline Emigh, Newsbytes. In a teleconference today, IBM [NYSE:IBM] announced the formation of an independent, entrepreneurial software venture, to focus on producing suites in the CRM (customer relationship management) arena, and to be . . .

EDS Unit Partners to Sell Ads for Online Magazines—July 31, 1998

WASHINGTON, D.C. (NB)—By Stacy Collett, Integration Management. Always looking to drill deeper into the infinite possibilities of the Internet, systems integrators are finding that the most important alliance partners for electronic commerce are their own . . .

Cyberliability Gap Opens Wider in U.K.— July 10, 1998

LONDON (NB)—By Steve Gold, Newsbytes. An independent study into the changing habits of U.K. companies has revealed that many will have to cross a huge chasm before they are technologically safe, legally sound and properly insured against the risks of business use of . . .

Softbank and IBM Team for E-Business—

Reports—July 6, 1998

TOKYO, JAPAN (NB)—By Bob Woods, Newsbytes. Japan-based Softbank Corp. [TOKYO:9984] and IBM's [NYSE:IBM] IBM Japan Ltd. said that they would jointly market electronic business, or e-business, software and services. Press reports said Softbank will bring its sales network . . .

IBM Finds E in E-Business a Legal

Headache—July 2, 1998

NEW YORK (NB)—By Bob Woods, Newsbytes. A battle is shaping up between computing giant IBM [NYSE:IBM] and a two-person French-American start up over the right to use a specially shaped "e" that's similar to the "@" or at symbol used in e-mail . . .

DCI Launches ICON Show, For Quick

Adaptability—June 25, 1998

BOSTON (NB)—By Jacqueline Emigh, Newsbytes. DCI, a major producer of high-tech trade shows, is instituting a new offering called Information Architecture Conferences (ICON), designed around the concept of quick adaptation to the rapidly . . .

IBM Unveils Starter Network Systems—

June 17, 1998

RESEARCH TRIANGLE PARK, N. C. (NB)—By Sylvia Dennis, Newsbytes. IBM [NYSE:IBM] has unveiled two E-Business systems that it says will allow firms to get their networks up and running more quickly and efficiently than before. Both systems push pricing levels, Big . . . .

IBM and Cisco Launch E-Business Networking Systems—June 17, 1998

NEW YORK (NB)—Networking Roundup. IBM [NYSE:IBM] and Cisco Systems Inc. [NASDAQ:CSCO] have announced networked business systems that the companies say provide high- performance local area networking capabilities and fast access to the Internet. . . .

Calico Targets Europe for E-Commerce— June 9, 1998

SAN JOSE, Calif. (NB)—Networking Roundup. E-business software and services company Calico Technology Inc. has opened a full-service European office, headquartered in the U.K. The company says that the new facility will work in partnership with strategic resellers to . . .

IBM Transaction Servers to Sip More Java— June 9, 1998

BOSTON (NB)—By Jacqueline Emigh, Newsbytes. IBM [NYSE:IBM] plans to add more Java support to its CICS transaction processing (TP) server later this year, to give World Wide Web sites in arenas like finance and travel the industrial strength mainframe . . .

Networking for the Future—June 7, 1998

HONG KONG (NB)—By IT Daily. To find out what the future of networking is, you shouldn't call your cable salesman, don't even think about scanning the Web. The best place to catch a glimpse of what's to come is in the laboratories where scientists are charting the course and where you . . .

IBM Shows Off E-Business Solutions—

June 4, 1998

HONG KONG (NB)—By Staff Reporters, IT Daily. Thousands of people from all corners of business poured into the Hong Kong Convention and Exhibition Centre this week to see IBM show off its electronic commerce solutions. The two-day seminar, called "e-metropolis: A New Business . . ."

Bank of China Plans Hong Kong's First SET

Gateway—June 3, 1998

HONG KONG, CHINA (NB)—By Staff Reporters, IT Daily. Online commerce is nothing new to Hong Kong, but coming this year, Hong Kong will have its first secure payment gateway for credit card transactions over the Internet. BOC Credit Card and IBM [NYSE:IBM] have . . .

CSC Posts Record Results, Takes Charge—

May 4, 1998

NEW YORK (CNNfn)—Shaking off the effects of a failed attempt to take it over, Computer Sciences Corp. Monday posted record quarterly earnings and beat Wall Street estimates by a penny. El Segundo, Calif.-based CSC, an information systems and consulting firm, recorded . . .

PC Price War Hurts IBM—April 20, 1998

NEW YORK (CNNfn)—Computer giant IBM Corp. reported its first quarterly decline in almost two years Monday, reflecting a bitter price war in the computer industry, a stronger dollar, and weakness in Asia. Big Blue earned just over $1 billion, or $1.06 a diluted share, on revenues of $17.6 . . .

IBM Sets 'e-business' Focus—April 15, 1998

NEW YORK (CNNfn)—IBM Corp. unveiled a range of business products Wednesday as part of the company's "e-business" focus. IBM said the new tools are designed to help businesses ranging from small operations to large enterprises conduct business over the Internet and corporate networks. Among the . . .

Netscape Unveils Software—

August 18, 1997

NEW YORK (CNNfn)—Netscape Communications Corp. on Monday introduced a stand-alone version of Navigator 4.0, its Internet browser software. Netscape also announced commitments by companies such as IBM to distribute the software. IBM said it would include the browser with its software, . . .

Zapata Scraps 'Net Plans

NEW YORK (CNNfn)—October 15, 1998 | October 14, 1998 | October 13, 1998 | October 12, 1998 October 11, 1998 | October 9, 1998 October 15, 1998

Zapata scraps 'Net plans—11:01 A.M. ET Zapata Corp., the fish processing company that created a splash in the spring when it announced it would transform itself into an . . .

Appendix C
Miscellaneous E-business Information

....

This is an extended list of miscellaneous industry e-business information, which the reader may choose to research for more details regarding specific events related to e-business. This list is also directly or, in some cases, indirectly related to fields of e-commerce.

THE NUMBERS

According to Forrester Research, Inc., American companies did $43 billion in business over the Internet in 1998, a figure that is expected to reach $1.3 trillion in 2003 (9 percent of total U.S. business). Globally, Internet commerce will reach $3.2 trillion–5 percent of worldwide sales—by 2003. —*The Journal News*, April 26, 1999.

What's in store for online shopping? While there is a mania around e-commerce, there are still questions about whether it will affect real-time shopping. The growing list of customer complaints makes it clear that e-commerce is tougher than expected. Customers are citing that they can't find the product they want on the Internet site, even though it may be in the catalog, as well as complaints about shipping and handling. For consumers, the Internet experience can be disappointing, but it is still a powerful shopping tool. —*The Wall Street Journal*, April 26, 1999.

There are more than 100 million publicly addressable Internet sites. It is suggested that this year, $43 billion worth of retail sales will be made over the Internet. This number is expected to double by 2003. Business-to-business e-commerce is expected to grow to $1.3 trillion by 2003, up from $8 billion this year. Another gigantic market will be Internet-based advertising. Revenues from Internet telephony are expected to reach $14.7 billion by 2003. It is also expected that AOL will have 18 million subscribers when its fiscal year ends in June 2000. By 2004, AOL should have 39 million. —*The Wall Street Journal*, April 26, 1999.

According to International Data Corporation, worldwide corporate spending on outsourcing corporate desktops and networks is expected to more than double within four years, driven by the IT staff shortage and potential budget savings. Network and desktop outsourcing services grew almost $2 billion between 1997 and 1998 to reach $14.3 billion. By 2003, spending will reach $30.7 billion. In addition, two areas, Latin America, and Eastern Europe, the Middle East, Africa, and parts of Asia are other fast-growing areas that are expected to increase their outsourcing spending at an annual growth rate of 20 percent and 21 percent, respectively. —*CNET*, April 30, 1999.

Australia's Internet users have doubled to 1.7 million in 1998, and according to Australia's largest consulting firm, www.consult.co, the number is expected to reach 5.7 million, which is about 30 percent of the population, in 2003. —*Bloomberg*, May 3, 1999.

According to the Internet Advertising Bureau, revenues for Internet advertising hit $1.92 billion in 1998, which more than doubled the $907 million spent in 1997 and surpassed the $1.58 billion spent on outdoor advertising in 1998. —*The New York Times*, May 4, 1999.

A mere 0.1 percent of groceries and health-and-beauty items are bought online in the United States vs. 4 percent of airline tickets and books and 9 percent of software, says Jupiter Communications. This trend may not last long. In recent months, at least four cyberdrugstores have opened their doors. Peapod, the closest thing to a national online grocery service, has moved into Long Island, N.Y. Borders Books' co-founder Louis Borders will soon launch a rival to Peapod starting in Northern California, while Amazon.com is in talks to join the grocery game as well. —*BusinessWeek*, May 10, 1999.

Senior-level management support for electronic commerce may get a boost as top corporate executives around the world log on to the Internet more frequently, according to an Andersen Consulting survey. Andersen surveyed more than 1700 executives at Fortune 1000 companies as well as leading government entities in 24 countries. What Andersen found is that senior executives in the world's major markets are going online more often and are becoming more comfortable using the Internet.

- More senior executives in Australia, Spain, and the United Kingdom logged on to the Internet in 1998 than in 1997, and they did so more frequently, Andersen said.

- Access to the Internet increased slightly from 1997 to 1998, Andersen said, pointing out that 92 percent of CEOs, chief financial officers, and CIOs around the world had Internet access in 1998, compared to 90 percent in 1997. Of those with access, 83 percent went online at least once per week in 1998, compared to 71 percent in 1997. One-half of the surveyed executives said they "feel comfortable" online, which is up from one-third in 1997.

• Corporate executives in Canada and the United States are the most connected to the Internet, Andersen said, followed by executives in the United Kingdom, Australia, France, and Spain. —*Infoworld*, May 13, 1999

WHAT'S NEW ON THE INTERNET

In an effort to promote itself as a "tech savvy" state, Pennsylvania has announced plans to be the first to replace its license plate motto with the state's Internet address—www.state.pa.us. This proposal is getting a mixed reception. If the tag line is changed, it will be the first time in 23 years. —*Business Week*, April 19, 1999.

With about 8000 youngsters in need of homes, the federal government has announced plans to create an Internet site to list children who are up for adoption. The site will include photos and descriptions of children awaiting adoption through public agencies across the nation. The number of U.S. children free for adoption is expected to soar in the next few years, and a national Internet site will give children a greater pool of families to draw from. —*USA Today*, April 20, 1999.

Online currency is a new effort to coax customers to buy on the Internet. Beenz Company Ltd., a New York-based startup, has launched the Internet's first universal currency. It works very simply: Surfers need to register a "bank account" through Beenz Company. A counter of Beenz earned is displayed whenever a surfer enters a site that dispenses Beenz. Users earn Beenz by completing tasks at a site, such as questionnaires. Beenz can be spent immediately to buy goods and services on any participating Internet site, and the Beenz Company keeps a complete record of each user's transactions. —*Report on Business*, April 22, 1999.

In recent weeks, there has been a great enthusiasm for Internet banking. The industry has found its stocks rising—and those of little-known financial companies have jumped as much as 300 percent in a single day after the companies publicized their intentions to provide banking services over the Internet. —*The New York Times*, April 23, 1999.

It is estimated that some 10 million children spend time online, and kids are making up the fastest-growing segment of Internet users—the first generation to grow up online. Many kids spend their time chatting, but more and more are publishing online personal pages on the Internet that broadcast their likes and dislikes. Adolescence can be hard, and researchers who study teen Internet habits say the online personas teens choose reflect that, as some teens develop romantic relationships by e-mail. —*The Washington Post*, April 24, 1999.

As more corporations turn to the Internet for marketing and sales, long waits on the Internet are becoming bad for business. Companies can improve service somewhat by buying more powerful computers for their sites; however they have less control over the network traffic jams that can develop between their sites and the users. Sandpiper Networks Inc. and Akamai Technologies Inc., both startup companies, are pioneering a way to distribute material over the Internet that avoids much of the congestion that is found on the Internet. Their Internet page distribution system could unclog Internet traffic jams, and both sell their service directly to Internet content providers, automatically distributing the content to servers, updating the material as necessary, and keeping track of the number of visitors. —*The New York Times*, April 26, 1999.

Ford Motor Co. has announced the formation of a business selling used auto parts primarily through the Internet. Ford's new business will serve as a clearing house for auto parts, becoming a "junkyard" of sorts on the Internet. Insurance agents and adjusters have said that such a service would be useful to them because they could search quickly for parts, price them, and require repair shops they work with to buy online. —*The Wall Street Journal*, April 26, 1999.

Starbucks Corp. has announced its plans to build a new and significant e-commerce business. While Starbucks already maintains an Internet site where it sells coffee beans, coffee-making paraphernalia, and compact disks, it is speculated that their new 'cyber business' will involve gourmet foods. —*The Wall Street Journal*, April 26, 1999.

Elliot Maxwell, the Clinton administration's e-commerce czar, has announced that the government will play a role in Net-based business and has outlined 16 areas where the government will play a role in e-commerce. In addition to bandwidth and consumer protection, they include privacy, taxation, and opening global markets. —*CNET News*, April 26, 1999.

Amazon.com, the Internet seller of books, movies, and videos, has announced three new acquisition agreements that will propel Amazon into the rare-book business, Internet navigation, and new e-commerce technology. In addition, Amazon is starting an electronic greeting card business that will be free to visitors of their site. —*The Wall Street Journal*, April 27, 1999.

Big brokers are set to launch a counterattack to head off their low-cost Internet trading rivals. Prudential Insurance Co. of America, Citigroup, and Merrill Lynch & Co. are all moving toward giving more clients access to e-trading through "fee-based" accounts. Investors will pay a set annual charge for a package deal including an allotment of trades, rather than pay commissions for each trade. However, nobody expects the big brokers to offer online trading at the rock bottom rates of Internet upstarts. —*The Wall Street Journal*, April 27, 1999.

Yahoo! Inc. has recently attached a warning on its popular stock-chat message boards: Don't believe what you read. A spokesperson for Yahoo! says the notice is just a reminder of information that has always been explained in the service's terms of use. Yahoo!, along with others, has lately been faced with increasing scrutiny to uncover scams. Securities regulators say the warning is a step in the right direction. —*The Wall Street Journal*, April 27, 1999.

WH Smith, a book and stationary retailer, has announced that it will launch WHSmith Online, which will provide free access to the Internet. To differentiate itself from other free Internet service providers, WH Smith has focused on offering educational content and a family-friendly service. —*Financial Times*, April 27, 1999.

Citigroup has launched an electronic-commerce service in the Asian-Pacific area allowing companies to place orders, monitor invoices, and arrange payments online. It will eventually be introduced in Europe, the United States, and Latin America. E-commerce is expected to become increasingly important with this particular type of business forecast to reach as much as $400 billion by 2002. —*The Wall Street Journal*, April 27, 1999.

Time Warner has formally announced that it will shut down its Pathfinder Internet site. This is part of a plan to develop Internet hubs that group its existing Internet sites into different subject areas, including sports, finance, and entertainment. For the past year, Time Warner has been deemphasizing the Pathfinder Internet site, which accessed the Time Warner Internet sites. It has had well documented problems since its beginning in 1994. —*The Wall Street Journal*, April 27, 1999.

The Internet has become a convenient and easy-to-use tool for the hearing impaired to do some shopping. The Internet can accommodate many different customers than might venture into a store. E-mail has been a helpful way for buyers to communicate with sellers. —*USA Today*, April 27, 1999.

Toys "R" Us Inc. has announced that it intends to become a dominant force in e-commerce by overhauling its Internet site. The revamped Internet site and distribution center are expected to be up and running within the next few months. —*The New York Times*, April 28, 1999.

There has been much discussion whether or not the Internet should be available to anyone, of any age. How much protection should Internet "speech" receive under the First Amendment? The Internet allows nearly anyone to obtain or transmit information instantaneously to and from anywhere. Does it deserve more—or less free speech protection than older media? These are just some points made in the debate over free speech on the Internet. —*The New York Times*, April 28, 1999.

The National Science Teachers Association has launched www.scilinks.org, an Internet site to sell textbooks on the Internet. A student can now go to the site, type in the code published next to the key phrase in the textbook, and link to appropriate recommendations. —*The New York Times*, April 28, 1999.

Budget Rent a Car will allow its customers to bid online to get the best price available, a move that extends the growing Internet auction business further into the travel industry. The service will begin in May 1999. —*Newsday*, April 29, 1999.

A computer glitch at least three days old at online bill processor CheckFree Holdings Corp. snarled some electronic-banking services for customers at about 20 large banks, including First Union Corp. and Wells Fargo & Co. The affected customers pay their household bills through Microsoft's Money product and Intuit's Quicken. The banks were recently switched to a new CheckFree processing system. —*The Wall Street Journal*, April 29, 1999.

Debates over online privacy have led to the proliferation of seal-of-approval programs designed to signal privacy protection. Like the presence of a Good Housekeeping seal, which is supposed to designate a worthwhile product, the privacy seals are displayed by Internet sites to indicate that they have met standards of trustworthiness. Three main seal programs have popped up in the last few years: Truste (pronounced trustee), which was founded in 1997 by the Electronic Frontier Foundation, the Boston Consulting Group, and a trade association called Commercenet; CBA WebTrust, which was developed last year by the American Institute of Certified Public Accountants and the Canadian Institute of Chartered Accountants; and BBB Online, which was unveiled in March by the Better Business Bureau. —*The New York Times*, April 29, 1999.

Internet Call Manager, a service developed by Infointeractive, based in Halifax, Nova Scotia, is offering a pop-up menu that identifies incoming callers and offers a chance to complete the voice connection through the Net itself. The service, which costs between $4 and $7 a month, diverts incoming voice calls to a special Internet server that in turn sends caller ID messages to the user's computer screen. A user can then instruct the server to ignore the call, take a voice-mail message, or disconnect the modem and put the caller through to a conventional phone almost instantly. —*The New York Times*, April 29, 1999.

In a second major lawsuit by a Massachusetts company against anonymous chatters on the Internet, Stone & Webster is seeking damages against 20 people it charges made false statement about the company or disclosed inside information online. Stone & Webster believes at least some of the defendants are employees. Such cases are becoming more common as investors turn to the World Wide Web for information. Lexington-based Raytheon Co. began a similar action in February. —*The Boston Globe*, April 29, 1999.

Concerned that online pharmacies are biting into its growth, CVS Corp. plans to begin selling pharmaceuticals through its own Internet site. CVS, which has seen its stock dip as much as 25 percent this year, plans to expand CVS.com by the fourth quarter to sell vitamins and personal-care products as well as prescription drugs. The site, which had been mainly for corporate and investor information, also will offer consumers a wide array of medical and health care information. —*Newsday*, April 30, 1999.

Andrew Tyler didn't actually have the money to buy a 1955 Ford convertible or a Van Gogh painting or an antique bed. But that didn't stop the 13-year-old boy from bidding more than $3 million for the merchandise via the Internet auction house eBay. In fact, the eighth-grader was the winning bidder on $952,012 worth of merchandise. Andrew's shocked parents suspended his Internet privileges after an auction house called last week to discuss a winning $900,000 bid their son made. eBay said Andrew's account has been suspended, and the sellers who accepted bids from Andrew have been notified of the fictitious offers. "To him, it was like a game," said Andrew's mother. "He didn't know it was for real." —*USA Today*, April 30, 1999.

The Congressional Management Foundation released a report last week that claimed few congressional offices have succeeded at effectively communicating with their constituents online. They evaluated all of the Internet sites on Capitol Hill from July 1998 until April 1999. The most common mistakes that congressional offices made included gearing the site toward the press, rather than toward constituents, promising but not delivering, and failing to update content. —*The Washington Post*, May 3, 1999.

With the recent shootings at Columbine High School, many parents are becoming more and more skeptical about their children on the Internet. There are many good reasons for their apprehension: Unlike other forms of media, the Internet is inevitably a "mixed bag." Efforts to regulate its content have been challenged by free speech arguments. —*The New York Times*, May 3, 1999.

National Australia Bank Ltd., Asia's fifth largest bank, has launched its Internet banking service. The bank expects savings from increased customer use of Internet bank services to offset the development costs. An online banking transaction costs between 15 Australian cents and 40 cents, while over-the-counter transactions cost an average of $3.00. *Bloomberg*, May 3, 1999.

German software maker SAP has announced an initiative to create an Internet marketplace where businesses can buy and sell each others' products. The effort would allow SAP users to access its business software via the Internet as well. SAP will be providing an interactive online directory linking corporate buyers with potential suppliers of goods, and enabling companies to trade over the Internet more easily to reduce costs. —*Reuters*, May 3, 1999.

Analysts and executives have agreed that a vast majority of e-commerce sites are secure, but many speculate that a trend may be heading in the opposite direction. It is obvious that some companies lack the technical knowledge to use security safeguards, while others claim they can not afford security products and advice. Experts claim that those most vulnerable to security flaws are small and medium-sized sites. —*The New York Times*, May 3, 1999.

Fast Search & Transfer Inc. has teamed up with Dell Computer Corp. to create a new Internet search engine that they claim will be the most comprehensive ever. The new site, www.alltheweb.com, already has 80 million indexed Internet pages, and claims to be up to 200 million by summer. —*The Boston Globe*, May 4, 1999.

The Securities and Exchange Commission has announced plans to require online brokers to disclose trading risks as part of a campaign to make the industry more responsible for education investors. This, essentially, would be the e-commerce version of a warning label on a pack of cigarettes. —*The Wall Street Journal*, May 4, 1999.

All auctions on eBay were suspended temporarily on Monday, May 3, 1999, when the popular Internet site experienced a computer system outage. Because of the outage, eBay was unable to host scheduled auctions of *Star Wars* merchandise. —*USA Today*, May 4, 1999.

Universal Music, the largest record company, has announced that it will invest in technology to sell and distribute music over the Internet by the end of the year. This announcement signals impatience with the efforts of the Recording Industry Association of America to agree on a standard for selling recordings as data that arrives on a customer's computer hard drive, instead of standard cassettes or tapes. Accepting the fact that the growing likelihood that tomorrow's record store will be on the computer, the recording industry is looking for a standard for delivering music electronically. —*The New York Times*, May 5, 1999.

Vice President Al Gore and representatives from the high-tech industry have announced new online resources to help parents protect their children from objectionable material on the Internet. This Internet initiative is meant to serve a dual purpose— to protect children from pornographic and violent content, as well as blunt further public criticism of the Internet. Each company that is involved (AOL, Walt Disney, and AT&T, to name a few) has committed to maintaining a separate Internet site that will contain tips on safe Web surfing. —*The Wall Street Journal*, May 5, 1999.

Most companies in Hong Kong are currently behind the curve in the Internet, but more and more Hong Kong companies are getting caught in the frenzy. Analysts say that the insatiable demand for technology stocks has helped fuel the remarkable rally in the Hong Kong market, which has risen more than 20 percent since March. —*The New York Times*, May 5, 1999.

MCI WorldCom has shelved its glossy annual report and instead is telling shareholders to go online for the details. The company sent about a million slimmed-down reports to shareholders—on plain white paper with no color photos. Bernard J. Ebbers, MCI WorldCom's CEO wrote in a letter than online reports can be updated more frequently (the company will do so quarterly) and save more than $800,000 in printing, production, and mailing costs annually. —*The Wall Street Journal*, May 6, 1999.

What's the next medium that America Online Inc. hopes to conquer? Try radio. The online giant is negotiating to buy an equity stake in Dallas-based Chancellor Media Corp. and gain rights to broadcast Chancellor programming across the AOL system on the Internet. The talks come just weeks after AOL's main Internet portal rival, Yahoo! Inc., agreed to pay $5.6 billion for Broadcast.com Inc., the top provider of audio and video programming over the Internet. —*BusinessWeek*, May 10, 1999.

Worried about the Internet's potential to invade people's privacy, politicians around the globe are considering new laws to prevent the Internet from being misused. In turn, many businesses are worried that their dream of a worldwide electronic marketplace will be ruined by local regulations. There are many issues and problems revolving around Internet regulation, and businesses are pleading with the government to conduct business on their own and police themselves. —*Business Week*, May 10, 1999.

New companies are flocking to online investment banking. Even though most are small and designed for the Internet, they may very well be the banks of the future. Investment banking may be a tougher business for e-commerce to overhaul than books, auction, or even trading stocks. The Internet no doubt will enable banks to process transactions more cheaply than they do now—but the Internet could also increase costs for traditional banks if customers demand service on the Internet and in the branch. —*Business Week*, May 10.1999.

Hewlett-Packard is cutting deals with an eye toward the future rather than the present. Under an innovative strategy for the conservative computing giant, HP is seeding companies with investments or offering business agreements that create long-term clients and even sales conduits. HP wants to make sure it gets a cut of the money changing hands because of the Internet—either by getting HP hardware into the infrastructure or by garnering HP a percentage of the proceeds. —*CNET News.com*, April 29, 1999.

Goodyear Tire & Rubber is trying to tread new ground. In an effort to use the Internet to help its dealerships, Goodyear wants to get all 2500 of its sales sites across the country hooked into a massive extranet. The system, called Xplor, has been running since April 1998. All 750 Goodyear-owned dealerships are tied in. However, only 800 of the 2500 independently owned outlets use it. The goal is to get the remaining 1700 independent shops logged on by the end of 1999. Xplor, developed in conjunction with IBM, is Internet-based so dealers get to it by using an Internet browser and typing in their password. Once inside, they can get real-time information about technical data, return policies, product availability, price, and delivery times. They can also place orders—with "tire dolly" shopping carts—and later check the shipping status. The system is supported by a variety of IBM software including Lotus groupware and its MQSeries messaging and information infrastructure. —*Interactive Week*, May 3, 1999.

The SETI@home program, run by the University of California at Berkeley, is part of a worldwide effort known as Search for Extraterrestrial Intelligence, or SETI. SETI@home collects and analyzes data from a giant 1000-foot diameter radio telescope. The project's Internet site (setiathome.ssl.berkely.edu) began distributing software that will enable home-computer users to help the scientists analyze data. —*The New York Times*, May 20, 1999.

Genealogy research has become a popular use of the Internet, and as a result, the LDS Church has built the world's largest archive of genealogical information. The site, www.FamilySearch.org, provides a new search engine that hunts for specific names and relationships throughout the church's online database. It will also provide an online family history library catalog, as well as listings of other family history resources, such as books and software. —*Desert News* (Salt Lake City), May 24, 1999.

America Online is suing a small Internet software company, Tribal Voice, Inc., over its use of the popular AOL trademark, "buddy list". AOL uses the phrase to describe one of its popular features—a window that shows users which of their friends are online and available for electronic conversations. Tribal Voice claims that "buddy list" is a common term and that this is another case of a large company picking on the "little guy." —*The Wall Street Journal*, May 24, 1999.

Macromedia Inc. has announced plans to spin off its free content Internet site into a new company that will enable users to create personalized entertainment centers on the Internet. The new site, called Shockwave.com, will be launched this summer. —*The Wall Street Journal*, May 24, 1999.

Federated Department Stores has announced its partnership with WeddingChannel.com, in an effort to boost a lucrative wedding gift business. Currently, WeddingChannel.com is a one-stop Internet site that offers the prospective bride and groom a variety of wedding-related features, including an online gift registry for brides to be. This hasn't been particularly successful, so the partnership with Federated will hopefully boost business—giving WeddingChannel.com access to the 300,000–400,000 brides that Federated registers with them every year. —*The Wall Street Journal*, May 25, 1999.

In recent months, the most favored targets for e-commerce have been kids and teens. Currently, eToys is the leading Internet toy retailer, but the industry is expected to heat up in the next year. FAO Schwartz and Toys R Us Inc. have both reported that they will up their presence on the Internet. —*The Washington Post*, May 25, 1999.

DriveOff.com, a new Internet site developed by Navidec Inc., is designed to compete against more traditional car-buying sites such as CarsDirect.com and Autobytel.com. DriveOff.com is slated to begin operation this summer and will work with a national alliance of automobile dealers now being organized. Dealers that participate will pay DriveOff.com a set-up fee and a monthly marketing fee. —*The Wall Street Journal*, May 25, 1999.

Universal Music Group and BMG Entertainment, two major music labels, have announced that they will join AT&T and Matsushita Electric Industrial Co., in developing technology for a large-scale system for distributing music over the Internet. The companies will band together to develop an electric media distribution system. This technology will give consumers an easy and convenient way to play music in digital formats. —*The Wall Street Journal*, May 26, 1999.

iMall, the Internet-shopping site, has recently redefined itself as an e-commerce "enabler"—a company that strives to help businesses get online and begin to make sales within a few hours. iMall has also announced plans to step up its marketing, which will bring it more visibility. —*The Wall Street Journal, California Edition*, May 26, 1999.

The regulation of transactions over the Internet raises complex questions. The U.K. government has announced that it will drop its plans to force companies to entrust third parties with keys to encryption software they use to protect electronic messages. The government claims that it can do little to prevent advanced encryption technology hampering police efforts to combat crime by intercepting electronic communications. —*Financial Times*, May 26, 1999.

As more kids go online every single day, it is imperative to ensure their safety. With this in mind, the House has recently passed legislation that would triple funding for Customs Service pursuit of Internet sex predators and other cybercriminals. —*USA Today*, May 26, 1999.

Montgomery County has announced plans for eMontgomery, which will enable residents to use the Internet to pay parking tickets and property taxes, to apply for plumbing permits, or to register at Montgomery College. They will also have the capability to select courses and buy books. Montgomery is believed to be the first municipality in the area to announce such a venture. —*The Washington Post*, May 26, 1999.

Buying and selling stock options just got a little easier, thanks to the Internet. Top Silicon Valley companies, such as Cisco Systems and Oracle Corp., have rolled out new Internet-based stock option plans this spring. The new programs give employees quicker access and makes things easier for those running stock option plans. —*Investor's Business Daily*, May 26, 1999.

Once reluctant to get too deep into the Internet services business, commercial banks are being pulled toward helping merchant clients set up online storefronts. The demand is emanating from technology vendors who view banks, because of their credit card processing expertise, as natural candidates to boost the new generation in retailing. In the last two months, coalitions of well-known vendors have stepped forward with what amount to paint-by-the numbers Internet packages for banks to sell to merchants. These programs, combined with the evident popularity of electronic commerce, have piqued more bankers' interest. First Data Corp.' merchant division has teamed up with IBM and iMall Inc. to offer what they describe as "one stop e-commerce services" for banks and merchant customers. First Data handles the card processing. IBM provides Internet design through its HomePage Creator software. iMall does the Internet hosting and traffic-driving and offers gateway links to the payment system. —*American Banker*, May 27, 1999.

There has been a surge in demand for songs that can be downloaded off the Internet, often referred to MP3s, after the type of computer file that's usually used to encode them for use on computers. While the popularity of online music has been exciting for most fans, it has alarmed the music industry. Record companies worry about the availability of illegal online MP3 copies of copyrighted recorded music. Two most trusted music publications, *Rolling Stone* and the *Source*, have begun to organize and review uploaded songs from artists without record contracts. The Internet site, Tunes.com, has organized the new MP3 effort for the two magazines. —*The Wall Street Journal*, May 27, 1999.

Coping with sudden explosions of Internet activity has become a touchy and growing problem for Internet sites and their service providers. Traffic jams are likely to get worse as growing number of consumers move onto the Internet, making traffic management one of the hottest parts of the industry. Currently, many big Internet-net-working software companies cope with such massive traffic loads in different ways, such as "caching" information at various server sites—which makes sites seem fresh, while requiring less bandwidth than would be needed to constantly update a site's entire information load. —*The Wall Street Journal*, May 27, 1999.

Walgreen Co., the largest U.S. drugstore chain, has said that prescription drugs will be the first products sold over its Internet site. Currently, the site allows customers to log on and check the status of drug refills. The expansion of the site, allowing the sale of prescription drugs, could be completed as early as August. Walgreen has said that the prescriptions sold online will be cheaper than those offered in stores. —*Bloomberg*, May 27, 1999.

The FBI and the National White Collar Crime Center have recently announced their plans to create an Internet Fraud Complaint Center online. Anyone who sees signs of online identity theft, e-mail pyramid schemes, or any other Internet-based criminal activity, will be able to file a report on the Internet site. —*The New York Times*, May 27, 1999.

An around-the-clock technical center to help crack secret Internet and e-mail systems used by criminals is being set up by the computer industry and the police. The center will open encrypted messages for officers who have a warrant. If the codes cannot be cracked it will call in computer specialists. —*The New York Times*, May 27, 1999.

Inmate Internet sites, where the incarcerated can post pictures and messages, are provoking outrage and frustration among victims' rights and groups and prison officials. Many inmates post Internet personal ads on prisonpenpals.org, describing themselves, while leaving out few key details—such as why they are in prison. Prisoners do not have direct access to the Internet, but friends or relatives generally post photos or messages on behalf of the inmates. —*The Globe and Mail*, May 27, 1999.

A recent attack from computer hackers forced the FBI to shut down its Internet site last week. Federal Internet sites are increasingly becoming targets for hackers who are upset with government policies or actions. FBI field offices around the country have begun several investigations of hacker groups, and they have confirmed that homes of suspected hackers have been raided. —*The Wall Street Journal*, May 28, 1999.

Matria Healthcare Inc., a disease management company, has launched an Internet-based consumer information service called NetNurse. NetNurse.com will focus on pregnancy issues and will then be expanded to include general women's health, pediatrics, diabetes, and respiratory-related topics. —*The Wall Street Journal*, May 28, 1999.

Merrill Lynch & Co. has unveiled a radical new Internet-brokerage strategy, one of the boldest moves in its 85-year history. The nation's largest full-service securities firm will offer online trading for as little as $29.95 a trade. Currently, Merrill customers pay commissions of as much as several hundred dollars a transaction. To do this, the firm must essentially build a large-scale, discount-trading operation. Within months, Merrill has to streamline and add key features to its computer systems, hire hundreds of technical staff, and expand its existing customer service centers. The company has given December 1 as the launch date. —*The Wall Street Journal*, June 2, 1999.

Three years ago, E*Trade Group helped spark a revolution with Internet stock trading. Yesterday, the company predicted a similar market revolution—in online banking—as it announced plans to acquire Telebanc Financial Corp., an Internet banking company. The company will be a formidable new rival to the big banks. It has marketing expertise and once the deal closes, it can extend banking services to its one million-plus online trading customers. —*The Wall Street Journal*, June 2, 1999.

Charles Schwab, the largest U.S. discount broker, and Tokio Marine and Fire, Japan's largest property and casualty insurer, announced they would create an online brokerage business in Japan. It marks a significant expansion of Schwab's international strategy. Foreign growth is increasingly important for U.S. brokers, as fears grow of increased competition in the United States after Merrill Lynch's announcement that it would offer online trading. Schwab will take a 50 percent stake in the new venture and will control day-to-day operations. —*Financial Times*, June 3, 1999.

PaineWebber Group is wading into online trading for less affluent investors, but the full-service brokerage giant won't likely go as far as rival Merrill Lynch & Co. Instead, PaineWebber will test new trading programs later this year that offer a mishmash of services for low, annual fees. Such programs are separate from PaineWebber's already announced plans to offer online trading to wealthy customers in its Premier Asset Account in the third quarter of this year. —*The Wall Street Journal*, June 4, 1999.

In the past year, a growing number of distinguished companies, including Provident American Life & Health Insurance, Co., have been shedding their brick-and-mortar operations and remaking themselves as a cyber-only business. While only 5 percent of the companies on the Internet are taking this radical leap, more are expected to follow as e-commerce explodes. Struggling companies may see the Internet as a way to start anew or a chance to one-up rivals. The strategy can be risky, though since online consumers account for only a small fraction of total consumers. —*Business Week*, June 7, 1999.

Financials

Yahoo!, Inc., the No. 1 Internet search directory, is looking into possibly buying CheckFree Holdings Corp., an electronic-commerce service company. The acquisition is said to cost an estimated $3 billion and makes sense for Yahoo!, giving it a provider of online bill-payment services. —*MSNBC*, April 27, 1999.

Amazon.com, the Seattle online merchant, jolted stock traders with a warning that wide operating deficits are likely this year, even as it reported breakneck sales growth and a smaller-than expected first-quarter loss. Amazon also said it has begun a search for a chief operating officer, a new post. The company's founder, chairman, and chief executive officer, Jeffrey Bezos, indicated that his company is expanding so quickly that he needs a deeper management team. —*The Wall Street Journal*, April 29, 1999.

iVillage Inc., which produces a network of Internet sites for women, reported major loses in its first quarter as a publicly traded company, largely because of steep sales, marketing, and production costs and one-time items. For the first quarter, the company said its net loss widened to $17.6 million from $8.5 million in the same period. —*The Wall Street Journal*, April 29, 1999.

MSNBC reported on a recent study that found Internet executives sold 500,00 or more shares of their firm's stock in public Internet companies. Seven of those firms had million-share sellers. Those amounts are high compared to insider selling at other firms. Analysts call it minor profit-taking. —*Investor's Business Daily*, April 29, 1999.

The RCN Corporation, a provider of telecommunications services based in Princeton, NJ, acquired a 47.5 percent stake in the Juniornet Corporation, a commercial-free online learning service for children for about $47 million in cash. At the same time, Juniornet bought RCN's Lancit Media Entertainment subsidiary, which creates children's television programming, for about $25 million in cash. Juniornet, based in Boston, uses a technology combining a CD-ROM and an online connection, which increases bandwidth and reduces download time, while preventing access the Internet at large. —*The New York Times*, April 29, 1999.

Seagram Co.'s Universal Music Group is enlisting powerful allies including AT&T, BMG Entertainment, and Matsushita Electric Industrial Co. to back its digital music-delivery system in an aggressive push to become the de facto standard for delivering music over the Internet. A deal to collaborate on a digital delivery platform, code-named "Nigel," could be signed as early as next week, although people close to the talks caution it could still fall apart, or the closing could be delayed by AT&T's intense focus on the pending acquisition of MediaOne Group. —*The Wall Street Journal*, May 6, 1999.

During the last month, Amazon.com has been storming into new areas of electronic commerce, ranging from online auctions to electronic greeting cards. But the bigfooting is sending shudders throughout the venture capital community, which is trying to choose start-ups that could someday become powerful cyberspace merchants in their own right. Nobody wants to end up competing with Amazon, said one venture capitalist. Just a few weeks ago, funding prospects looked bright for a half-dozen start-ups with plans to sell pet supplies online. Then Amazon.com announced it was buying a minority stake in Pets.com, a tiny San Francisco company with those exact ambitions. Financiers pulled back funding overtures to rival companies within a matter of days. —*The Wall Street Journal*, May 6, 1999.

Despite all the booksellers rushing to do business on the Internet, don't expect traditional bookstores to disappear any time soon. One interesting case in point is a small, family-owned book-selling operation that actually manages to turn a profit on its online sales, something Amazon.com has yet to accomplish. The outfit is Powell's of Portland, Oregon. It has seven stores, 420 employees, and it fills about 1000 Internet orders each day. That should be enough to bring in $3.5 million in revenues in its 1999 fiscal year. The secret: about 85 percent of the sales are used or out-of-print books, which have better profit margins. Also, Powell's store stocks all the books it offers on its site. Most important, Powell's doesn't discount. The company spends only about $100,000 on marketing and won't accept advertising on the Internet site. They buy surplus books from publishers and retailers, and from estate sales. —*Barron's*, May 31, 1999.

WebMD Inc. sued closely held Certifiedemail.com Inc., charging it with providing false financial information to deceive WebMD into acquiring it. —*Atlanta Business Chronicle*, May 31, 1999.

One of the hottest addresses in cyberspace, China.com, is set to float on Nasdaq as early as next month, according to bankers. The company, which boasts several international shareholders, is expected to raise about $50 million. According to one banker, China.com must be worth $500 million just for the URL. —*Financial Times*, May 31, 1999.

Rupert Murdoch is branching out from global media ventures into high-tech banking, becoming the latest heavyweight to take a minority stake in U.S. start-up investment bank W.R. Hambrecht. Epartners, the $300 million investment vehicle formed a month ago by Murdoch's News Corp., said its initial investment would be a stake in the pioneer of initial public offerings on the Internet. Terms of the deal weren't revealed, but earlier this month Reuters' Instinet said it paid $20 million to buy an 11.4 percent stake in Hambrecht. —*Daily News*, June 1, 1999.

America Online said it will buy Internet music companies Spinner Networks and Nullsoft Inc. for $400 million in stock, marking an aggressive move into the world of digital music. Closely held Spinner, based in San Francisco, operates a popular music service that functions essentially as an Internet radio station. Nullsoft, also closely held, develops and distributes software for listening to music online. The acquisitions represent AOL's first major plays in the online music space, which is enjoying explosive growth among Internet users but raising vexing copyright issues for music companies.

The deals also give AOL access to programming and technology likely to become even more valuable as consumers switch to high-speed broadband connections, which can deliver songs online with fewer glitches. —*The Wall Street Journal*, June 2, 1999.

CBS Corp. said it will acquire 35 percent of Internet-directory service Switchboard Inc. in exchange for advertising time on CBS media properties and other considerations that CBS valued at about $135 million. Switchboard, which is majority owned by Banyan Systems, is a search engine that allows visitors to search for friends, businesses, directions, and maps from a directory that includes 117 million business and residential listings. Under the pact, Switchboard will rename its Internet site "CBS Switchboard." —*The Wall Street Journal*, June 3, 1999.

EDITORIAL QUOTES

"Kids used to put posters up on their walls—now they put them up on a Internet page," said Esther Dyson, head of the Electronic Frontier Foundation. "It's how they express themselves." —*The Washington Post*, April 24, 1999.

"Web users have made it clear that they are concerned about privacy, and as Web publishers we need to address that concern." —Carol Perruso, President of latimes.com.

"If 1998 was the year of electronic commerce, 1999 will be the year of customer dissatisfaction." —Charles Wilson, managing director of AisleFive, in regards to the rise in complaints of consumers purchasing on the Web. *The Wall Street Journal*, April 26, 1999.

"Banks will wake up in three years and realize that their financial data are in the hands of the Yahoos of this world." —William Melton, the chairman and chief executive officer of Cybercash Inc., after his keynote address to the Comdex computer show in Chicago. He went on to say that bankers have no more than two years to act if they are to prevent Internet portal companies from stealing their business. *American Banker*, April 27, 1999.

"The federal government has rules. Every state has rules. Every country does, too. So, the question is, how do we adapt the rules to the new medium? In the Internet world, we need the private sector to take the lead in developing effective consumer protection practices." —William M. Daley, Secretary of Commerce at Amdahl Corp. *San Jose Mercury News*, May 2, 1999.

Thirty-nine percent of parents are worried about their kids surfing the Internet while 39 percent are gung-ho about it, says the Annenberg Public Policy Center. —*Investor's Business Daily*, May 5, 1999.

General Electric, second only to Microsoft in market value for U.S. companies, is currently selling about $1 billion in products over the Internet, but that number accounts for only about 1 percent of its $100 billion in annual sales. According to John F. Welch, CEO of GE, the Internet is the biggest "revolution to happen in the business in the last 100 years, since the Industrial Revolution..." —*The Journal News*, May 26, 1999.

Global Internet music sales are expected to reach $4 billion by 2004. This will account for 8 percent of all recorded music sold worldwide and is expected to be up to 20 percent by 2010. The United States is expected to dominate the digital music market by commanding $2.28 billion worth of online sales in five years. $228 million of that will be digital versions of recordings which are downloaded on to consumers' computers. —*Financial Times*, May 26, 1999.

Some e-commerce sites are costing more than initially anticipated. Getting a new e-commerce Internet site off the ground costs, on average, $1 million, according to Gartner Group. Labor was the biggest expense, making up 79 percent of costs. The biggest headache was noted as tailoring a vendor's packaged technology to a company's needs. —*The Wall Street Journal*, May 27, 1999.

Five years ago, when IBM asked U.S. small business owners their opinion about the Internet, the survey used the term "information highway" because the Internet was not in common use. This year, a follow-up poll of 206 entrepreneurs finds that almost all of them—93 percent—see the Internet as an asset. Still, just one-third of the sample are using it to sell products. Close to 60 percent use it to buy goods. Most of the small-business owners say the main value of the Internet is as an information source, and e-mail is the most commonly used online tool. The survey targeted businesses with fewer than 100 employees and annual revenue of between $5 million and $99 million.— *The Globe and Mail*, May 31, 1999.

Sixty-seven percent of online purchases are never completed, largely because top e-commerce sites have made few provisions for real-time, online customer service and support, a new survey shows. And, only 5.75 percent of the people who visit e-commerce sites even try to make a purchase, according to Net Effect, the software firm that conducted the study. The five-month poll includes two dozen companies that sell over the Internet, including Amazon, eToys, and Dell. —*USA Today*, June 1, 1999.

Banner, e-mail, and other forms of Internet marketing in Japan grew 89 percent in 1998, reaching almost $100 million. This number is expected to increase to $166 million in 2000 and $833 million by 2005, according to a report by DSA Analytics. The study also noted that the Japanese Internet user is increasingly familiar with banner ads, with over half of users clicking on them by the second half of 1998. —*eMarketer Newsletter,* No. 23, June 8, 1999.

Computer Economics estimates that 37.1 percent of organizations across all industry sectors now have e-business operations in place. According to their recent report, 46.8 percent are planning to move to e-commerce in the near future. Firms in the banking and finance, insurance and transportation sectors are the furthest along in developing e-business capabilities. —*eMarketer Newsletter,* No. 23, June 8, 1999.

According to the Australian Bureau of Statistics (ABS), there were nearly 1.1 million homes, 16 percent of total households, with Internet access in Australia in 1998. This number represents a 280 percent jump over the 1996 number of 286,000 connected households. Nearly 5.7 million Australians (34 percent of the population) over the age of 5 used a home computer frequently. In 1996, 4.0 million (24 percent of the population) did so. —*eMarketer Newsletter,* No. 23, June 8, 1999.

A recent report by Market Tracking International (MTI) argues that music suppliers and retailers are finally beginning to acknowledge the possibilities the Internet offers for music distribution. In 1998, online music sales were worth $169.9 million. By 2004, they will be worth over $3.9 billion. —*eMarketer Newsletter,* No. 23, June 8, 1999.

According to the study, "Internet User Trends: Yearend 1998" study release last week by The Strategis Group, females are closing the "Internet gender gap." The difference between men and women online has narrowed from 21 percent to only 8 percent in less than two years. While only 16 percent of U.S. adult females used the Internet in mid-1997, compared to 37 percent of males, female usage mushroomed to 38 percent by the end of 1998, while that of males grew to 46 percent. —*eMarketer Newsletter,* No. 23, June 8, 1999.

Protecting consumers in cyberspace presents new challenges for policymakers, especially as transactions cross traditional borders. To address some of the complex questions raised by the new global marketplace, the Federal Trade Commission and consumer and government representatives from around the world met in a two-day meeting. During the conference, a University of Utah professor, Rob Maher, presented the conclusions of a landmark survey that was financed by the European Union and coordinated by Consumers International, a federation of 245 consumer organizations in 110 countries. For the study, representatives of those groups bought more than 150 items from Internet sites based in 17 countries, and then tried to return them. Among the findings: 8 percent of the items ordered never arrived; many Internet sites did not give clear information about delivery charges; a minority disclosed whether the laws of the seller's country or the buyer's country would apply in the event of a dispute, and only 53 percent had a return policy. In addition, only about 13 percent of the sites promised not to sell customers' personal data to a third party and only 32 percent provided information on how to complain if there was a problem with a transaction. —*The New York Times*, June 8, 1999.

According to research done by NFO Interactive, 24.1 percent of online shoppers state that their online spending does indeed decrease the amount of money they spend in neighborhood and regional stores. In addition, it was reported that 23.8 percent of those surveyed stated that their Internet purchases have increased the amount they generally would spend annually on those products. —*eMarketer Newsletter,* No. 23, June 8, 1999.

The Internet pumped $301.4 billion into the economy last year and provided jobs for 1.2 million people. So says a University of Texas study that its sponsor—networking gear maker Cisco Systems Inc.—bills as the most comprehensive economic look at the Internet ever. Revenue attributed to the Internet has risen at an annual rate of 174.5 percent since 1995, when the young technology's impact was a mere $5 billion, says the study. In comparison, the nation's gross domestic product is growing at a 3.8 percent clip. According to the numbers, the Internet has almost caught up to the auto industry. Last year, the auto industry contributed $350 billion to the U.S. economy. Energy posted $223 billion in revenue, and telecommunications $270 billion, according to the study. —*Investor's Business Daily*, June 10, 1999.

The Internet's numbers are adding up. The 1.2 million jobs mean that about one in five people who work in U.S. technology work in Internet jobs. Though tons of young companies have created a booming market in Internet initial public stock offerings, a University of Texas study found that about one-third of Internet jobs come from the 15 largest Internet companies. Electronic commerce fed about $102 billion into the economy last year. Nearly 482,000 people have e-commerce to thank for their jobs. These players include companies that sell to consumers, such as Amazon.com Inc., as well as businesses that sell their products to other businesses over the Internet. —*Investor's Business Daily*, June 10, 1999.

Index

Back Forward Reload Home Search Guide Images Print Security Stop

http://www.phptr.com/

PRENTICE HALL

Professional Technical Reference
Tomorrow's Solutions for Today's Professionals.

Keep Up-to-Date with
PH PTR Online!

We strive to stay on the cutting-edge of what's happening in professional computer science and engineering. Here's a bit of what you'll find when you stop by **www.phptr.com**:

Special interest areas offering our latest books, book series, software, features of the month, related links and other useful information to help you get the job done.

Deals, deals, deals! Come to our promotions section for the latest bargains offered to you exclusively from our retailers.

Need to find a bookstore? Chances are, there's a bookseller near you that carries a broad selection of PTR titles. Locate a Magnet bookstore near you at www.phptr.com.

What's New at PH PTR? We don't just publish books for the professional community, we're a part of it. Check out our convention schedule, join an author chat, get the latest reviews and press releases on topics of interest to you.

Subscribe Today! **Join PH PTR's monthly email newsletter!**

Want to be kept up-to-date on your area of interest? Choose a targeted category on our website, and we'll keep you informed of the latest PH PTR products, author events, reviews and conferences in your interest area.

Visit our mailroom to subscribe today! **http://www.phptr.com/mail_lists**